BLUE RIDGE
MUSIC TRAILS

BLUE RIDGE MUSIC TRAILS

is a project of the Blue Ridge Heritage Initiative

Project Director:

Wayne Martin, North Carolina Arts Council

Published in association with

the North Carolina Arts Council,

the Virginia Commission for the Arts,

the Blue Ridge Institute and Museum of Ferrum College,

the North Carolina Folklife Institute, and the

Blue Ridge Parkway, National Park Service

BLUE RIDGE
MUSIC TRAILS

FINDING A PLACE IN THE CIRCLE

BLUE RIDGE

PHOTOGRAPHS BY CEDRIC N. CHATTERLEY

FRED C. FUSSELL

MUSIC TRAILS

The University of North Carolina Press   *Chapel Hill & London*

Designed by Richard Hendel and Eric M. Brooks
Set in Goshen, Charter, and Meta types by Eric M. Brooks
Maps by Victoria Cumbee
Photographs by Cedric N. Chatterley unless otherwise credited
Manufactured in China

The Blue Ridge Heritage Initiative gratefully acknowledges
the financial support of the following:
    National Endowment for the Arts
    North Carolina Arts Council
    North Carolina Department of Cultural Resources
    Virginia Commission for the Arts
    Z. Smith Reynolds Foundation
    Appalachian Regional Commission
    American Express Corporation

The paper in this book meets the guidelines for permanence and
durability of the Committee on Production Guidelines for Book Longevity
of the Council on Library Resources.

Library of Congress Cataloging-in-Publication Data
Fussell, Fred.
Blue Ridge music trails: finding a place in the circle / Fred C. Fussell;
photographs by Cedric N. Chatterley.
    p. cm.
Includes index.
ISBN 0-8078-5459-x (pbk.: alk. paper)
1. Folk music—Blue Ridge Mountains Region—History and criticism.
2. Musical landmarks—Blue Ridge Mountains Region—Guidebooks.
3. Blue Ridge Mountains Region—Guidebooks. I. Chatterley, Cedric N.,
1956– II. Title.
ML3551.7.B58 F8   2003
781.62'1307568—dc21   2002154136

paper   07 06 05 04 03   5 4 3 2 1

I believe that's the main thing, getting people to come

and listen to the music. The music tells a story — about

tragedy and love and death. And, you know, it just

explains things, really.

Larry Dean Pennington, traditional musician,

Ashe County, North Carolina

CONTENTS

FEATURED ARTICLES

PROFILES

Jam session at Old Fort Mountain Music

PREFACE: ENTERING THE CIRCLE

The Blue Ridge Mountains of North Carolina and Virginia form the heart of a traditional music-making legacy that is unique in America. This is a region where traditional music and dance are performed and celebrated as in no other place in America. Regular weekly square dances featuring live music are still popular in mountain communities. Many local radio stations throughout the Blue Ridge broadcast live performances of traditional music by local musicians. An annual fiddlers' convention featuring local players is probably taking place somewhere nearly every weekend during the summer, and homemade music competes favorably with the popular commercial offerings that dominate the music scene in most other regions of the United States.

A dozen musicians from western North Carolina and western Virginia have been awarded the National Heritage Fellowship, our nation's highest honor for traditional artists. Doc Watson, who has become a kind of national father figure for Southern Appalachian roots music, is among this group.

Traditional mountain music is an integral component of community celebrations and holiday festivities throughout the Blue Ridge. Fiddle bands play at molasses makings and at small-town festivals; singers gather to perform shape-note hymns and have dinner on the grounds; and residents of small communities gather at a hundred or more local venues to enjoy traditional music played by their friends and next-door neighbors.

All of this musical activity flourishes in a region that is one of the most popular tourist destinations in America. Tens of thousands of outsiders visit the Blue Ridge every year to enjoy mountain vacations. In springtime visitors hike the winding hillside trails, enjoy the grandeur of high-country vistas along the Blue Ridge Parkway, or fish for trout in the cold, clear waters of mountain streams and rivers. In summer residents of warmer climes come seeking relief from the lowcountry heat. Visitors crowd the narrow mountain roadways in autumn to enjoy the spectacle of colorful foliage. In winter families and church groups arrive by the busload to ski and to play in the snow at mountain resorts.

While they're in the area, many tourists stop to have a look at one or two

Shape-note sing at Mount Carmel Baptist Church, Alexander County, North Carolina

of the numerous roadside attractions that vie for their attention. Some pan for gold and jewels near Spruce Pine and Marion, North Carolina, sifting carefully through buckets of mountain dirt in search of semiprecious stones and anything else that glitters. Others search for and select that perfect Christmas tree from among the many thousands that dot the high-country hillsides. Still others watch woolly worms climb up lengths of cotton twine or shop in the quaint mountain gift shops and craft galleries.

Yet, down deep, most visitors sense that there's something more to this beautiful place than the superficial traces of community that they find on their own or with the aid of tourist brochures. And even though they may long for a more meaningful connection with mountain people and authentic mountain culture, they're often at a loss as to how to achieve it. It's not easy—or at least it doesn't seem to be—for strangers in an unfamiliar community to meet local residents and experience the essential life of the place they're visiting.

The problem is compounded by a lingering and misguided notion that the people of Southern Appalachia are actually akin to the many insulting comic-strip and TV-sitcom representations of them. Those exaggerated stereotypical images of mountain-eers live on, especially in the minds of some who are visiting the mountains for the first time. Visions of encountering Snuffy Smith, Li'l Abner, Daisy Mae, Jed Clampett, Ernest T. Bass, and those half-witted, dentally challenged, perverted, mean-as-a-snake characters in the movie *Deliverance* invade the minds of many who go there. More recently, the popular movies *Songcatcher* and *Oh Brother Where Art Thou?* have added more characters to the list. On the other hand, there's no

Jessie Lovell and Marsha Bowman practice at the Old Fiddlers' Convention in Galax, Virginia.

denying that the soundtracks of these and other such popular motion pictures have introduced mountain music to multitudes of people who might otherwise never have heard it.

Despite that, mountain residents are puzzled, angered, and wounded by the way they are, time and again, unfairly perceived by outsiders. They see themselves in a completely different light. They are rightfully proud of their musical heritage and proud of the cultural characteristics that distinguish them from other Americans. Many are very much aware, both as individuals and as members of traditional communities, that they have inherited an unparalleled and precious cultural legacy, and that it's their responsibility to maintain and to transmit that legacy forward to subsequent generations.

Some of them continue to sing traditional ballads that have been handed down for generations, ballads that reach far back into history. And even though those ballads may speak of people they've never seen and places they've never been, the traditional singers hold on to them. They're aware of the rarity and the importance of such songs. And, furthermore, they simply like to sing them.

Many Blue Ridge music makers play stringed instruments using techniques they learned from family members and neighbors. Making music is a vital social function for many people who live in the region. Some have grown from infancy to old age knowing traditional music as an integral part of their everyday lives—not just through CDs or radio or television, but as living music played by living people, both at home and out in the community.

And do they evermore play music out in public! The traditional music makers of the Blue Ridge—farmers, teachers, postal workers, barbers, architects, pharmacists, students, nurses, merchants, technicians, and other

Local musicians entertain diners at the Dairy Queen in Rocky Mount, Virginia.

ordinary folks—love nothing more than to get together, socialize, tell corny jokes, eat good food, and make music. They play in community centers, coffee shops, barbecue restaurants, music stores, fast-food joints, shopping malls, community festivals, street fairs, barbershops, school auditoriums, and town parks. They play traditional bluegrass, old-time, country-and-western, gospel, and blues, and they play with gusto, enthusiasm, and energy.

They will generously share their time-honored traditions and practice-honed skills with any who want to listen, all the while swapping tunes, techniques, and lyrics with their fellow players. They make their music with a fine humor and with light hearts, but at the same time they're serious about it. They pick, strum, frail, and bow strings of steel pulled tight across instruments of spruce, ebony, walnut, cherry, rosewood, mahogany, and maple. They beat pairs of metal or wooden spoons together in the palms of their hands, and they scrub their fingers across the ribs of metal or wooden washboards. They blow harmonicas. They tap out a rhythm with their dancing

Forming the circle at the Mountain Street Dance in Waynesville, North Carolina

feet. They unabashedly sing out with high-pitched tenor voices, creating the distinctive harmonies that are the backbone of American country music. They know that their music is distinctively southern, distinctively Appalachian, distinctively American, distinctively *theirs*—and theirs to share.

The circle, both literal and symbolical, is important to traditional Blue Ridge musicians, who gather naturally in a circle when they come together to make music. The greater the number of players, the larger the circle grows. Local dances often begin with a circle or round dance. Everyone present can participate in a round dance, and the joining of hands within the circle reinforces the sense of community.

It is my hope that the information provided in this book—tips, leads, directions, maps, and images—will help people discover traditional mountain music. In the process, visitors will learn more about Blue Ridge communities and perhaps—if they are fortunate—find their place in the circle. The music is there. The music makers are there. Hear the music. Dance the dance. Gather round, folks, and listen up. You'll be glad you did.

Buena Vista, Georgia
September 2002

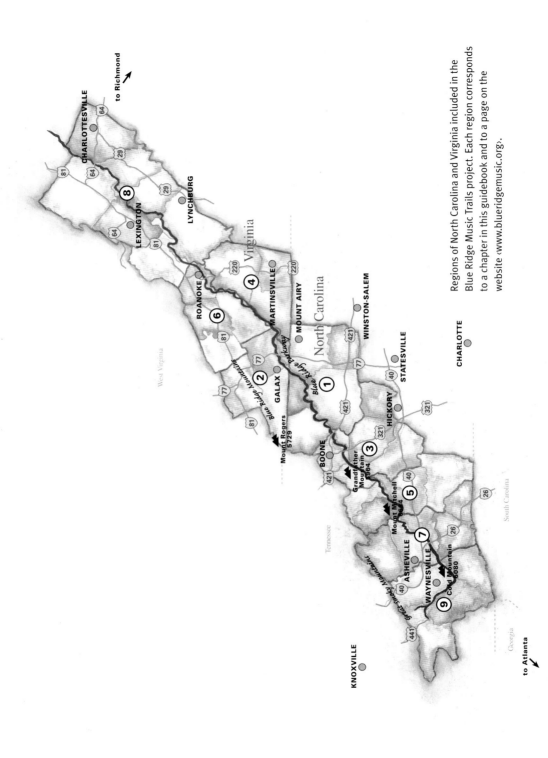

Regions of North Carolina and Virginia included in the Blue Ridge Music Trails project. Each region corresponds to a chapter in this guidebook and to a page on the website ‹www.blueridgemusic.org›.

ABOUT THIS GUIDEBOOK

The Blue Ridge Music Trails project focuses on a geographic region of the Southern Appalachian Mountains in western North Carolina and Virginia. Although the area encompasses five major mountain ranges, the project takes its name from the largest of these, the Blue Ridge Mountains, and from its close association with the Blue Ridge Parkway, the 469-mile scenic route that both traverses and links the region.

The Blue Ridge Music Trails connect traditional music venues and other resources to one another, to the Blue Ridge Parkway, and to major roads and byways of the region. The more than 160 sites included in this guidebook are public venues where traditional music is presented to general audiences; no new sites were created for this project. Sites were nominated by residents of the region or by folklorists who conducted fieldwork there between 1998 and 2001. The final selection of sites for inclusion in the project was based on criteria listed below, contingent upon written permission from those who own or run the venues.

Living traditions are not frozen in time, but change constantly to meet the needs of the local community. Traditional music is no exception. Music events in the Blue Ridge sometimes alter their schedules or locations, lose vitality, or even disappear altogether. New sites emerge when informal or private music gatherings move to public spaces, or when one or more determined individuals decide to create something new in their communities.

For these reasons, it is wise to contact sites in advance to verify the accuracy of the information presented here. A companion website, ‹www.blueridgemusic.org›, also supplements this guidebook. Website entries will be reviewed and updated on a regular basis and will therefore contain the most current information on sites. New music venues not included in this book will also be added if they meet the selection criteria.

Both the guidebook and the website are organized in a similar fashion. Western North Carolina and southwestern Virginia are divided into nine subregions, beginning with the counties that lie along the border between the two states. This area is home to the strongest and most visible musical traditions within the Southern Appalachians. From here the trails flow outward, alternately northward and southward, to the borders of the region.

As a matter of fact, no matter where he or she enters the region, a traveler cannot move systematically from one music venue to the next in order. Even though all of the events listed here occur on a regular basis, some are staged weekly, some monthly, and some annually, and some happen at the same time as others.

Each subregion corresponds to a chapter in this guidebook and a separate page on the website. The music and dance venues within each subregion are grouped under the counties in which they take place, and maps illustrate the locations of the communities where sites and venues are located. Note, however, that these maps do not show all secondary roads in the region. The website includes a link to Mapquest, which provides more detailed directions to many, though not all, of the sites.

The voices of musicians in the region occupy a prominent place in this publication. Through transcribed interviews, fourteen of these musicians tell the stories of their lives and explain what traditional music means to them and to their communities. These individuals speak on behalf of the thousands of residents who play and support traditional music in the Blue Ridge Mountains.

CRITERIA FOR SITE SELECTION

1. All the venues and sites are located in Southern Appalachian communities of North Carolina and Virginia where traditional music has been practiced for generations. Venues and sites are within twenty-five miles of the Blue Ridge Parkway or are situated within counties traversed by the Parkway. Certain exceptions to this rule were made where compelling reasons existed for doing so.
2. The music venues listed in this book are public venues that welcome visitors and have restroom and parking facilities.
3. All the venues display identifying signs or other recognizable means of identification.
4. The selected venues present programs of traditional music and dance that have been handed down in the region over generations, are characteristic of and deeply rooted in communities, or are practiced by recently settled immigrant communities.
5. The following types of music resources were deemed eligible for inclusion in this guidebook: performances and events that significantly feature traditional music and dance; public jam sessions and

Road leading to Jim and Jennie's Music Barn

performances; traditional music and dance instruction workshops and demonstrations; traditional music and dance displays, exhibits, and archival resources; local radio stations and programs that broadcast regional music; instrument makers and music shops that retail locally handmade instruments; shops that specialize in traditional music publications, recordings, and videos that are available for purchase; and landscapes and landmarks that are significant to traditional music and dance within the region.

ACKNOWLEDGMENTS

The Blue Ridge Music Trails is one of four heritage trails projects planned, implemented, and promoted through the Blue Ridge Heritage Initiative, a partnership among the states of North Carolina, Virginia, Tennessee, and Georgia. The other projects also focus on resources that reflect the region's unique cultural identity—the traditions and history of the Eastern Band of Cherokee Indians, mountain crafts, and the area's agricultural traditions. Taken together, these trails constitute a network of sites and venues that allow residents and visitors to explore the authentic living heritage of the region. In addition to education, the goals of the Blue Ridge Heritage Initiative are the conservation and perpetuation of cultural traditions and sustainable economic development.

The Blue Ridge Music Trails is a collaboration between the states of North Carolina and Virginia. The project brought together traditional musicians and other residents of mountain communities, the North Carolina Arts

Council and Department of Cultural Resources, the North Carolina Folklife Institute, the Virginia Commission for the Arts, the Blue Ridge Institute at Ferrum College, the Blue Ridge Parkway Division of the National Park Service, the North Carolina Department of Commerce, the National Endowment for the Arts, the Virginia Foundation for the Humanities, the Z. Smith Reynolds Foundation, the American Express Company, and numerous other organizations and individuals interested in preserving and sharing the traditional music of Southern Appalachia.

The field research that produced the data and information needed to plan this project was conducted by teams of professional folklorists. Sally Council and Amy Davis surveyed twenty-two counties in North Carolina and wrote the impressive resource inventory that preceded this guidebook. Council and Davis's deep interest in the music traditions of the region also created much goodwill for the project among musicians and other residents. The Virginia survey was conducted by Douglas Day, whose work was augmented by archivist Susan Stephenson of the Blue Ridge Institute.

Peggy Baggett of the Virginia Commission for the Arts and Roddy Moore and Vaughan Webb at the Blue Ridge Institute and Museum provided outstanding leadership in implementing the project in Virginia. Peggy's organizational skills and fundraising efforts kept the work moving forward. Roddy Moore and Vaughan Webb generously shared their knowledge of Virginia musical traditions and sites, created the website for the project, wrote directions to sites, loaned historical photographs for the guidebook, and made certain that sensitive sites were protected. Dorothy Kreyenbuhl at the Blue Ridge Institute provided administrative support, while webmaster Jinny Turman collected and managed information used in the guidebook and website.

We are honored that Joe Wilson of the National Council for the Traditional Arts contributed to the chapter on the history of music in the region. No one knows more about the subject or has had greater success in bringing national visibility to Blue Ridge musicians. Daniel W. Patterson and Beverly Bush Patterson's descriptions of religious folksong traditions are an important addition to the chapter on the history of Blue Ridge music. Both are outstanding scholars who are moved by the artistry of the performers and intrigued by the layers of meaning to be discerned in traditional music.

Mary Regan and Nancy Trovillion at the North Carolina Arts Council enabled the Blue Ridge Heritage Initiative to get off the ground and provided resources and encouragement. Betty Ray McCain, former secretary of North Carolina's Department of Cultural Resources, and Elizabeth Buford, former deputy secretary, supported the Blue Ridge Heritage Initiative throughout their tenures. David Long and David Quinn of the Division of Community Assistance at the North Carolina Department of Commerce served on the steering committee and helped guide the Heritage Initiative from its inception.

The staff of the Blue Ridge Parkway Division of the National Park Service deserve special acknowledgment for its help. Former superintendent Gary Everhardt, along with Joe Wilson, pushed for the development of the Blue Ridge Music Center on the Parkway and proposed the 1996 meeting that led to the creation of the Blue Ridge Heritage Initiative. Current superintendent Dan Brown has continued to support this unique collaboration. Gary Johnson, chief planner for the Parkway, is a member of the steering committee for the Heritage Initiative and was particularly helpful in determining how the trails system should interface with the Parkway. Laura Rotegard, formerly community planner and now management assistant, also serves on the steering committee and has provided expertise and encouragement in all stages of this work. Laura's optimism, dedication to public service, and love of music inspires all who have the privilege of working with her.

Becky Anderson and HandMade in America provided the model for this project with their groundbreaking guidebook, *Craft Heritage Trails of Western North Carolina*. Becky has shown the nation that a cultural resource can be the catalyst for sustainable economic and community development in rural communities.

Folklorist Molly Parsons assisted with the selection of documentary photographs to accompany the text, solicited additional photos and artwork, and wrote captions. She, along with folklorists William Lewis and Margie Crawford, wrote directions, verified contact information and schedules, and secured release forms from project participants. Melanie Rice helped gather artwork to supplement photos.

Katherine Reynolds of the Folklife Program at the North Carolina Arts Council organized and documented meetings of the task force and steering committee that convened to plan and monitor the project. Her efforts were supplemented by the work of folklorists Leila Childs and Ann Kaplan.

Victoria Cumbee designed the handsome maps featured in the guidebook. Visual artists Lenore De Pree and Willard Gayheart allowed their work to be reproduced. Documentary photographers Rob Amberg and Roger Haile and collector Robert S. Brunk contributed photographs.

Gary Poe and Paul Brown, whose knowledge of music traditions in the region is deep, served as consultants and advisors to the committee that made the final site selections.

Thanks to David Perry, editor-in-chief of the University of North Carolina Press, who counseled the steering committee as it grappled with the challenge of how to appropriately present the resources documented during the research phase of the project.

Behind it all, from start to finish, was Wayne Martin, who directs the North Carolina Folklife Program. His depth of knowledge and breadth of understanding of Southern Appalachian folk culture never fails to amaze any who are involved in researching and interpreting that region. Throughout the duration of this project, his affection for the people and places that are the subjects of this book established a pattern of personal sensitivity for all who were a part of the process, and his insightful guidance remained the enjoining positive force that inspired everyone—be they scholar, researcher, writer, or tradition bearer.

Most of all, thanks to the people of western North Carolina and Virginia who have played traditional music over many generations. This book commemorates their words, their communities, and their heritage.

BLUE RIDGE
MUSIC TRAILS

Overlook on the Blue Ridge Parkway

HISTORY OF BLUE RIDGE MUSIC

Joseph Wilson and Wayne Martin

Country dance, Woolwine, Virginia, ca. 1950s
(Photograph courtesy of the Blue Ridge Institute, Ferrum, Va.)

EARLY DAYS

Early settlers in the Tidewater lands of the New World could not have anticipated the flowering of new musical styles that would accompany the expansion of immigrant populations into the mountains that lay to the west. The powerful Cherokee nation inhabited the southernmost part of the region, and the Cherokees, Shawanos, and other native peoples used the middle and upper areas as hunting grounds. Some colonists feared conflict with the Indians and the dangers associated with isolation should they venture into this frontier territory. To others, however, especially those who sought land, the Blue Ridge represented opportunity.

It was approximately one hundred years after the founding of Jamestown before colonists began to immigrate en masse into the southern mountains. The Great Wagon Road—or Valley Road, as it was called in Virginia—provided the best way into the mountains. The Valley Road followed old Indian trails for some seven hundred miles, starting near Philadelphia and running down the Shenandoah Valley. Near what is now Roanoke, Virginia, some travelers turned south along the Carolina Road, which led into the Piedmont region of North Carolina and South Carolina. Others continued into the mountains of southwest Virginia, east Tennessee, and beyond.

A community of Germans settled an area near present-day Luray, Virginia, in 1730. The Germans were followed by English Quakers, who in turn were followed by Scots-Irish, French Huguenots, Irish, Welsh, and more English. Some African American slaves were brought into the Blue Ridge by these settlers. Others came with owners who migrated from the Tidewater when the lands there became worn out by the relentless planting of tobacco.

In 1805, when the population of the entire nation was only two million, as many as ten thousand travelers passed through Abingdon in the far southwestern corner of Virginia. By some estimates, fully one-fourth of the present population of the United States has ancestors who used this route to move westward.

Groups traveling the Valley Road brought with them cultural practices from their diverse homelands. A few of these survive today in forms that are recognizable as "old country" traditions. But most blended over time with those from other cultures and evolved into something altogether new as people from different backgrounds moved and settled together. Musical exchanges among these groups proved particularly fruitful and resulted in unprecedented ways of playing music.

In the Blue Ridge, fiddles are almost always the lead instrument in old-time music. The Hill Billies, a string band named by record producer Ralph Peer, donned overalls and kerchiefs for this publicity photo from 1926. (Photograph courtesy of the Blue Ridge Institute, Ferrum, Va.)

THE FIDDLE AND BANJO

The fiddle and banjo ensemble, the core of the mountain string band and the symbol of Blue Ridge music to many Americans, is a prime example of a new flavor that emerged from the cultural stew simmering in the southern mountains in the years before the Civil War.

When Europeans first brought it to North America during the late seventeenth century, the fiddle was a novel and exciting instrument that was beginning to replace the hornpipe, tabor, and harp at country dances and other rural social gatherings in the Old World. The excitement it generated resulted partly from improvements to the instrument and partly from its increased availability. European luthiers like Antonio Stradivari of Cremona and Jacob Stainer in the Tyrol pioneered construction techniques that gave the instrument a deeper tone and greater projection. New wealth accrued from the tobacco trade allowed Virginia planters to purchase violins by these makers, or at least good copies of their instruments. Perhaps one such fiddle was the prize described in an announcement appearing in the *Virginia Gazette* in 1736, in which spectators in Hanover County were invited to hear twenty fiddlers compete for a fine violin.

Black slaves and white indentured servants did much of the music making at Virginia dances, and the *Gazette*'s advertisements for runaways sometimes mentioned that the escapee was a fiddler. Virginians seeking to acquire slaves and indentured servants sometimes specified that, in addition to the usual qualifications, they wanted a musician.

By the beginning of the nineteenth century, fiddles could be found in settlements throughout the Southern Appalachians, including Cherokee communities. Captain John Norton reported in his 1809 travel journal that some Cherokees were playing fiddles and doing English dances. Fiddles were played in people's homes for dances and for pleasure, at community work gatherings like cornshuckings and bean stringings, for special celebrations such as the last day of the school year, and at contests and fiddlers' conventions where musicians vied for awards and recognition.

The banjo has a far different lineage. No one knows exactly when the instrument first came to North America, but there is no doubt about where it came from. Banjo-making skills were introduced by West Africans brought to America to work on tobacco and sugar plantations. Before that the instrument had existed in Africa, in a bewildering array of forms, for hundreds of years.

President Thomas Jefferson was a fiddler who also seems to have had his

A variety of banjo styles evolved in western North Carolina and Virginia. Carroll Best of Haywood County, North Carolina, developed a complex three-fingered picking technique.

hands on a banjo at some point because he was able to describe the instrument and how it was tuned. In his book *Notes on the State of Virginia*, Jefferson said of black residents of the Blue Ridge, "The instrument propoer [*sic*] to them is the banjar which they brought hither from Africa."

African Americans playing the African banjo and the European fiddle formed the first uniquely American ensemble—the root of the root, the beginnings of a sound that would eventually shape blues, bluegrass, and country-and-western music, among other genres. Generations of travelers reported that black fiddle and banjo players provided music for dancing in many areas of the Southeast.

It is uncertain when whites took up banjo playing, but after 1800 the instrument was used by white entertainers who impersonated black banjoists, creating racial caricatures by wearing ragged clothing and blackening their faces with burnt cork. They told jokes, sang comedy songs and performed tunes like "Turkey in the Straw" and "Arkansas Traveler" on banjo, fiddle, hand drum, and bones. Some of these performers worked in early circus troops and were playing for Blue Ridge audiences by the early 1840s. They initiated the first international pop music fad, the so-called minstrel-show era, which lasted until the end of the century. During the heyday of minstrelsy, the banjo, a traditional instrument once used solely by country people, was adopted by urban players who could afford fine instruments. Banjo construction improved, and the instrument as we know it today was created.

Like all fads, minstrelsy passed, but it left an enduring legacy behind in the Blue Ridge. The banjo, the main prop of the minstrel performer, had found its way into the region, and in tandem with the fiddle it formed the core of the mountain string band. A number of minstrel tunes, usually divorced from their original lyrics, continue to be performed by musicians in the region today.

THE MYTH OF ISOLATION

The Blue Ridge began to attract the notice of the popular press shortly after the Civil War. Unfortunately, journalists sometimes valued imagination above accuracy when writing about the people and events of the region. Feuds and moonshine were favored themes, and by the 1920s the term "mountaineers" conjured up a widely disseminated stereotype of uneducated, fiercely independent people living among clans in remote hollers.

This pervasive notion of geographic and cultural isolation still colors public perception of the region's traditional music. Many believe that the relative inaccessibility of mountain communities allowed them to preserve their music in an unchanged, even primitive, state over generations. The most romantic version of this theory imagines mountain music as a hold-

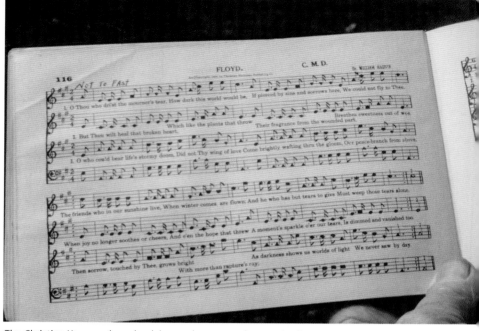

The *Christian Harmony* hymnbook is popular among shape-note singers in southwestern North Carolina. (Photograph by Mary Anne McDonald; courtesy of the North Carolina Arts Council)

over of the ballads, reels, and pipe tunes of the British Isles. But the influence of African American music and the minstrel stage demonstrates that the Blue Ridge was far from isolated, even in the early nineteenth century. Music in the region was shaped by other national events and trends as well. A few of these are worth noting.

At the beginning of the nineteenth century, a wave of religious revivals swept the South, reaching deeply into the Southern Appalachians. Songs associated with this "Great Awakening" entered the repertories of many church congregations in western North Carolina and Virginia. Shape-note hymns, named for the distinctively shaped musical notes that make sight reading easier, were brought around the same time to the Appalachians and other regions of the South by singing masters from New England.

The middle of the nineteenth century witnessed one of the cataclysmic events of American history, the Civil War. In the mountains of western North Carolina and Virginia, loyalties were sharply divided, and communities witnessed bitter conflicts among families and between neighbors who had chosen opposite sides. Traditional songs express this division, with bal-

Many different styles of religious songs and congregational singing developed in Blue Ridge churches throughout the 1800s, and many of them continue in use today. One of the older styles—practiced by whites, blacks, and Cherokees—involved unaccompanied congregational singing of hymn texts to traditional ballad melodies. Where congregations had few hymnbooks or could not read, a song leader would "line out" or chant a line or two of the text, then pause while the congregation repeated that text singing the familiar hymn tune, sometimes in a highly ornamented version. Such singing is practiced still by Primitive Baptists and German Baptist Brethren.

Participants in the shape-note singing at Morning Star Methodist Church in Canton, North Carolina, take a break to share dinner on the grounds.

Early Methodists developed another style of unaccompanied song that could be caught easily by ear. Their campmeeting and revival spirituals featured repeated lines and choruses and often used melodies derived from traditional dance tunes. Shape-note hymnbooks, which used a special shape for each note of the scale to facilitate sightreading, picked up both of these repertories but arranged them for three- or four-part unaccompanied choral performance. Singing masters taught rural people how to read this musical notation, and the song settings came into use both in church worship and in periodic singing conventions. The most popular shape-note books in the Blue Ridge were William Walker's The Southern Harmony and Musical Companion *(1835) and* The Christian Harmony *(1867); the latter is still used in "singings." Among the oldest Christian Harmony sings in the Blue Ridge region are the ones at Morning Star Church in Canton and at Etowah Elementary School in Etowah, North Carolina.*

In Primitive Baptist churches still, and in Methodist and other churches for many years, musical instruments were not allowed. The churches either did not find them authorized by the New Testament or disliked their association with dissolute behavior, so church singing was unaccompanied and stood in contrast to much of the music in the secular world outside. By the twentieth century, yet another style of singing entered both black and white churches in the Blue Ridge: up-tempo gospel songs performed with pianos, guitars, and other instruments, together with solo performances by featured groups.

The more mainstream congregations, rural and urban, have shifted from local Blue Ridge traditions to singing from hymnals issued by the national or regional printing houses of their denominations. The indigenous music has been little noticed by outsiders and overshadowed by national trends, but the older religious songs and traditional singing styles have been pervasive nevertheless. Well known to many longtime residents, they continue to enrich the musical landscape of the region.

—*Daniel W. Patterson and Beverly Bush Patterson*

lads such as "Going across the Mountain" promoting the Union's perspective while "Bright Sunny South" conveyed Southern sympathies.

Despite its divisiveness, the war did serve to expand the repertories of Blue Ridge musicians. Soldiers from the mountains traded tunes with fiddlers and banjo players from other parts of the South and learned pieces from regimental bands. After the conflict ended, mountain musicians brought home these tunes along with other songs composed to commemorate battles or convey the experiences of wartime.

In the late 1800s, logging and mining companies expanded their operations in the mountains of western North Carolina and Virginia, hiring laborers from across the region to mine coal and log the forests. Camps constructed to house and feed these workers became fertile swapping grounds for tunes. Large-scale mining and logging also required the building of railroads. The employment of African American work crews to lay track and drill tunnels introduced work songs and ballads like "John Henry" and "Swannanoa Tunnel" to mountain musicians.

By the turn of the twentieth century, mountain residents could buy merchandise made available to national markets by large mail-order companies. In addition to tools and clothing, they ordered musical instruments from Sears Roebuck and Montgomery Ward. Guitars, mandolins, autoharps, and cellos, now easily accessible, joined fiddles and banjos to form larger string-band ensembles, the precursors to the old-time and bluegrass bands so pervasive in the region today.

The invention of sound recordings and the birth of the recording industry in the 1920s and 1930s brought Blue Ridge music to the attention of a na-

A guitarist (in doorway) and an accordion player (at right) were part of this African American work crew that helped construct the Clinchfield Railroad through the Blue Ridge, ca. 1900–1930. (Photograph courtesy of the Blue Ridge Institute, Ferrum, Va.)

tional audience. To their surprise, urban record company executives discovered that a sizable market for stringband music existed among rural residents. The vitality of fiddle and banjo traditions in the Southern Appalachians inspired companies to set up temporary recording studios in towns like Asheville, Roanoke, and Bristol. The promotional campaigns devised to sell the recordings of Appalachian musicians often drew upon the stereotype of isolated mountaineers who had preserved the "old-time" music.

Most of the musicians from western North Carolina and Virginia who auditioned made only a handful of recordings, but a few, such as Ernest ("Pop") Stoneman of Galax, Virginia, J. E. and Wade Mainer of Buncombe County, North Carolina, and the Carter Family of Maces Springs, Virginia, had prolific recording careers and helped shape the development of country-and-western music. The influence of these groups proved so powerful that their playing styles and repertories began to supplement—and sometimes replace—local styles and tunes within the region.

About the same time that commercial labels were recording Blue Ridge musicians for profit, collectors interested in cultural preservation were

The late Evelyn Ramsey of Madison County learned ballads from family members who were documented by Cecil Sharp and his assistant, Maude Karpeles. Mrs. Ramsey's niece, Donna Ray Norton (right), is carrying on the family's singing tradition.

scouting the region to document traditional music. British scholar and folksong collector Cecil Sharp was one of the first. Sharp journeyed to the Blue Ridge around the time of the First World War to take down the words and music of the ballads he heard there. Sharp was captivated with the quality of the music he encountered and was surprised by the fact that people of all ages knew the songs. In his *English Folk Songs of the Southern Appalachians*, Sharp described some communities in the Blue Ridge as places where "singing is as common and almost as universal a practice as speaking."

Other music scholars and collectors followed Sharp. Their field recordings, along with those made by record companies, constitute a treasure trove of ballads and love songs, dance tunes, children's songs, hymns, spirituals, and gospel songs. Over the years, many people have plumbed this archive. Aaron Copland, perhaps the nation's best-known composer, interpreted traditional fiddle tunes in his classical works as a way to express the American spirit and cultural identity.

In 1957 a performing group called the Kingston Trio drew upon an obscure ballad collected from singer Frank Proffitt of western North Carolina for their hit recording "Hang Down Your Head, Tom Dooley." The success of this song helped launch the folksong revival of the fifties and sixties. Some Americans who were part of this movement became interested in the sources of songs performed by popular artists like the Kingston Trio and Joan Baez. Young urbanites began to visit the Blue Ridge to locate old-time and bluegrass musicians. They made recordings and documentary films of traditional artists and introduced mountain musicians to college and city audiences. Some were inspired to learn to play the music they heard performed in concerts or issued on recordings.

During the late 1960s, large numbers of outsiders began to attend music events in the Blue Ridge region. Fiddlers' conventions held in Union Grove, North Carolina, and Galax, Virginia, attracted crowds of young people motivated by the desire to hear music, learn tunes, or just to be part of a huge party.

Fiddler Tommy Jarrell and friends make music for a dance, 1980. (Photograph by Lyntha Eiler, Blue Ridge Parkway Project, BR8-LE1-19, American Folklife Center, Library of Congress)

Aspiring musicians from across the nation and from Europe and Japan continued to visit Blue Ridge music venues during the last quarter of the twentieth century. Some musicians like Tommy Jarrell and Fred Cockerham of Surry County, North Carolina, became musical role models for thousands of people who had grown up outside the region, a phenomenon noted by the *New Yorker* magazine in 1987.

BLUE RIDGE MUSIC TODAY

In the Blue Ridge, as in nearly all places in America nowadays, one can find fans and performers of almost any type of classical, contemporary, pop, and alternative music. In addition, recent immigrants from Mexico, Central America, and Asia are bringing their own musical tastes and styles to the region. In this mix, however, the established traditions of the Blue Ridge continue to thrive and evolve.

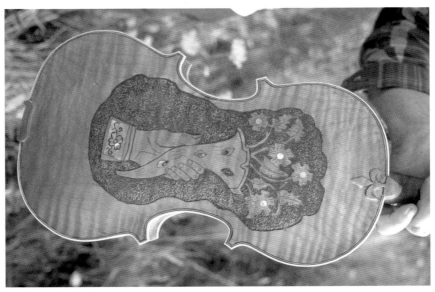

Audrey Hash Ham of Ashe County, North Carolina, carves ornate designs on her fiddles.

With guidance from local musician Emily Spencer, students at Mount Rogers High School in Grayson County, Virginia, formed a string band to perform at school functions and community events.

The Blue Ridge harbors a fine array of string bands. Old-time bands perform largely from an older dance music repertory. Bluegrass bands, which evolved in part from that old-time tradition over the last sixty years, play music intended more for listening than for dancing. Singers of the older Anglo-Irish ballads still live and perform in the region, and some historic forms of religious music survive as well. There's a vigorous tradition of making musical instruments—mainly fiddles, banjos, guitars, mandolins, and dulcimers. Some of the finest of these are made in small woodworking shops in the region.

Performers from the Blue Ridge—such as Doc Watson, Etta Baker, and Wayne Henderson, among others—are taking their music to audiences across the country and around the world. At the same time, visitors are making the journey to western North Carolina and Virginia to hear the music in its homeplace. Many young people growing up in mountain communities are playing the music passed down by their families and neighbors. They learn through informal apprenticeships with relatives and friends, by attending community musical events, or by taking more formal lessons offered in afterschool programs in some of the public schools. Several area colleges that offer traditional music camps and workshops provide scholarships to promising young musicians from the region. People from outside of the mountains have moved to Asheville, Blacksburg, and smaller communities in the Blue Ridge in order to get closer to music traditions and to a growing community of revivalist musicians. They bring new musical ideas and styles that are attracting an enthusiastic young audience.

The music of the Blue Ridge continues to inspire nontraditional art forms and to influence popular culture. Fiddle and banjo music of western North Carolina plays a prominent role in Charles Frazier's national best-selling novel *Cold Mountain*, while films like *O Brother Where Art Thou?* and *Songcatcher* are introducing regional musical styles, and outstanding Blue Ridge musicians, to new audiences.

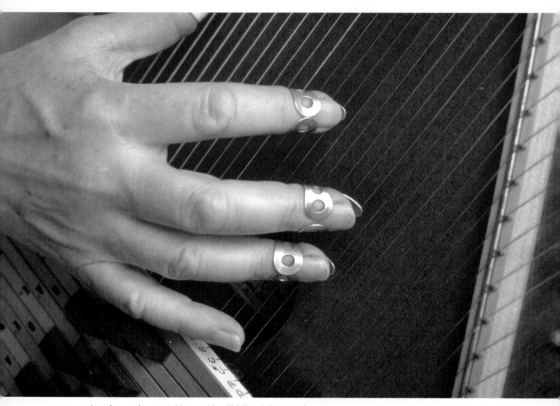

Autoharp player at Mount Airy Fiddlers' Convention

REGION ONE

MUSIC IN THE HEART OF SOUTHERN APPALACHIA

SURRY COUNTY

Roads leading north out of Mount Airy, North Carolina, toward Galax, Virginia, link a series of small communities that can claim some of the richest music-making traditions in the Blue Ridge. Round Peak, Pine Ridge, Skull Camp, Lowgap, and Beulah all have been home to generations of master musicians who evolved a local fiddle and banjo ensemble tradition into a powerful brand of stringband music—music that continues to be played at dances, fiddlers' conventions, and fundraising events held in these communities. In addition, old-time music enthusiasts throughout the world now acclaim this tradition.

In contrast to these small rural communities, Mount Airy, a large town of 10,000 residents, has become a center for traditional music in recent decades. It is also an economic hub for the region, the home of industries that produce granite products, textiles, and furniture. The vigorous local economy helps to support the malls, restaurants, and motels that have grown up around the edges of Mount Airy and the theaters and museum that flourish closer to downtown.

Despite the ongoing activity, Mount Airy maintains a reputation as a sleepy southern hamlet. This image is a lingering effect of the success of the town's most famous native son, actor Andy Griffith, and the idealized small town of Mayberry that he created for his television program, *The Andy Griffith Show*. Griffith drew heavily from the character of Mount Airy in depicting his fictional town, at times even incorporating actual places, such as the Snappy Lunch Café that he frequented as a youth, into the series.

Griffith was also well acquainted with local music traditions. In some of the early episodes he would take up his guitar and sing such songs as "Riding on That New River Train." In episodes that featured the fictional "hill-

Charles Dowell prepares breakfast at the Snappy Lunch Café.

billy" clan, the Darling family, Griffith and his co-writers often included bluegrass music, albeit performed by a Missouri band, the Dillards.

Due to the long-standing national popularity of Andy Griffith and his show, the Mayberry theme is highly visible in the commercial life of Mount Airy. The name "Mayberry" appears frequently on business marquees, on restaurant menus, and in storefront window displays. Visitors come to Mount Airy, sometimes by the busload, hoping to find the places where myth and reality intersect. Although little about the present-day town resembles Mayberry, the Surry County musical traditions that influenced a young Andy Griffith remain strong.

❇ WPAQ *Merry-Go-Round*

One particular weekly radio program in the Blue Ridge—the WPAQ *Merry-Go-Round* on Saturday morning—has an exceptionally long history of presenting the best of live traditional mountain music. In fact, WPAQ station owner Ralph Epperson has kept traditional music at the forefront of his radio programming for more than fifty years now. Back when Epperson's newly inaugurated radio station first went on the air, live and recorded music performed by native Southern Appalachian musicians immediately became the cornerstone of his broadcasts. Over the years a host of regional and national music legends, including Tommy Jarrell, Benton Flippen, The Carter Family, Mac Wiseman, Lester Flatt and Earl Scruggs, and Bill and Charlie Monroe, have gathered before the microphones for the Saturday morning broadcast. The program's popularity and proven devotion to regional music has resulted in WPAQ's *Merry-Go-Round*'s becoming the third-longest-running live radio show in the nation.

The Downtown Cinema Theatre, where the *Merry-Go-Round* broadcast originates, is a vintage movie theater that will seat up to 450 people. An ornate marquee on the theater's facade looms over the sidewalk of Mount Airy's Main Street, announcing the day and time of the WPAQ *Merry-Go-Round*, of other upcoming performances and concerts, and of the current motion picture attraction being shown there. The place remains an active movie house as well as a venue for live performances. A street-front ticket

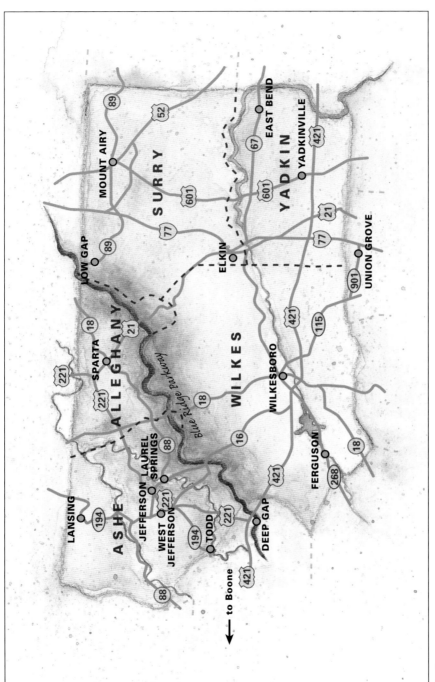

Region 1

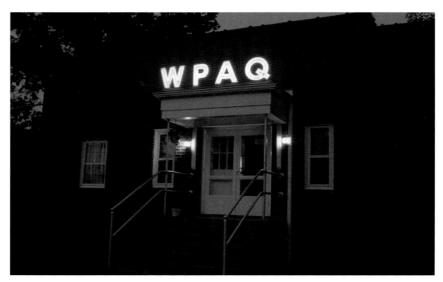

WPAQ in Mount Airy, North Carolina, began live broadcasts of local musicians in 1948.

booth is situated to the left of the front entrance to the theater, but since the *Merry-Go-Round* is a free event, the booth is empty on that day.

The small lobby of the Downtown Cinema Theatre is reminiscent of many found in surviving 1930s-era movie houses. There's a snack bar where Arts Council volunteers sell snacks and soft drinks, and the heavy smell of freshly popped and buttered popcorn permeates the entire building. To the left and right of the snack bar are curtained doorways that open into the theater auditorium. Another pair of doors, located on opposite sides of the lobby, lead up twin stairs to a mezzanine and to the balcony seating.

A typical Saturday morning visit to the *Merry-Go-Round* might go something like this: When you first enter from Main Street and pass from the brightly lit lobby into the auditorium, the theater auditorium seems very dark. It takes a second or two for your eyes to adjust to the darkness, but after a moment you're able to discern a stage and rows of seats. At the rear of the theater, on the right, a technician sits behind a dimly lit sound control panel. He greets visitors with a friendly nod as they enter the room. A few patrons are seated randomly in twos and threes around the house. In front of the stage, at floor level, is a small open area for dancing. The theater is comfortable, clean, and well maintained.

A group of musicians, five or six, are playing onstage. Each takes a turn leading as they perform an extended medley of old-time mountain tunes. They play banjos, fiddles, and guitars. The audience members applaud politely after each song is completed. The time is ten minutes before eleven, and the final moments of the weekly Saturday morning jam session are passing by. At eleven o'clock, the WPAQ *Merry-Go-Round* radio show will begin another of its live broadcasts from the Downtown Cinema Theatre.

Once the final number from the jam session is completed, the house lights brighten a bit and some of the musicians drift offstage and into the auditorium to talk with friends and visitors who are there in the audience. A few minutes later Clyde Johnson, the host and master of ceremonies of the *Merry-Go-Round*, appears onstage. Assisted by several of the musicians who have just finished playing, Clyde rearranges the microphones and stands, sets up a small table and chair off to one side, and takes his appointed seat there. An unseen something trips a release and suddenly a large bright banner reading "WPAQ's Saturday Morning Merry-Go-Round" is unfurled on the rear wall of the stage. A trio of young women armed with banjo, fiddle, and guitar walk quietly in from the back of the theater, nod in Clyde's direction, and take up their positions onstage behind the microphones, facing the audience.

Ralph Epperson, founder of WPAQ and champion of traditional mountain music.

After a short pause, the house lights dim, a bright red "on the air" electric sign lights up on the proscenium, and Johnson welcomes the theater and radio audiences to the program. He quickly introduces the trio of musicians and they immediately take off with a bright rendition of "Boil Them Cabbage Down." Just like that, another episode of Appalachia's longest-running live radio program is on the air. The music is fine, the scene is friendly and comfortable, and the famous pork-chop sandwich of the Snappy Lunch Café awaits you right across the street. It's a good day.

LOCATION: To find the Downtown Cinema Theater, take US 52 toward Mount Airy. When the highway splits into US 52 Business and US 52 Bypass, stay on US 52 Bypass. Exit at NC 89 and turn east toward the downtown. Follow NC 89 until you reach Renfro St. and turn left. Turn left again when you reach Moore Ave., and left yet again on Main St. The Downtown Cinema will be on your left.

CONTACT: Kelly Epperson, WPAQ, 316 Robin Rd., Mount Airy, NC 27030, (336) 786-6111, (336) 789-8332; or Greater Mount Airy Chamber of Commerce, PO Box 913, 200 N. Main St., Mount Airy, NC 27030, (800) 948-0949, (336) 786-6116, ‹tourism@visitmayberry.com›, ‹www.visitmayberry.com›

Performers on WBLT in Bedford, Virginia, ca. 1950 (Photograph courtesy of Shirley Hunter and the Blue Ridge Institute, Ferrum, Va.)

"You just can't find any music when you leave out from around here," says musician Tom Barr of Galax, Virginia. His is a complaint heard frequently from natives of the Blue Ridge who leave the mountains. "What they call country music outside of here—well, that ain't country!" is often next. What they mean, of course, is that very few local radio stations outside the Blue Ridge regularly, if ever, play recordings of truly traditional southern mountain music, be it old-time, bluegrass, or gospel. Even fewer have regular programming that features live musicians playing mountain music.

The long tradition of broadcasting live and recorded regional music on the radio is an all but unequalled factor in the continued widespread popularity of traditional music in the Blue Ridge. Numerous musicians who grew up in the region acknowledge that, as youngsters, they learned their very first old-time songs "off WPAQ or the Grand Old Opry.*" Hillsville, Virginia, banjo player Jim Marshall, speaking of the influence of radio on his early development as a musician, said, "We always played music on Saturday nights. Then we got a radio. [Our friends would] come to our house and listen to the* Grand Ol' Opry. *Didn't many people have radios then. Mama got one though, and everybody would come to listen to it. That's where I picked up the Mainer style of picking."*

Like Jim Marshall, but a number of years later, Caldwell County, North Carolina, native Glenn Bolick and his family were also radio fans. "We had a battery-powered radio at our house," said Bolick. "That was before we got electric power. We listened to the Grand Old Opry *on the radio sometimes on Saturday night. Hickory, North Carolina, had a station back in those days. The Blue Sky Boys, Bill and Earl Bolick, were distant cousins of ours, and they were on the radio."*

When asked about the contemporary influence of radio programming on the music of the region in which he lives, Tom Barr declared, "If you go away from around here on vacation somewhere and you want to hear any good music, you have to take it with you. So we carry our guitars with us."

Whether the programming is recorded or live, vintage or contemporary, radio stations featuring traditional music and musicians are an important and popular aspect of the music scene in the Blue Ridge region today.

A scan of your radio dial while you're driving through northwestern North Carolina or southwestern Virginia will reveal to you what the local folks are talking about when they speak of finding or not finding "real good" music on the radio. You can get station WPAQ in Mount Airy by tuning your radio dial to 740 AM.

❄ Downtown Cinema Theatre Jam Session

From 9:00 to 11:00 A.M. on Saturdays, just before the live radio broadcast of WPAQ's *Merry-Go-Round*, there's a jam session on the stage of the Downtown Cinema Theater. This stage presentation showcases—on a first-come, first-seen basis—the talents of any local bands and individual traditional musicians who show up to play that morning. The jam session, like the radio broadcast that follows, is free and open to the public. Arts Council volunteers sell popcorn, candy, and soft drinks in the theater lobby to help cover operating expenses. The musicians perform for free. At the same time that the stage show is unfolding in the theater auditorium, there's often a second, less formal, jam session taking place upstairs on the mezzanine level. Be sure to hear both.

LOCATION: To find the Downtown Cinema Theatre, follow the directions given above for WPAQ's *Merry-Go-Round*.

CONTACT: Tanya B. Rees, Surry Arts Council, PO Box 141, Mount Airy, NC 27030, (800) 286-6193, (336) 786-2222 ‹surryarts@advi.net›, ‹www.surryarts.org›; or Greater Mount Airy Chamber of Commerce, PO Box 913, 200 N. Main St., Mount Airy, NC 27030, (800) 948-0949, (336) 786-6116 ‹tourism@visitmayberry.com›, ‹www.visitmayberry.com›

❄ Blue Ridge Jamboree

The Blue Ridge Jamboree is a monthly performance of old-time, bluegrass, gospel, and country music presented in the auditorium of the Andy

RADIO STATIONS ALONG THE TRAILS

The following Blue Ridge radio stations are among those that produce programs featuring traditional live or recorded music played by regional musicians.

REGION 1
WDSL 1520 AM, *Mocksville, N.C.*
WKSK 580 AM,
  West Jefferson, N.C.
WPAQ 740 AM, *Mount Airy, N.C.*
WSGH 1040 AM, *East Bend, N.C.*

REGION 2
WBRF 98.1 FM, *Galax, Va.*
WMEV 93.9 FM, *Marion, Va.*
WMEV 1010 AM, *Marion, Va.*
WVTR 91.9 FM, *Marion, Va.*

REGION 3
WCIS 760 AM, *Morganton, N.C.*
WETS 88.9 FM, *Boone, N.C.*
WKJX 1080 AM, *Lenoir, N.C.*

REGION 4
WAKG 103.3 FM, *Danville, Va.*
WKDE 105.5 FM, *Altavista, Va.*

REGION 5
WFMX 105.7 FM, *Statesville, N.C.*
WKYK 1450 AM, *Burnsville, N.C.*
WNCW 88.7 FM, *Spindale, N.C.*
WTOE 940 AM, *Burnsville, N.C.*
WWOL 780 AM, *Forest City, N.C.*

REGION 6
WGFC 1030 AM, *Floyd, Va.*
WJLM 93.5 FM, *Salem, Va.*
WKEX 1430 AM, *Blacksburg, Va.*
WPSK 107.1 FM, *Pulaski, Va.*
WUVT 90.7 FM, *Blacksburg, Va.*
WVRU 89.9 FM, *Radford, Va.*
WVTF 89.1 FM, *Roanoke, Va.*

REGION 7
WCQS 88.1 FM, *Asheville, N.C.*
WHKP 1450 AM,
  Hendersonville, N.C.
WJFJ 1160 AM, *Columbus, N.C.*

REGION 8
WAMV 1420 AM, *Amherst, Va.*
WKDE 105.5 FM, *Altavista, Va.*
WREL 96.7 FM, *Lexington, Va.*
WTJU 91.1 FM, *Charlottesville, Va.*
WVTU 89.3 FM,
  Charlottesville, Va.
WYYD 107.9 FM, *Amherst, Va.*

REGION 9
WBHN 1590 AM, *Bryson City, N.C.*
WCQS 89.7 FM, *Waynesville, N.C.*

Benton Flippen (left) and Verlen Clifton warm up in preparation
for a live radio performance. (Photograph by Rob Amberg)

Griffith Playhouse. Three local musicians started this event in the mid-1980s
as the Mount Airy Hometown Opry. The Surry Arts Council later assumed
responsibility for the event and changed the name. At the Blue Ridge Jamboree, a master of ceremonies introduces local and regional bands that play
for listeners as well as for flatfoot and clog dancers. Dancing is seen as an integral part of the music and is encouraged from the stage.

The Jamboree happens the third Saturday evening of each month beginning at 7:30 P.M. An admission fee is charged.

LOCATION: The Andy Griffith Playhouse is located at 218 Rockford St. in
    Mount Airy. Take US 52 toward Mount Airy. When the highway splits into US 52

Business and US 52 Bypass, stay on US 52 Bypass until it intersects with US 601. Take US 601 North, which turns into Rockford St. At the second traffic light, you will see the Andy Griffith Playhouse on your left. Turn left into the parking lot.

CONTACT: Tanya B. Rees, Surry Arts Council, PO Box 141, Mount Airy, NC 27030, (800) 286-6193, (336) 786-2222, ‹surryarts@advi.net›, ‹www.surryarts.org›; or Greater Mount Airy Chamber of Commerce, PO Box 913, 200 N. Main St., Mount Airy, NC 27030, (800) 948-0949, (336) 786-6116, ‹tourism@visitmayberry.com›, ‹www.visitmayberry.com›

✵ Thursday Evenings at the Andy Griffith Playhouse

On Thursday evenings, there's a jam session on the ground floor of the Andy Griffith Playhouse in Mount Airy. This jam spotlights the talents of the many veteran musicians who reside in or around the Mount Airy community. At the same time that the old-timers are gathering indoors, it's not unusual to find a more spontaneous gathering of younger musicians outside in an adjacent courtyard and parking area. Many visitors and regular listeners can be seen alternating between the two performance areas, trying to take in as much music as possible from both scenes.

The sessions begin at 7:00 P.M. and wind down around 11:00 P.M. This is a free event.

LOCATION: To find the Andy Griffith Playhouse, follow the directions given above for the Blue Ridge Jamboree.

CONTACT: Tanya B. Rees, Surry Arts Council, PO Box 141, Mount Airy, NC 27030, (800) 286-6193, (336) 786-2222, ‹surryarts@advi.net›, ‹www.surryarts.org›; or Greater Mount Airy Chamber of Commerce, PO Box 913, 200 N. Main St., Mount Airy, NC 27030, (800) 948-0949, (336) 786-6116, ‹tourism@visitmayberry.com›, ‹www.visitmayberry.com›

✵ Annual Music Events at the Andy Griffith Playhouse

In the fourth week of September each year, Mount Airy hosts a three-day event (Thursday through Saturday) called Mayberry Days in Downtown Mount Airy that includes bluegrass music and traditional storytelling. On the Thursday of Mayberry Days, there's a free jam session at the Andy Griffith Playhouse from 5:00 to 10:00 P.M. A similar free event called the Bluegrass Picnic takes place on the playhouse lawn the Thursday before the Fourth of July each year. This one also runs from 5:00 to 10:00 P.M.

LOCATION: Follow the directions given above for the Blue Ridge Jamboree.
CONTACT: Tanya B. Rees, Surry Arts Council, PO Box 141, Mount Airy, NC 27030, (800) 286-6193, (336) 786-2222, ‹surryarts@advi.net›, ‹www.surryarts.org›; or Greater Mount Airy Chamber of Commerce, PO Box 913, 200 N. Main St., Mount Airy, NC 27030, (800) 948-0949, (336) 786-6116, ‹tourism@visitmayberry.com›, ‹www.visitmayberry.com›

❈ Mount Airy Bluegrass and Old-Time Fiddlers' Convention

One of the more significant music festivals held in the Blue Ridge every summer is the annual Bluegrass and Old-Time Fiddlers' Convention at Mount Airy, an event that is now more than three decades old. Because the fame of Surry County musicians has spread throughout the nation and the world, the event attracts hundreds of musicians and thousands of mountain music fans.

The Mount Airy Fiddlers' Convention was originated by G. F. Collins, who with Kyle Creed, Paul Sutphin, Verlen Clifton, Earnest East, and Fred Cockerham formed a legendary band called the Camp Creek Boys. This band, which for years won blue ribbons at fiddlers' conventions around the region, recorded a now-famous record album in the late 1960s that was singularly important in sparking a national interest in Blue Ridge music.

Other local musicians who have had a considerable impact on the revival and perpetuation of old-time musical styles and repertories throughout the Blue Ridge and beyond include Tommy Jarrell, Benton Flippen, Mac Snow,

Participants wait in line for their chance to compete.

Fiddler Earnest East, who grew up in the small community string band of Round Peak north of Mount Airy, helped to develop the powerful stringband music now associated with Surry County. (Photograph by Rob Amberg)

and Chester McMillan. After these music makers were documented on records, aspiring musicians from beyond the region began traveling to Surry County to learn from them. Tommy Jarrell, in particular, welcomed many visitors into his home and became the focus of a great deal of attention and adulation from revivalist fiddle and banjo players.

During its early years, the Mount Airy Fiddlers' Convention was mainly a local event, but gradually outsiders began showing up to hear the performances of their mentors and to take advantage of the opportunity to associate with the Surry County players they admired. As more and more revivalist musicians emulated the local musical styles, the Fiddlers' Convention gained participants who wanted to perform alongside the old-timers. Even now, after many of the original master artists have died, younger musicians continue to gather at Mount Airy. Many of them look upon the event as a kind of homecoming or reunion.

This two-night convention is sponsored by the Mount Airy American Legion and the local VFW. Appropriately, it's staged at the Mount Airy Veterans Memorial Park, a broad, grassy, ten-acre field that contains the festival stage, a huge camping area, and parking for three thousand cars. The park is surrounded on three sides by low wooded hills that lend the event a feeling of isolation from the nearby town.

Umbrellas, ice cream, and good music keep the audience happy in the midst of a summer shower.

The single stage is basically an open-sided truck trailer outfitted with stage lights and a sound system. Participating musicians line up and socialize beneath a large backstage tent while they're waiting their turn to perform. Contestants compete in a number of categories, including bluegrass and old-time band, bluegrass and old-time fiddle, bluegrass and old-time banjo, guitar, mandolin, bass, dobro, dulcimer, autoharp, folksong, and dance. More than two thousand dollars in prize money is awarded each year, along with a long list of ribbons and trophies. A platform near the stage allows for dancing, and there's lots of open space out front on the grassy lawn where audience members can spread out their blankets and set up their folding chairs. A limited quantity of public seating, shaded by a large canvas canopy, is available near the performance stage.

As with other fiddlers' conventions in the region, a compelling feature of the Mount Airy Bluegrass and Old-Time Fiddlers' Convention is the preponderance of freewheeling jam sessions that take place all around the campground—and all around the clock. Activities on the main performance stage are broadcast live over WPAQ 740 AM radio. In 2000 the convention was attended by more than four thousand people, despite a thunderous rainstorm that disrupted the Saturday proceedings.

The Mount Airy Bluegrass and Old Time Fiddlers' Convention is held annually on the first full weekend in June. The music starts at 7:00 P.M. on Friday evening and again on Saturday at 9:30 A.M. There is an admission charge, though preschoolers are admitted free.

Camping is available at the festival site on a first-come, first-served basis, and the owners of many of the more than one thousand campers and RVs that show up every year arrive as early in the week as possible to better their chances of landing their favorite parking spot. There is a fee for camping. The festival grounds are well furnished with restrooms, concession stands, and picnic shelters.

LOCATION: To find Veterans Memorial Park, take US 52 toward Mount Airy. When the highway splits into US 52 Business and US 52 Bypass, stay on US 52 Bypass until you come to the NC 89 exit. Take this exit and turn east toward the downtown. Follow NC 89 east to Renfro St. and turn left (this street turns into N. Main St.). Go to the next traffic light at the intersection of N. Main St. and Lebanon St. Take a left onto W. Lebanon and proceed through one traffic light. Veterans Memorial Park is on the left at 691 W. Lebanon St.

CONTACT: Jack Jones, 116 W. Poplar St., Mount Airy, NC 27030, (336) 786-6830, (336) 786-2551; Greater Mount Airy Chamber of Commerce, PO Box 913, 200 N. Main St., Mount Airy, NC 27030, (800) 948-0949, (336) 786-6116, ‹tourism@visitmayberry.com›, ‹www.visitmayberry.com›

❉ Autumn Leaves Festival

This festival was started to celebrate the end of the tobacco and apple seasons in the Mount Airy area. Now it has become a celebration of the

Vendor Jack Chapman dips candy apples at the Autumn Leaves Festival.

magnificent fall colors that decorate the Blue Ridge every autumn. The old-time, bluegrass, and gospel music featured at this festival is broadcast live over station WPAQ 740 AM. It's a special treat to listen to the live music on the radio as you approach the festival grounds in your car, and then to reach the music stage and find it all happening there before you.

The festival is held on Main Street in downtown Mount Airy on Friday, Saturday, and Sunday of the second weekend in October. The festivities begin at 1:30 P.M. on Friday, at 8:30 A.M. on Saturday, and at noon on Sunday.

LOCATION: Take US 52 toward Mount Airy. When the highway splits into US 52 Business and US 52 Bypass, stay on US 52 Bypass. Exit at NC 89 and turn east toward the downtown. Follow NC 89 to Renfro St. and turn left. Turn left again when you reach Moore Ave., then left yet again onto Main St.

CONTACT: Yvonne Nichols, Greater Mount Airy Chamber of Commerce, PO Box 913, Mount Airy, NC 27030, (800) 948-0949, (336) 786-6116 ext. 5, ‹admin@mtairyncchamber.org›; or Greater Mount Airy Chamber of Commerce, PO Box 913, 200 N. Main St., Mount Airy, NC 27030, (800) 948-0949, (336) 786-6116, ‹tourism@visitmayberry.com›, ‹www.visitmayberry.com›

❄ Sonker Festival at the Edwards-Franklin House

West of Mount Airy, on Haystack Road in the community of Lowgap, you can attend a festival honoring a distinctive Appalachian deep-dish fruit or sweet-potato pie called a "sonker." Sponsored by the Surry County Historical Society on the first Saturday in October, this festival benefits the preservation of the two-hundred-year-old Edwards-Franklin House in Lowgap. There's plenty of old-time music and lots of tasty food.

LOCATION: The Edwards-Franklin House is located seven miles west of Mount Airy. Take NC 89 West out of Mount Airy. Turn left onto Beulah Rd. about one mile after you pass under I-77. Drive approximately one mile on Beulah Rd. and turn west onto Haystack Rd. Follow Haystack Rd. for approximately three miles. You will cross a bridge immediately before reaching the Edwards-Franklin House on the right.

CONTACT: Cama Merritt, 832 E. Country Club Rd., Mount Airy, NC 27030, (336) 786-8359, ‹rmerritt@infoave.net›; or Greater Mount Airy Chamber of Commerce, PO Box 913, 200 N. Main St., Mount Airy, NC 27030, (800) 948-0949, (336) 786-6116, ‹tourism@visitmayberry.com›, ‹www.visitmayberry.com›; or Mount Airy Visitors Center, (336) 789-4636

❄ Alleghany Jubilee

On Friday and Saturday evenings year round in the town of Sparta, the seat of North Carolina's Alleghany County, mountain dancing takes place on Main Street. By 7:00 P.M. small groups of people can be found standing around outside the Old Spartan Theater, waiting not so patiently for the band to strike up its first tune of the evening. Others find a seat inside the theater and change from their usual footwear into their stark-white, steel-tap-bottomed dancing shoes. Others quietly converse over a cup of coffee. The scene is the weekly Alleghany Jubilee—where flatfooting, clogging, buck dancing, and the mountain two-step are the order of the evening.

The Spartan Theater is a narrow building located about midway along downtown Sparta's Main Street. Its exterior is that of an old storefront and its interior is an interesting mix of snack bar, dance floor, performance stage, and sporadic groupings of wall-mounted memorabilia. The miscellany of objects displayed on the interior walls of the hall includes snapshots of patrons dancing, eating, and having fun, group portraits of various bands that have appeared there over the years, a few reproductions of paintings depicting vintage musical instruments, several large plywood silhouettes of dancing couples, and a variety of other mountain music- and dance-related decorations.

Three groups of vintage folding theater seats are fixed in rows near the rear of the long rectangular room, creating two narrow aisles that lead forward to the open dance floor. Additional rows of seats and chairs line the side walls, and at the far end of the room is the bandstand—a raised wall-to-wall platform crowded with a sound system and the usual stage paraphernalia—mic stands, stools, speakers, lights, drapes, and so on. By far the greater part of the room is its cavernous center, which is meant for dancing.

Suddenly, at eight o'clock sharp, the band (which has been quietly tuning up onstage for the past twenty minutes or so) lets go with a fast-paced mountain favorite—"Old Joe Clark"—at considerable volume, fiddle and banjo in the lead. Just as suddenly, sixty or more dancers hit the floor and begin rhythmically shuffling around the rooms, clogging or flatfooting. Their white leather shoes have hard steel taps affixed to heel and toe, and the dancers stamp loudly and with great zeal on the hardwood floor in unison with the rhythm of the old-time fiddle tune. For the uninitiated, it's a stunning moment.

The two-step is danced to slower tunes.

The White Top Mountain Band is a favorite of dancers in the region.

A covered-dish supper precedes the music and dance on Tuesday nights.

On Tuesday nights there's a free bluegrass and old-time picking session, with dancing, inside the Spartan Theater from 7:00 to 9:00 P.M. This event, which is attended primarily by local folks, ends with a "potluck" supper, the components of which are brought in by attendees. The public is welcome to join in, but everyone attending is expected to contribute a dish to the spread if they intend to eat supper.

The Old Spartan Theater is open year round on Friday and Saturday nights from 8:00 to 11:00 P.M. There is an admission fee, but children under twelve get in free. There is plenty of on- and off-street parking nearby. Coffee, soft drinks, and snacks are available inside the theater.

LOCATION: To get to the Old Spartan Theater, take US 21 into downtown Sparta. The theater is on Main St. opposite the courthouse.

CONTACT: Ernest and Agnes Joines, PO Box 891, Sparta, NC 28675, (336) 372-4591; or Alleghany County Chamber of Commerce, 348 S. Main St., Sparta, NC 28675, (800) 372-5473, (336) 372-5473, ‹allegcofc@skybest.com›, ‹www.sparta-nc.com›

✵ Alleghany County Fiddlers' Convention

The Alleghany County Fiddlers' Convention, which takes place on the third Friday and Saturday in July, is a relatively young competition that has quickly gained popularity among regional musicians. Located in this cradle of old-time music, the competition attracts a large gathering of exceptional players and knowledgeable music fans. Many people arrive early to set up their campsites and to join one of the many jam sessions happening at the festival site, the Higgins Agricultural Fairgrounds north of Sparta.

By Friday evening, when the competition begins, the festival grounds have become home to a new tent and RV community that hums with the continuous sounds of old-time and bluegrass music. Music shared at the impromptu jam sessions among the campsites is generally as significant as the music that's performed onstage. And throughout the weekend dancers

A group of young musicians practices for the band competition.

crowd onto a large wooden floor at the side of the stage, where they clog or flatfoot to the rhythm of the contest tunes. Live radio coverage of the event is broadcast on WCOK 1060 AM in Sparta.

The convention begins at 7:00 P.M. on Friday evening and continues on Saturday starting at noon. Playoffs begin at 7:00 P.M. on Saturday. There is an admission fee. Camping is free unless you need an electrical hookup.

LOCATION: The Alleghany County Fiddlers' Convention is sponsored by the Sparta-Alleghany County Volunteer Fire Department and is held at the Higgins Agricultural Fairgrounds. From Sparta, travel west on US 21 for approximately one mile. The fairgrounds are located on your left.

CONTACT: Lynn Worth, 334 Reynolds Rd., Sparta, NC 28675, (336) 372-8809, ‹savfd@skybest.com›, ‹www.Ls.net/~fiddler/›; or Alleghany County Chamber of Commerce, 348 S. Main St., Sparta, NC 28675, (800) 372-5473, (336) 372-5473, ‹allegcofc@skybest.com›, ‹www.sparta-nc.com›

❋ Hog Stomp

Every Thursday evening in Sturgills, North Carolina, there's a social gathering, dance, and jam session that's locally called the Hog Stomp. This friendly and fun event is held at the Old Helton School, a small brick-and-frame building in the northern section of Ashe County that serves as a community center. Led principally by tobacco farmer and bluegrass banjo player Larry Pennington and his fiddler friend Dean Sturgill, this weekly event is truly a community-based entertainment venue. It's very popular with the local folks, and the small classroom-turned-concert-hall is frequently filled to overflowing as soon as the seven o'clock starting time clicks by.

Despite the fact that the participating musicians are numerous—as many as fifteen at times—the event is really more a performance than it is a jam session. There is a clear delineation between the performing musicians and the appreciative audience members who show up to listen and to dance to the music.

The musicians stand together at one end of the room as they play. A vari-

The jam session at Helton School

ety of secondhand chairs and sofas, two deep, line the walls around the room. A small closet-sized kitchen on the end of the room opposite the players is furnished with a countertop that holds a pot of fresh coffee, home-baked cakes, and storebought cookies that have been brought by ladies from nearby communities.

While the musicians play, a small number of individual dancers may occasionally flatfoot dance inside the circle of listeners. Otherwise, most simply sit comfortably to the side, watch the musicians, and listen to the music. At times, Larry Pennington and several others will demonstrate a bit of "showbiz" trickery in which three musicians play a pair of banjos together. The first player works the fretboard of banjo number 1 with his left hand, and a second musician plays the same instrument's strings with his or her right hand while at the same time fretting banjo number 2 with the left. Yet a third player strums the strings of the second banjo with his or her right hand. Together, the three musicians play a blindingly fast and precisely coordinated bluegrass tune on the two instruments at once, with amazingly good results. The trick is quite clever and probably needs to be seen to be fathomed.

The music at the Old Helton School is typically performed in two sets, each lasting about an hour or a little more. If the weather isn't too cold or

Banjoists Larry Pennington and Trish Kilby play a tune together using one instrument.

rainy, the musicians will often move their second set out-of-doors into an adjacent parking area or onto the elongated concrete porch that borders the south side of the building. Music making and dancing continue until around 10:00 P.M.

LOCATION: Take US 221 to West Jefferson. In West Jefferson, take NC 194 North approximately ten miles to Lansing. Turn right at the only traffic light in Lansing. Continue on 194 until you come to a small intersection beside Evans Country Store in the Sturgills/Helton community. Turn right at this intersection, pass one house, and turn right again—just before the concrete bridge—into the Old Helton School driveway. The school is located at the end of the driveway.

CONTACT: Dean Sturgill, 1941 Spencer Branch Rd., Lansing, NC 28643, (336) 384-3895; or Ashe County Chamber of Commerce, 6 N. Jefferson Ave., West Jefferson, NC 28694, (336) 246-9550, ‹ashechamber@skybest.com›, ‹www.ashechamber.com›

❋ Mountain Music Jamboree

Not far from Sparta, near the community of Glendale Springs, a popular celebration of mountain music and dance is held every Saturday night from October through May and on Friday and Saturday nights from June through September. This event features old-time and bluegrass music played for the benefit of the many flatfoot dancers, cloggers, buck dancers, two-steppers, and square dancers who crowd into the place every week. Folks arrive early—the music starts at 7:00 P.M.—and dance until 11:00.

Local musician and caller Arvill Scott began the Mountain Music Jamboree fifteen years ago in a former schoolhouse in nearby Laurel Springs. After five years he moved the event to Burgiss Barn, a restaurant and bed-and-breakfast built from trees felled in 1989 by Hurricane Hugo. In 2002 the Jamboree moved again to the current location near Glendale Springs to accommodate a growing audience of dancers and listeners. Attendance currently averages two hundred per night, but the new and spacious building on NC 16 has room for more.

The music at the Jamboree features many of the region's most accomplished old-time and bluegrass musicians. On most nights two groups—one old-time and one bluegrass—alternate sets. Bands that perform with extraordinary skill are sometimes rewarded with a "dance ovation," in which the dancers refuse to abandon the dance floor even after the last tune is finished and the band has left the stage. The appreciative dancers simply continue to dance unaccompanied until the musicians return to the stage and perform an encore.

LARRY DEAN PENNINGTON
I HAD THE SOUND IN MY HEAD

Larry Pennington of Ashe County, North Carolina, a founding member of the popular and well-traveled band Big Country Bluegrass, is a remarkably skilled and highly regarded bluegrass banjo player. Pennington is also a tobacco farmer.

My name's Larry Dean Pennington. I live at Warrensville, North Carolina. I was born in Ashe County in 1946, the fourth day of August. I growed up around music. By the time I was big enough to know anything, I was listening to music. Back years ago people didn't have that much to do, so they made their own entertainment. Everybody went to their neighbors' houses and played music. It just seems to be bred into the people around here. And they pass it down. My daddy, he played a little bit of what I guess you'd call a 1940s-something style—which is just a finger and a thumb, you know. He didn't have the three-finger roll.

We enjoyed the music. My mother, she was a great inspiration to me on my music. She'd say, "That's 'Pretty Polly,'" or "that's so-and-so." That really helped me. I knew from the first what I wanted to play was a banjo. I started plunking on a banjo when I was about eleven years old. I had the sound in my head. I listened to Earl Scruggs, Ralph Stanley, and Don Reno. That was about the main three influences on the banjo. So I got me a pick and I put it on. I kinda drove 'em all crazy for a while. I'd put that pick on that third finger and try to make it work. One day it went to working. From there on, I could just hear that sound in my head, the different rolls. I can't explain it. I just do it the way I feel it. I do what they call traditional bluegrass. It's not the hippity-hoppity bluegrass. One time I might play a tune one way, and the next time it might be a little bit different.

When I got on up in my teens, I started playing at the Galax Fiddlers' Convention. I believe it was about 1962 the first time I ever played down there in competition. I played the "Lonesome Road Blues." I got about halfway through it, and I kinda messed up. So I just quit and started again. Everybody give me a hand 'cause I stopped and started again, you know? By 1963 I got to where I could do pretty good so I got a little band together with a fellow around West Jefferson there. His name was John Richardson. He said, "Let's get on a radio show." So we started playing on WKSK in 1963. We played there for a couple of years. So I got good enough to go back to Galax. That was in 1965. I won the first place in the bluegrass banjo competition! That tickled me real good, you know.

Up into about the early eighties, I was just playing around wherever I could. Then I got to getting around Dean Sturgill over here, and he said they was gonna open the Hog Stomp here at Sturgills school. It's a good place to come if you want to enjoy some good bluegrass and old-time music. A lot of tourists drop in here, and they seem to enjoy it very much. It's an open thing to the public.

Wayne Henderson give it its name, the Hog Stomp, back when it was over at Rugby. It's went by that ever since. We really enjoy it. We've saw people from all over the United States here, and from some foreign countries. It's not the biggest place in the world, but we have fun. We want to make everybody welcome. A lot of older folks come here. The ladies always bake some cakes, and we make coffee. Everybody gets along real good.

I play now with a band named Big Country Bluegrass. We play mostly at bluegrass festivals. I've met a lot of people over the years who say that they don't like bluegrass and old-time music. I always say, "How do you know you don't? You ought to come and try it sometimes." You've got to really understand what's going on before you can make an opinion. I believe that's the main thing, getting people to come and settle down and listen to the music. The music tells a story—about tragedy and love and death and, you know, it just explains things, really.

At the Jamboree, every imaginable style of mountain dance is enjoyed, and even though many in the audience are there primarily to watch and listen, most—including some folks who have never danced before—hit the floor clogging, flatfooting, two-stepping, and joining in on the various square dances, Virginia Reels, and cakewalks that are performed there. During the evening Arvill Scott often calls a broom dance, which is similar to musical chairs. The odd person out finds himself or herself dancing with a broom, a scenario that those in attendance find highly amusing.

The Jamboree is a multigenerational gathering, and visitors from throughout the United States and from many places around the world find their way there. Arvill Scott tracks the origins of visitors with pushpins in a large world map that hangs prominently on the wall of the place. There is an admission charge, but children under fourteen who come with adults are admitted free.

Dance bands featured at the Jamboree are among the best in the region.

Two young dancers take a break to view the sunset.

LOCATION: When traveling south on the Blue Ridge Parkway, exit at milepost 259 onto Trading Post Rd. Continue straight to NC 16 and turn left. Continue for two miles and look for the Mountain Music Jamboree on the left side of the road. When traveling north on the Parkway, exit at milepost 261 onto NC 16. Go north for one mile and you will see the Jamboree on your right.

From West Jefferson, take US 221 to NC 16. Travel south on NC 16 for seven miles to Glendale Springs. The Jamboree is located on your left two miles beyond Glendale Springs on NC 16.

From North Wilkesboro, travel west on US 421. Turn north on NC 16 and travel approximately fifteen miles. Pass under the Blue Ridge Parkway and proceed one mile to the Jamboree. It will be on your right.

CONTACT: Arvill Scott, (800) 803-4079, ‹atscott@fastransit.com›, ‹www.mountainmusicjamboree.com›; or Ashe County Chamber of Commerce, 6 N. Jefferson Ave., West Jefferson, NC 28694, (336) 246-9550, ‹ashechamber@skybest.com›, ‹www.ashechamber.com›

❄ Christmas in July

The town of West Jefferson is located in the heart of the Christmas tree farming enterprises of northwestern North Carolina. An unusual three-day craft and music festival held there every summer is called Christmas in July.

The North Carolina Christmas tree farming business began in the late 1950s in neighboring Avery County. The vegetable row crops and beef cattle that had sustained local farmers for decades were becoming less profitable, and something was needed to take their place. As an experiment, one of the signature tree species of the southern highlands, the Fraser fir, was cultivated and marketed as Christmas trees. A new, economically viable agri-industry was born. Now there are literally hundreds of thousands of mountainside acres in the high country of North Carolina that are planted in Fraser fir and other evergreen species that make nice-looking Christmas trees.

In celebration of that success, the Ashe County Arts Council has created an annual festival that takes place on Friday and Saturday of the weekend nearest to the Fourth of July. It's held in July because everyone connected with the tree business is too busy during the months before Christmas to participate in a festival. The main music stage, which features an impressive slate of highly regarded regional bluegrass and old-time musicians, is situated right in the middle of West Jefferson's Main Street.

LOCATION: Take US 421 to US 221 North at Deep Gap. Continue north on US 221 for approximately fourteen miles to the intersection of US 221/NC 163/NC 194 by the Ingles grocery store and Kentucky Fried Chicken. Turn left on NC 194

GARY POE AND THE *OLD-TIME AND BLUEGRASS MUSIC SHOW*

On Saturdays at 11:00 A.M., at the precise moment that WPAQ's Merry-Go-Round *goes on the air from the Downtown Cinema Theatre in Mount Airy, eighty miles away (by mountain road) in West Jefferson Blue Ridge native Gary Poe begins an hour-long music program on radio station WKSK 580 AM. Poe, a retired public school science teacher and a devoted advocate of traditional music, produces a program that features both vintage and contemporary recordings of mountain music. Poe's thoughtful and expert commentary on the history and cultural significance of Blue Ridge music*

Public mural in West Jefferson

traditions are worthy of close attention. From time to time, Poe also conducts live interviews with guest musicians, and his show features live performances as well. For the most up-to-date information on the show, go to ‹www.porchpickin.com› and click on "Area Radio." Station WKSK also features live gospel music on Sunday mornings.

headed north. This takes you into downtown West Jefferson where the festival is located.

CONTACT: Jane Lonon, Ashe County Arts Council/Christmas in July Festival, PO Box 353, Jefferson, NC 28640, (336) 246-ARTS (2787), ‹jlashearts@skybest.com›, ‹www.ashecountyarts.org›; or Ashe County Chamber of Commerce, 6 N. Jefferson Ave., West Jefferson, NC 28694, (336) 246-9550, ‹ashechamber@skybest.com›, ‹www.ashechamber.com›

❄ Bluegrass and Old-Time Fiddlers' Convention at Ashe County Park

This one-day bluegrass and old-time music competition is staged at the Ashe County Park in Jefferson, North Carolina, on the first Saturday in August. Most of the contestants are local musicians and dancers who attend the event faithfully from year to year. The Jefferson Rotary Club sponsors the convention. There is an admission fee. Advance tickets are available from the Ashe County Chamber of Commerce.

Fiddlers' Convention is artist Lenore De Pree's depiction of activities that take place at the Bluegrass and Old Time Fiddlers' Convention. (© 1998 by Lenore De Pree)

LOCATION: From Independence, Virginia, take US 221/21 South. When US 221 and US 21 split, continue on US 221 South to Jefferson. As you enter Jefferson, veer right onto NC 88 going west through downtown Jefferson. At the second stoplight, turn right onto Old NC 16. The Ashe County Park will be a quarter of a mile ahead on the left and is well marked.

From Winston-Salem or Boone, North Carolina, take US 421 to the intersection with US 221 at Deep Gap. Drive north on US 221 for approximately fourteen miles to the intersection of US 221/NC 163/NC 194 by the Ingles grocery store and Kentucky Fried Chicken. Go straight through this traffic light. You will pass Mount Jefferson State Park on the right. At the next traffic light, turn left onto Long St. and follow it for a very short distance to the end. At the stop sign, turn right onto N. Main St., which turns into Old NC 16. Continue straight through the traffic light (crossing NC 88) onto Old NC 16. The Ashe County Park will be a quarter-mile ahead on the left.

CONTACT: Mary Anne Moore, PO Box 847, West Jefferson, NC 28694, (336) 219-0074, ‹sterlinginc@skybest.com›; or Ashe County Chamber of Commerce, 6 N. Jefferson Ave., West Jefferson, NC 28694, (336) 246-9550, ‹ashechamber@skybest.com›, ‹www.ashechamber.com›

❄ Ashe County Arts Council Coffee House Talent Night

The Fellowship Hall of the Jefferson United Methodist Church hosts this bimonthly event that showcases both musical and storytelling talents from the surrounding area. The *Prairie Home Companion*–style program features four or five local individuals or groups who perform two 10- to 12-minute sets of old-time, bluegrass, Celtic, pop, or classical music, or who tell stories. The spacious fellowship hall will accommodate audiences of three hundred or more. The shows are festive and are popular within the community.

Talent nights are held on the third Saturday evening of every other month and are open to the public. Visitors are welcome, and this event is an excellent place for outsiders to experience a hospitable introduction to local culture. The program begins at 7:30 P.M.

LOCATION: Take US 221 North to West Jefferson. Once you reach West Jefferson, continue straight on US 221 North through the first traffic light at the McDonald's and the Ingle's shopping center. When you reach the second traffic light, turn left onto Long St., which dead-ends in one block. Where the road ends, turn right onto Main St. Jefferson United Methodist Church is a half block down on the left. Parking is located in front and behind the church.

CONTACT: Jane Lonon, Ashe County Arts Council, PO Box 353, Jefferson, NC 28640, (336) 246-ARTS (2787), ‹jlashearts@skybest.com›, ‹www.ashecountyarts.org›; or Ashe County Chamber of Commerce, 6 N. Jefferson Ave., West Jefferson, NC 28694, (336) 246-9550, ‹ashechamber@skybest.com›, ‹www.ashechamber.com›

❄ Greenfield Restaurant Bluegrass and Old-Time Music

The Greenfield Restaurant is a year-round popular dining establishment for local residents in Ashe County. On Friday and Saturday nights, regional musicians perform bluegrass and old-time music there. The music starts at 6:00 P.M. and lasts until around 10:00. Generally, one band is booked for each weekend evening. The setting is informal and neighborly.

LOCATION: Take US 221 until it intersects with NC 163 in West Jefferson. Turn east onto NC 163 and travel approximately a half-mile to Mt. Jefferson Rd. Turn left onto Mt. Jefferson Rd. and follow it behind the Wal-Mart. Greenfield's will be on the right at 1795 Mt. Jefferson Rd.; it is well marked.

CONTACT: Dick Copus, Greenfield Restaurant, PO Box 1304, West Jefferson, NC 28694, (336) 246-2900, ‹Greenfield@skybest.com›; or Ashe County Chamber of Commerce, 6 N. Jefferson Ave., West Jefferson, NC 28694, (336) 246-9550, ‹ashechamber@skybest.com›, ‹www.ashechamber.com›

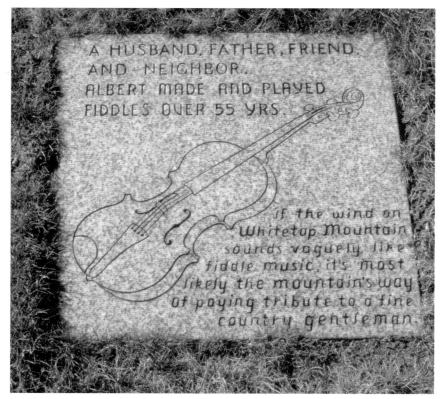

Commemorative stone marking the grave of Albert Hash
(Photograph by Sally Council; courtesy of the North Carolina Arts Council)

✤ Albert Hash Memorial Festival

The Albert Hash Memorial Festival is held on the grounds of the Ashe Civic Center on the southern edge of the town of West Jefferson, North Carolina. This festival is presented in memory of a legendary local fiddler and instrument maker, Albert Hash. Hash served as the principal mentor for many of the region's finest contemporary musical instrument makers, including Wayne Henderson, Tom Barr, and Hash's own daughter, Audrey Hash Ham. He was also the longtime leader of the White Top Mountain Band and inspired that band's current leader, Thornton Spencer.

The concrete platform of the civic center's loading dock serves as a makeshift stage for the Albert Hash Memorial Festival, and audience members sit scattered around in folding chairs on the adjacent paved parking area. The music, by a variety of regional bluegrass and old-time bands, starts at 2:00 in the afternoon and ends around 11:00 P.M. Inside the lobby

Contrary to its name, the New is one of the oldest rivers in North America.

of the civic center are displays on the life of Albert Hash and an exhibit featuring several of his finely crafted fiddles.

LOCATION: Take US 421 to the intersection with US 221 at Deep Gap. Follow
US 221 North for approximately twelve miles to West Jefferson. Continue on
until you see the high school and Wal-Mart on your right. Proceed three-tenths
of a mile past Wal-Mart. The Ashe County Civic Center is located at the entrance
to Mt. Jefferson State Park just below the Lowe's grocery store.

CONTACT: Maude M. Calhoun, Albert Hash Festival, 962 Mt. Jefferson Rd.,
West Jefferson, NC 28694, (336) 246-4483, ‹ashecivicctr@skybest.com›,
‹www.ashecivic.com›; or Ashe County Chamber of Commerce, 6 N. Jefferson
Ave., West Jefferson, NC 28694, (336) 246-9550, ‹ashechamber@skybest.com›,
‹www.ashechamber.com›

DOROTHY HESS
I'M REALLY A FIGHTER

Dorothy Hess of Ashe County, North Carolina, lives in a small house surrounded by a yard full of carefully maintained flowers and shrubs. She continues to sing and play the dozens of love songs she learned from her mother as a child.

I didn't take my first step until I was five years old. I'll always remember that day. I stood up and I cried, "I can't do it!" But the doctor said, "Just take one step. If you fall, I'll catch you." I took one step and over I went. But he caught me! I got brave then and I started walking a little bit more each day.

I was born in Lebanon, Virginia, in 1929. I was born with a bone deformity, and I guess being able to sing and strum on my guitar kind of compensated for that. My legs were bent backwards against my bottom and my feet turned under till my toes touched my heels. I spent most of my first seventeen years in the crippled children's hospital in Richmond, Virginia. When I'd get to come home, Mother would sing for me. I loved to hear the music. She would sing all these folksongs, real sad things. I loved them. When I'd go back to the hospital, I would try all of those songs out. I knew them right down pat. I'd lay there and sing all the time. That was just my thing.

Mom and Dad always tried to get me to make a recording when I was just a young-ster. They said I was really good. And I would just yodel as hard as I could. I'd have the nurses piled around my bed saying, "Do that again!" But getting out in front of the public was another story. I had been teased so much at school—the other children gave me a hard time. You would think that they would understand that I couldn't help how I was but, you know, children can be cruel. They were cruel.

Mother played the banjo. My sister played guitar. They were on the radio in Bris-tol, Virginia. They had a Saturday night jamboree there in a huge auditorium, and it was always packed full of people. My mom and my sister, they had these old, old out-fits with black bonnets and black dresses, and they went as "Liza and Kate." Sort of comedians, you know. They really took the shows! Mama played banjo, clawhammer style. My younger sister took up the banjo. My older sister taught me to play the guitar. One day she said, "Do you want to learn to play?" And I said, "Yes, I do, but I don't think I can do it." But I did. I sang on the radio. I was just a little thing, and I was in my braces. The crowd loved it.

Sometimes I'd stay there at the hospital for a year and a half at a time without ever coming home. To a child, that's a long time. I'd be so homesick. While I was in the hospital, I cried every night. *Every* night. I'd lay in the bed and I'd hear a train way off somewhere, and I'd lay there and cry. It was probably just a freight train, but I didn't care, I'd wanted to be on it headed home. It was a hard life, but I think it has made me see things a lot different from other people. Things look a lot better to me than they might to somebody else, because of the things that I have endured. I'm a fighter. I'm really a fighter.

Now I've started going to the fiddlers' conventions, singing all of Mama's songs that she had taught me. I love to sing around in the background at the fiddlers' conventions after the stage part is over, and entertain people. You really meet a lot of people that way. And they love the songs. I want this music to be passed on to the younger generation. And I'm seeing more of it now than I ever have. It pleases me. I don't want it to be forgotten.

✤ Todd New River Festival

Todd, a historic community located near the line between Ashe and Watauga Counties, is the scene of an early October festival on the banks of the New River. Once a bustling train town, Todd is now a quiet mountain hamlet. The New River Festival is presented at the town's main visitor attraction, the Todd General Store. The event offers an old-fashioned gospel sing, a checkers playoff, a horseshoe toss, craft displays, storytelling, and a fishing tournament. It takes place on the second Saturday in October, from 9:00 A.M. to 6:00 P.M.

LOCATION: NC 194 intersects with US 421/US 221 in Boone. Turn north onto
NC 194 and follow it for approximately twelve miles until you cross the Watauga/
Ashe County line. Take a right at the T-intersection onto Todd Railroad Grade Rd.
The store will be on the left.
From West Jefferson, take US 221/NC 194 South. Follow NC 194 when it
splits with US 221. Just before you reach the Watauga/Ashe County line, turn left
at the T-intersection onto Todd Railroad Grade Rd. The store will be on the left.
CONTACT: Joe Morgan, Todd General Store, Todd Railroad Grade Rd., Todd, NC
28684, (336) 877-1067, ‹sjmorgan@skybest.com›; or Ashe County Chamber

of Commerce, 6 N. Jefferson Ave., West Jefferson, NC 28694, (336) 246-9550, ‹ashechamber@skybest.com›, ‹www.ashechamber.com›

YADKIN COUNTY

❊ O'Henry's Restaurant

O'Henry's Restaurant is a Yadkin County site that specializes in home cooking and mountain music. Owned and operated by Joseph Henry and Judy Bowman, the restaurant features house specialties such as pork ribs, seafood, homemade soup, fried apple pies, and Judy Bowman's famous biscuits. At 7:00 P.M. on Fridays and Saturdays, local musicians gather there to play bluegrass, gospel, and country music. As patrons finish eating their suppers, the tables in the dining area are pushed back to make additional room for dancing — clogging, flatfooting, two-stepping, and buck dancing.

LOCATION: O'Henry's is located several miles east of East Bend near the Yadkin River. From the southeast, take NC 67/Reynolda Rd. out of Winston-Salem and cross over the Yadkin River. Continue approximately a quarter of a mile. O'Henry's is the first business on the right after the bridge.
   Traveling south from Mount Airy on US 52, take exit 123, marked "King/Tobaccoville." Take a right at the stoplight and proceed for a quarter-mile to Spainhour Mill Rd. Proceed approximately three miles and turn left onto Donnaha Rd. Go two to three miles until you come to NC 67. Turn right onto NC 67 and cross over the Yadkin River. Continue approximately a quarter of a mile. O'Henry's is the first business on the right after the bridge.

CONTACT: Joseph or Judy Bowman, PO Box 326, East Bend, NC 27108, (336) 699-8693; or Yadkin County Chamber of Commerce, 205 S. Jackson St., Yadkinville, NC 27055, (336) 679-2200, ‹BTODD@yadtel.net›, ‹www.yadkinchamber.org›

❊ Hall's Barbecue

Hall's Barbecue, located at Yadkinville, North Carolina, specializes in pit cooked barbecue — pork and chicken — and homemade everything else, including "the best pecan pie you ever ate." Formerly an old garage, this place has been a popular landmark restaurant in Yadkinville for decades. The musicians who perform at Hall's Barbecue on Friday and Saturday evenings are usually bluegrass or gospel players — sometimes both. The dining area seats 200 people. There's a stage on one end for the performers. The music starts

O'Henry's Restaurant entertains its patrons with bluegrass, gospel, and country music.

Hall's Barbeque in Yadkinville

at 6:30 P.M. and continues until around 10:30. There is no dancing here, but diners are welcome to stay around after eating just to enjoy the music.

LOCATION: Hall's Barbecue is located about six miles west of Yadkinville on US 421. Look for the flashing sign and the big pig out front.

CONTACT: Holbert Hall, 1232 Reavis Rd., Yadkinville, NC 27055, (336) 468-4449; or Yadkin County Chamber of Commerce, 205 S. Jackson St., Yadkinville, NC 27055, (336) 679-2200, ‹BTODD@yadtel.net›, ‹www.yadkinchamber.org›

❈ Yadkinville Bluegrass Contest and Fiddlers' Convention

This daylong bluegrass music competition is held annually on the third Saturday in April at the Yadkinville Elementary School, north of Yadkinville. It's sponsored by the Yadkinville Jaycees.

LOCATION: From US 421, take US 601 north to Yadkinville. When you have passed through the traffic light downtown, the Yadkinville Elementary School will be on the left within one mile.

CONTACT: Robert Steelman, 2224 Lone Hickory Rd., Yadkinville, NC 27055, (336) 463-5624, ‹rbsteelman@yadtel.net›; or Yadkin County Chamber of Commerce, 205 S. Jackson St., Yadkinville, NC 27055, (336) 679-2200, ‹BTODD@yadtel.net›, ‹www.yadkinchamber.org›

❈ Friday Night Music at Windsor's Crossroads

The old Union Grove Schoolhouse at Windsor's Crossroads is home to a weekly Friday night jam session from 7:00 to 11:00 P.M. The jam features a variety of musical forms including bluegrass, old-time, country, and gospel. There's lots of clogging, flatfooting, and buck dancing, too. The music is all acoustic at this place, so the dancers don't wear taps on their shoes. The rooms of the old building, constructed around 1915, have high ceilings and wonderful hardwood floors. The sound quality there is excellent. Typically there are two hundred or more musicians, dancers, and listeners there every week, although the number may vary according to the weather and the season. When it's warm and pleasant, the event spreads out onto the spacious surrounding grounds.

LOCATION: Take US 421 East from Wilkesboro or west from Winston-Salem. About a half-mile east of I-77, you will see a flashing light. Turn left here onto Asbury Church Rd. and continue until you cross under I-77 and come to a stop sign. At the stop sign, turn left onto Buck Shoals Rd. and continue until you

Roadside near Windsor's Crossroads

reach Windsor Rd. The Union Grove Schoolhouse is located at the intersection of Buck Shoals Rd. and Windsor Rd.

CONTACT: Bud Martin, Windsor's Crossroads Friday Night Jam Sessions, Windsor's Crossroads Community Building, 5101 Windsor Rd., Hamptonville, NC 28677, (336) 468-9690, ‹bud_martin@hunt-corp.com›; or Yadkin County Chamber of Commerce, 205 S. Jackson St., Yadkinville, NC 27055, (336) 679-2200, ‹BTODD@yadtel.net›, ‹www.yadkinchamber.org›

WILKES COUNTY

⚘ Whippoorwill Academy and the Tom Dooley Museum

The Tom Dooley Museum is part of a complex of restored buildings called Whippoorwill Academy and Village. The museum, which is housed on the

Whippoorwill Academy and Village features a restored
schoolhouse, store, smokehouse, and cabin.

upper story of an old hewn-log cabin, features artifacts, photographs, and
written information about Tom Dula, who was hanged in 1868 for the mur-
der of a woman named Laura Foster. A historic marker at the intersection of
NC 268 and SR 1134 in Wilkes County calls attention to the murder and to
Dula's subsequent capture and punishment. Dula's grave is located about a
mile from the Whippoorwill Academy on Tom Dooley Road, overlooking the
Yadkin River. Laura Foster is buried about five miles away in Caldwell
County.

The enduring legend of Tom Dooley has inspired several books, a video
program, the museum exhibit at Whippoorwill Academy, and the hit recording, "Hang Down Your Head, Tom Dooley," by the Kingston Trio. Additional
information on the Tom Dooley saga is available at the Old Wilkes County
Jail, a local history museum located behind the old county courthouse in
Wilkesboro, North Carolina.

Whippoorwill Academy and Village and the Tom Dooley Museum is open
to the public Saturdays and Sundays from 3:00 to 5:00 P.M. and during the

THE LEGEND OF TOM DOOLEY

Many Americans—maybe most—have probably never heard an Appalachian ballad sung by a traditional singer from the Blue Ridge. A few mountain ballads, however, have been popularized. "Tom Dula," released on record in 1958 as "Hang Down Your Head, Tom Dooley," remains perhaps the most widely known.

Laura Foster's solitary grave is located in a pasture near the banks of the Yadkin River

According to traditional North Carolina ballad singer Bobby McMillon, the Tom Dooley story is based on a murder committed by Tom Dula (sometimes pronounced locally as "Dooley"), a Confederate army veteran from Wilkes County. The song gained national popularity after it was recorded by a folk revivalist group known as the Kingston Trio. The trio based their rendition on a ballad sung to folksong collector Frank Warner by Frank Proffitt of Beech Mountain, North Carolina. Warner documented Proffitt's song on a field recording in 1940 and later shared the ballad with Alan Lomax, who included it in his collection titled Folk Song USA. According to Frank Proffitt Jr., his father unexpectedly learned about the Kingston Trio's success when he heard them perform his distinctive version of the ballad on the Ed Sullivan Show. It was quite a shock to him. Proffitt and Warner filed a joint lawsuit for legal claim to "Tom Dooley" and eventually received a portion of the royalties. The Kingston Trio's adaptation of the song included the following verses:

Hang down your head, Tom Dooley,
Hang down your head and cry;
Hang down your head, Tom Dooley,
Poor boy, you're bound to die.

I met her on the mountain,
There I took her life;
Met her on the mountain,
Stabbed her with my knife.

Hang down your head, Tom Dooley,
Hang down your head and cry;
Hang down your head, Tom Dooley,
Poor boy, you're bound to die.

This time tomorrow,
Reckon where I'll be;
Hadn't a-been for Grayson,
I'd a-been in Tennessee.

This time tomorrow,
Reckon where I'll be;
Down in some lonesome valley,
Hanging from a white oak tree.

Hang down your head, Tom Dooley,
Hang down your head and cry;
Hang down your head, Tom Dooley,
Poor boy, you're bound to die.

After that song reached the height of its national popularity, claims Bobby McMillon, a local story arose that the basis for the song was "that there was a guy named Bob Grayson who was in love with Laura Foster. And Tom was in love with Laura, too. And they got in a fight and some-how Laura was accidentally killed. They said Tom was hanged because of a misunderstanding. That was the story that came out when the Kingston Trio popularized the song." McMillon continued,

In reality what happened was that before Tom Dula went to the war, he had an affair with a girl named Annie Melton. Old man Wade Gilbert, he's the one who told me the story of Tom Dooley, said his grandmother was with Ann Melton the night she died. While Tom was gone to the war, Ann Melton married. When he come back and saw that she was married, he started seeing some of the other ladies in the community. One of them was Ann's cousin, Laura Foster. She lived up here in Caldwell County. But he kept up the affair with Ann Melton while he was at the same time seeing Laura Foster. It's been said that Ann Melton was jealous of Laura Foster.

One morning Laura took her daddy's mare and disappeared. Somebody saw her leaving home that morning and she told them she was running away from home to marry Tom. Two days later the mare come home, but she never did.

They went hunting for her and couldn't find her for several months. The body was finally found in a shallow grave in the woods down there close to where she was killed, in Wilkes County. Tom, in the meantime, had left the state. He went to Tennessee to work for a man named James Grayson. That's how the Grayson name got in it. Tom had worked for him for several days when two deputies came out of Wilkes County hunting for him. They actually came hunting for him before her body had ever been discovered.

Grayson took the deputies and some other men and they located Tom. By the time they brought him back, they'd found her body. They accused him of the murder. They had one trial in Wilkesboro, the county seat, and I don't remember for what reason, but they threw it out. Then they bound it over to the court in Statesville, a couple of counties away, probably because they couldn't get a fair trial in Wilkes County, and they found him guilty.

Artifacts and memorabilia associated with Tom Dula are displayed in the loft of Whippoorwill Academy

Most people in this area believe he was hanged in Wilkesboro on the Tory Oak, which goes back to the Revolution, but he wasn't. The second trial was in Statesville, and Ann Melton was in jail there, too, accused with him. That jail's still standing. The night before they hanged him, he wrote a note exonerating Ann Melton from having had anything to do with it. But I think if she didn't do it, she had a hand in it.

Tom was a fiddle player and they say that he sat on his coffin and rode it from the jail to the place of execution, a-playing the fiddle. They said when he got there he looked up at the scaffold and said, "Boys, if I'd a-known you was gonna hang me with a new rope, I'd a-washed my neck this morning." Then he got up and made his little speech. He held out his hand and said, "Gentlemen, you see this hand as it trembles? I never hurt a hair on that girl's head." And that was it. His sister and her husband, they was there, so they claimed the body and took it back to Wilkes county for burial. They've got a grave up there somewhere, but I can't pinpoint it. (Personal interview with Bobby McMillon, December 1, 1999)

week by appointment. It's closed January through March except by appointment. Admission is free, but donations are appreciated.

LOCATION: From Wilkesboro, take NC 268 West toward Lenoir. Whippoorwill Academy is on the right, twelve miles from the Hampton Inn. Watch carefully for a sign on the right marking the entrance.

From Lenoir, take US 321 North to NC 268. Turn right onto NC 268 and go approximately twelve miles until you come to Elkville, located just beyond the Caldwell/Wilkes County line. Once you have passed through Elkville, watch carefully for a sign on the left marking the entrance to Whippoorwill Academy.

CONTACT: Edith Carter, Tom Dooley Museum, PO Box 458, Ferguson, NC 28624, (336) 973-3237, ‹whippoorwill@wilkes.net›; or Wilkes Chamber of Commerce, 717 Main St., PO Box 727, North Wilkesboro, NC 28659, (336) 838-8662, ‹info@wilkesnc.org›, ‹www.wilkesnc.org›

❀ Merlefest

This internationally acclaimed event is an annual four-day acoustic and traditional music festival staged in memory of Merle Watson, the late son and former playing partner of festival host Doc Watson, the acclaimed master of Blue Ridge guitar and vocal styles. Merle Watson was fatally injured in a tractor accident in 1985.

Merlefest offers a seemingly endless menu of musical offerings that are presented on twelve different stages scattered all around the spacious campus of Wilkes Community College in Wilkesboro, North Carolina, reflecting the eclectic musical interests of Doc Watson, whose own musicianship covers a range of genres including bluegrass, old-time, blues, rockabilly, country, and jazz. Workshops are offered in guitar, banjo, fiddle, blues, dobro, bass, vocals, and several of the technical aspects of recording and producing music. Additional activities include a picking tent, contests for various instrument players, a dance tent, and various children's entertainments such as a petting zoo, playground areas, storytelling, sing-alongs, face painting, and pony rides. This festival has grown to become one of the top five acoustic events in the nation and draws over 50,000 fans.

Merlefest was started in 1988 to benefit the establishment and maintenance of a memorial garden at Wilkes Community College. Now the Eddy Merle Watson Memorial Garden for the Senses is a reality—a space designed to appeal to the senses of smell and touch. The garden contains a collection of diverse plant species that have been chosen for their strong fragrances or unusual textures. The garden complex includes a series of

Musician and artist Willard Gayheart's rendering of MerleFest pays homage to Merle Watson, Merle's son Richard, and Doc Watson, pictured top left to right, and other nationally known performers who participate in the event. (© by Willard Gayheart)

distinctive relief brick wall panels. The various features of the garden are labeled in Braille.

Merlefest opens each year on the last Thursday in April and runs through the following Sunday. The gates open at 3:00 P.M. on Thursday and at 8:00 A.M. on Friday, Saturday, and Sunday. Limited tent and RV camping is available on the community college campus. Public parking is located near the campus, and a shuttle bus runs from there to the festival site.

LOCATION: Take the NC 268 exit off US 421 in Wilkesboro. Continue a half-mile west past the entrance to Wilkes Community College to Blue Lot parking. Shuttle service runs from there to the campus.

CONTACT: "B" Townes, Merlefest at Wilkes Community College, PO Box 120, Wilkesboro, NC 28697, (800) 343-7857, ‹merlefest@wilkes.cc.nc.us›, ‹www.merlefest.org›; or Wilkes Chamber of Commerce, 717 Main St., PO Box 727, North Wilkesboro, NC 28659, (336) 838-8662, ‹info@wilkesnc.org›, ‹www.wilkesnc.org›. For additional details or for advance ticket purchases, call (800) 343-7857, or go to ‹www.merlefest.org›.

REGION TWO

A FIDDLERS' CONVENTION IN VIRGINIA

GALAX

Old Fiddlers' Convention

Vacationing family members enjoying a slow and scenic Sunday afternoon drive travel north along the Blue Ridge Parkway on a day in early August. They cross over the North Carolina–Virginia state line—literally, a white stripe painted diagonally across the paved surface. After a minute or two, they turn off the Parkway at milepost 215 and head north on VA 89 toward Galax. They ride for seven or eight miles along the open road, pass Brenda's Hub Restaurant, and cross a short concrete bridge. Reaching the summit of a long, low incline, they come to a sudden stop at the top of the hill. To their right, below the roadway and down a steep embankment, a broad, flat plain stretches before them for a half-mile or more. Within that plain is situated a virtual city, a transitory suburb of Galax that's been created by the aggregation of hundreds of RVs, campers, trailers, buses, vans, and tents, all neatly arranged in parallel rows along grass-covered avenues. The travelers have just arrived at Felts Park, the site of the Old Fiddlers' Convention in Galax, Virginia. It's a sight to behold.

The enormous campground at Felt's Park has been described by the local news media as "a city within a city." At campsites all around the park, charcoal grills are fired up and hamburgers sizzle away as parents hang out their children's clothes to dry on rope lines stretched between poles or vehicles. Other campers readjust the anchors on the awnings of their tents or RVs, and groups of children run around looking for new ways to entertain themselves. Small crowds of teenagers migrate to and from the nearby community swimming pool, while the older folks sit around in the shade and drink coffee, talk quietly, read, strum guitars, or take short naps.

Galax Old Fiddlers' Convention

There are scores—no, hundreds—of mountain musicians and music fans who spend practically every weekend from April through August attending the near-weekly fiddlers' conventions, festivals, street fairs, jam sessions, and other celebrations of mountain music that abound throughout the region. But of them all, none are more highly anticipated—or more popular—or bigger—than the Old Fiddlers' Convention at Galax.

The contest originated in the spring of 1935 as a fundraiser for Galax Moose Lodge No. 733, and it has gone on every year since then, except for one year during World War II when everyone was too busy with other matters. It's about the oldest such event in Appalachia and, without a doubt, the largest. Galax is normally a town of around 7,500 people, but it will double and perhaps more than triple in size by week's end during the fiddlers' convention. The many music lovers who go to Galax for this annual event travel from all over Appalachia—and from all around the globe—to play and to listen to bluegrass and old-time mountain music.

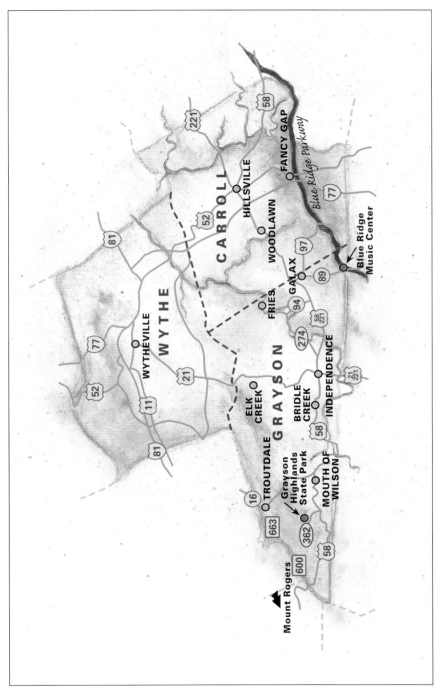

Region 2

A fiddler from New Mexico catches a nap.

Galax, Virginia, is a regional center for commercial furniture making, upholstering, and mirror manufacturing. In addition, Galax has long been associated with highly developed instrumental and vocal music traditions. An intricate and charming fiddle style could be heard here for many years after it disappeared in other places. Many believe that the clawhammer banjo style reached its apogee in the hands of musicians living around Galax and in nearby communities in Surry County, North Carolina.

The Galax area was a focal point for early and noted music collectors including John and Alan Lomax, Charles and Pete Seeger, and scores of others who visited there from the 1930s onward. The attention that they paid to Galax, along with the distribution of the recordings they made there, has contributed to the reputation of the Old Fiddler's Convention and the sizable increase in attendance over the years.

The list of notable regional musicians who have performed and won awards at Galax reads like a who's who of traditional mountain music—Kyle Creed, Charlie Higgins, Evelyn Farmer, Pop Stoneman, J. E. Mainer, Wade Ward, Uncle Eck Dunford, Fred Cockerham, Kilby Snow, Otis Burris, and on and on. An interesting illustrated history of the event, describing who played when and who won what, is *The First Forty Years of the Old Fiddlers Convention*. This little booklet, compiled by Galax native Herman K. Williams, is available at Barr's Fiddle Shop and other locations in Galax.

On Monday afternoon of the second week in August each year, at 6:00 P.M., the Old Fiddlers' Convention begins quietly with an evening of fiddle, mandolin, banjo, and guitar competitions for children. There is little indication that night of what is to follow in the days ahead. On each subsequent evening all that week and all day long on Saturday, many hundreds of musicians and dancers will compete for cash prizes totaling $20,000. It's an amazing competition. At the 2000 convention, registered musicians included 163 old-time fiddlers, 152 bluegrass fiddlers, 66 dulcimer players, 85 dobro players, 177 mandolin players, an incredible 369 guitarists, 238 bluegrass banjo pickers, 129 clawhammer banjo pickers, 81 autoharpists, 105 old-time string bands, 218 bluegrass bands, 224 singers of folksongs, and 168 flatfoot dancers—a total of 2,175 registrants!

"THE FIDDLERS'"

If it's early to mid-summer and you happen to be around traditional musicians or music lovers in western North Carolina and Virginia, it's very likely that you'll hear someone ask: "When are y'all going to Galax?" If, however, the questioner happens to be from Galax, and is speaking to another who's also from Galax, then you're more likely to hear, "When are y'all going to the Fiddlers'?" "The Fiddlers'" is Galax code for the Old Fiddlers' Convention and, if you're hip to it, there's no mistaking what's being talked about. Despite the fact that there are another dozen or more fiddlers' conventions every year around the Blue Ridge, "The Fiddlers'" is the granddaddy of them all—no questions asked and no ground given.

For the first six or more decades of this event, participation by women was pretty much confined to the folksong competition and, occasionally, to the autoharp contests. But in the last twenty years or so, that has changed. Today, female players are full participants in every category of the event—and frequently are winners in the full range of categories.

As the competition proceeds, category after category, the contestants are invited onstage one at a time and introduced by name and number to an audience seated before them in permanent bleachers or on folding chairs they've brought with them for the occasion. The festival stage is an open-fronted, tent-covered platform centered on what would appear, under normal circumstances, to be the infield of a baseball park. Competing musicians stand in line, sometimes for hours, awaiting their moment of glory. Each evening of the convention, Monday through Saturday, musician after musician after musician is introduced. Each plays his or her selection for the allotted maximum two-and-a-half minutes (no more, or they're disqualified) and then retreats to the sound of applause as the next contestant is brought forth by the announcer. Sometimes the competition can go on until as late as three or four o'clock in the morning. It lasts as long as it takes. It lasts until everyone has played, and that can be a long time, especially if the parade of musicians is sporadically interrupted by thunderstorms, as so often happens.

Meanwhile, the even bigger—and in the opinion of many, the better—part of the show is happening elsewhere. All around the festival grounds, in and among the hundreds of campers, tents, and RVs that have been set up

Contestants embrace backstage following their performance.

there for the week, musicians are playing and listening to each other play. A walk up and down and through the maze of campsites reveals music, and talk of music, everywhere. Someone has said that life on the campgrounds at Galax is 20 percent music and 80 percent talk. It seems so. The parallel parking arrangement of the many RVs, tents, and tent canopies that have been positioned on the campground creates a series of narrow lanes, and an afternoon or evening stroll up and down those lanes gives you a sensation not unlike that of rapidly flipping through radio stations. Every time you turn another corner or pass by another camp, a different tune can be heard streaming from the jam session that's happening there. The place is an un-qualified round-the-clock buffet of old-time and bluegrass music. It's hard to know what to listen to next.

As you wander the park, don't be reluctant to walk over close to the action to see what's happening and to listen. If you're a musician and you're carrying an instrument, you may be invited to join in. You'll quickly find that you are only one of scores of other music lovers and musicians who are doing the same thing. Listen in one place for a while, then move along to find another gathering and enjoy the scene and sounds there for five or ten

Barbara Poole and Larry Sigmon, who have a large
following in the region, perform in the parking lot.

minutes, then move on again. Everyone has come to Galax for the same reason: a love of hearing, discussing, performing, and just being around finely
played traditional old-time and bluegrass mountain music.

All week long around the campground there is much discussion of, trying
out of, and trading of various musical instruments. If you're looking for a
vintage Gibson guitar or a beautifully handcrafted mountain fiddle, or if
you've decided to bite the bullet and buy that bluegrass banjo that you've
always dreamed of owning, you're at the right place. Instrument traders
and dealers are plentiful at Galax. There's also a broad and informal amateur network of instrument swapping, trading, and selling among the participants. If you don't happen to see that exact mandolin you've been looking for, spread the word. Someone will get back to you, usually in an
amazingly short period of time, and often with a satisfactory answer to your
inquiry.

During its many years of existence, the Old Fiddlers' Convention at Galax
has been, and is still, many things to many people. To some, it's nothing
less than an annual pilgrimage to what they perceive as the Mecca of real
mountain music. To others, it's a place to indulge in and, they hope, to sur-

Night revelers.

vive a weeklong, twenty-four-hour-a-day party. It's a place where aspiring young musicians can easily find, associate with, and learn from esteemed and recognized elders of the mountain fiddle, banjo, and guitar. It's a musical family reunion for the many in attendance who are lifelong devotees and practitioners of traditional playing styles and who regularly attend musical events all around the region. It's where rising new talents are first recognized and where seasoned players confirm the mastery of their art. The Old Fiddlers' Convention at Galax—there just ain't nothing else like it in the world.

The festival runs Monday through Saturday, and there's plenty of food available on site all week. Keep in mind that this event is famous for its sudden and torrential summer thunderstorms, so bring along your foul-weather gear. Wear shoes that are suitable for walking in the inevitable mud that coats the campgrounds and the festival infield.

Camping on the festival grounds is available for competing participants only, and even they must register in advance. The grandstands at Felts Park seat more than 1,000 people, but it never hurts to bring along your own folding chair to this or any other outdoor musical event in the Blue Ridge. At the height of the event on Friday and Saturday evenings, an audience of 10,000 or more may be in attendance, so plan to arrive early and stay late—very late. Nearby parking is at a premium by 6:00 P.M. when the music begins, so plan ahead.

LOCATION: Follow I-77 to exit 14 and take US 58/221 to Galax. After you pass a Lowes Hardware Superstore on the left, proceed through eight traffic lights to the intersection of E. Stuart Dr. and Main St. (VA 89). Turn left onto Main St. at the light and drive through downtown. Look for Felts Park on the left.

CONTACT: Tom Jones, Annual Galax Old Fiddlers' Convention, PO Box 655, Galax, VA 24333, (276) 236-8541, ‹www.oldfiddlersconvention.com›; or Debbie Robinson, Director of Tourism, City of Galax, 111 E. Grayson St., Galax, VA 24333, (276) 238-8130, ‹drobinson@galaxcity.org›

Barr's Fiddle Shop

Tom Barr re-hairs a fiddle bow.

Saturday afternoons are usually the busiest time of the week for Tom Barr, the owner of Barr's Fiddle shop, located on Main Street in Galax. Barr's customers, many of them working people, have a free afternoon on Saturdays to spend as they wish, so they drop by the fiddle shop to see who's there and what's happening. They gossip, they tell jokes, they run their fingers through the wooden barrel full of guitar picks on display in the store, and they check out the banjos, fiddles, mandolins, and guitars that have been added to Barr's inventory since the last time they were there.

Barr's fiddle shop has a solid reputation for supplying the very best instruments available for playing mountain music. Tom Barr himself is a long-time traditional musician and a native of Galax. He understands traditional music. His wife, Becky, and their son, Steve, are also musicians. Tom Barr repairs musical instruments and builds fine guitars, fiddles, and banjos. He knows what's required by mountain musicians who want to play old-time and bluegrass music the way it's played around Galax.

There's always lots of talk of music and music makers and lots of music at Barr's Fiddle shop. But nothing is planned there. There's no set time in the afternoon for things to start, and there's no predetermined number or kind of players. There's no list of who will play what or when. But unless there's a heavy snowstorm, or a flood, there will almost certainly be a jam session on Saturday afternoon at Barr's Fiddle Shop, and afternoons sometimes begin there as early as ten in the morning.

Typically, someone—perhaps a fiddler—will come into the shop and spot an instrument that looks interesting. He (or she) and Tom, Tom's assistant Kyle Smith, or another person will exchange a few words regarding the quality of the instrument. They'll talk for a while about its look, its maker, its style, its age, its origin, the kind of wood the back and sides are made of, the way it feels in the hand, and on and on. The fiddler will then tentatively pull the bow across the strings a time or two to get the feel of things, and then suddenly will cut loose with "Whiskey before Breakfast" or "Chicken Reel," just to quickly check out how the fiddle holds up under pressure. That's

TOM BARR
A WAY OF LIFE

*Tom Barr of Galax,
Virginia, owns and
operates Barr's Fiddle
Shop, a center for musical
activity within the center
of musical activity in
Southern Appalachia.*

I was born in 1941, and raised out here about a mile south of Galax. My mother played music. A lot of our neighbors did, too. I used to hear them a lot as a kid. They used to gather up at our house, and they would play music until one or two o'clock in the morning. Once a year they'd have a fiddlers' convention out here where they played mountain music. Old-time music we call it today—old-time music with a little flair. They had autoharps, ukuleles, banjos, guitars, fiddles, all kinds of things like that.

Back in the forties when WBOB, the AM radio station here, signed on the air, they started having live music on a show called *The Saturday Afternoon Jamboree*. The musicians would get together down there in the yard near our house on Saturdays and practice—getting ready to go on the radio show. They'd be drinking white liquor out of half-gallon jars. There'd be twenty-five or thirty people, all sitting out in the yard. Later that day, you could hear them on the radio, live over the air. That was around 1948 or 1949, somewhere in there. You could listen to them live on the radio, if your batteries were any good.

Nobody had any money back then. The Depression went on through until the upper forties around here. They claim that the Depression was over in the thirties, but ours was still going on. You could go everywhere and it was hard to find a rabbit, cause everybody was hunting them to eat. There was one family that lived up above us, they'd eat possum. If you caught a possum, I tell you, there was somebody around who would eat it. There were lots of people around here then who didn't really have anything. The only entertainment they had was what they done for themselves. That's why all the families played music. That's the only thing they had. Everybody was poor. It was a way of life.

I started playing music—bluegrass music—in the early sixties, around 1962. You could go to the fiddlers' conventions back then, and if you didn't have a group, somebody would invite you to play with them. Anywhere you went, you could always find a group to play with. It was that type of situation. They'd say, "Come on, pick with us." We would play sometimes on WPAQ, and we had a show every Saturday afternoon on WBOB—an afternoon jamboree. Then I met the New River Ramblers. They were from up in Independence and they had a pretty good band. They needed somebody to play the bass, and they needed a fiddle player, too. So me and Thornton Spencer—I'd known Thornton Spencer for a good while—started playing with them. Albert Hash had played at one time with Thornton's brother-in-law. Albert had played a lot of music back in the forties, back in the thirties, and all. He used to play with Henry Whitter, back after G. B. Grayson died. That was in 1973 or 1974 and we started a band. The White Top Mountain Band was the name of it.

Albert Hash was a good man. I still miss him. Albert, he started out just about everybody in this part of the country that makes musical instruments. Wayne Henderson and most of the other people that's here now making musical instruments, Albert helped 'em get started. Albert could make mandolins, he could make guitars, he made fiddles, he could just do just about any kind of that work. He was the best craftsman that's ever been in this part of the world. Albert made fiddles for fifty-six years. His instruments—if you see one, it'll be fancy. I played music with Albert Hash for about twenty years. Then Albert, he passed on. After Albert passed away, it just wasn't the same thing anymore. Now we just mostly jam—just get together for the fun. Most of the time we just sit around the store here and jam.

If you go away from around here on vacation somewhere, if you want to hear any good music, you have to take it with you. We always take along a couple of guitars, and if we're out camping, we'll just sit there and pick music. And you know, that's enjoyable. It never gets old—and I hear it everyday. It's a way of life.

---

when Tom Barr will grab his upright bass, someone else will pick up an old banjo, and two or three others will reach for guitars or mandolins from the walls of the shop. Well, there you go—the jam at Barr's Fiddle Shop in Galax, Virginia, is on!

LOCATION: Follow I-77 to exit 14 and take US 58/221 to Galax. After you pass a Lowes Hardware Superstore on left, proceed through eight traffic lights and look for the intersection of E. Stuart Dr. and Main St. (VA 89). Turn left onto Main St. at the light and go through three stoplights. Look for the shop at 105 S. Main St.

CONTACT: Tom Barr, Barr's Music Shop, 105 S. Main St., Galax, VA 24333, (276) 236-2411

❄ *Blue Ridge Backroads*

Like the Downtown Cinema Theatre in Mount Airy, the historic Rex Theater in Galax is a venue for a popular weekly radio music show that features live performances by old-time and bluegrass musicians. Every Friday night from 8:00 to 10:00 P.M., *Blue Ridge Backroads* is presented on the theater's stage in front of an audience. The show is free and open to the public and is usually very well attended both by local folks and by tourists visiting the Galax area.

Although the Rex Theater only seats about 450 people, WBRF-FM broadcasts the show at 98.1 on your radio dial. The station's 100,000 watts of transmitting power enable a potential audience of about 300,000 additional listeners to hear this live broadcast. The partially restored Rex Theater also stages community productions, films, and workshops. The Galax Downtown Association owns the building, and although some of its supporters say it needs additional renovation, it's clean, it's comfortable, and it's a great place to enjoy live performances of mountain music.

LOCATION: Follow I-77 to exit 14 and take US 58/221 to Galax. After you pass a Lowes Hardware superstore on left, proceed through eight traffic lights and look for the intersection of E. Stuart Dr. and Main St. (VA 89). Turn left onto Main St. and proceed to the third stoplight at the intersection of Main and E. Grayson Sts. Turn left onto E. Grayson St. and the theater will be on the right.

CONTACT: Debbie Robinson, Director of Tourism, City of Galax, 111 E. Grayson St., Galax, VA 24333, (276) 238-8130, ‹drobinson@galaxcity.org›, ‹www.rextheatergalax.org›, ‹www.ingalax.net›

❄ Downtown Street Festival in Galax

Since 1993, on the second Friday and Saturday of August each year, the Galax Downtown Association has staged a street festival featuring crafts, food, storytelling, and bluegrass music. The event is an effort by the Downtown Association to attract people who are attending the Galax Old Fiddlers' Convention to the downtown area by creating some daytime activities. Festival hours are 10:00 A.M. to 5:00 P.M. both days.

LOCATION: Follow I-77 to exit 14 and take US 58/221 to Galax. After you pass a Lowes Hardware superstore on left, proceed through eight traffic lights and look for the intersection of E. Stuart Dr. and Main St. (VA 89). Turn left onto Main St. at the light and you will see the festival along Main St.

The Rex Theater in Galax (Photograph courtesy of Debbie Robinson)

STEVE BARR
YOU GOT TO HAVE SOMEONE TO FOLLOW

Steve Barr of Galax, Virginia, is the son of Tom and Becky Barr. Steve (or Stevie, as he is affectionately called by family and friends) recently took part in a national tour of traditional musicians sponsored by the National Council for the Traditional Arts.

When I was real little, I started out playing ukulele. Just messing around with it. Then I started with the banjo, just a cheap, old-time banjo. Tom, my father, made me a new one—a walnut banjo. But then we went to Italy and one of the government officials in Florence, Italy, bought it. So as soon as we got back, Tom made me a new one out of maple. Albert Hash turned the resonator for it out of a piece of an old stump, a burled maple stump. That's the one I play now.

When I started out, we had a music shop out at west Galax, and there was these two guys out there who played a lot—Beverly Davis and Charles Hawks. Charles, he was more of a standard picker, and he played the Scruggs style. Beverly Davis, he played more like the Boston style. We'd get down there at their barber shop and pick around. When one of 'em wasn't cutting hair, he'd be over there showing me something to play on the banjo. Then whenever the other one would get through with a haircut, he'd come in there and show me something else. They had such different styles. Charles, he was strictly a straight style. After Beverly would show me something, Charles would come in and say "That's the wrong way! No!"

I don't see how in the world they worked together. And they never would play together. While one of them would be playing, the other one would just stand over there and look. It was the funniest thing you've ever seen! They'd sit out there at that barbershop and fuss. It was the funniest thing. They was always a-bickering, but they helped me out more than anything. And because it happened that way I learned the straight style and I learned the more fancier style, too.

There's a lot of older musicianers around this area that's contributed a lot to the music. Young people like me have got to have someone to follow—older musicianers like Kyle Creed—he played old-time banjo—and Albert Hash—he played old-time fiddle. You got to have people that play music that you can look up to. You don't exactly copy. You just take their style, and you add your own style to it. If it wasn't for the older musicianers, I wouldn't even be playing. I wouldn't have had nothing to go on. If they wouldn't have kept it going, and passed it on to people like me, the music wouldn't still be alive. That's one good thing about this area, it just keeps getting passed down from generation to generation. You can get one style from one person, and another style from another. That's what carries it on to another generation. That's what keeps it going.

CONTACT: Debbie Robinson, Director of Tourism, City of Galax, 111 E. Grayson St., Galax, VA 24333, (276) 238-8130, ‹drobinson@galaxcity.org›

GRAYSON COUNTY

✸ Fairview Ruritan Club Fiddlers' Convention

This springtime celebration in the Virginia Blue Ridge kicks off the annual season of regional fiddlers' conventions. The Fairview Ruritan Club Fiddlers' Convention is a competition at which regional musicians vie for best old-time and bluegrass band honors as well as for individual awards. The Fairview convention occurs on the last weekend in March each year.

The Fairview Ruritan Club also sponsors a varied schedule of old-time and bluegrass musical entertainment year-round, featuring such well-known musicians and bands as Big Country Bluegrass, Ralph Stanley, the Clinch Mountain Boys, and Lost and Found.

LOCATION: Travel south from Galax on VA 89 for four miles. Turn left onto Fairview Rd. and proceed for half a mile. The club is located on the right.
CONTACT: Betty Scott, Fairview Ruritan Club Fiddlers' Convention, Grayson County Tourist Information Center, PO Box 336, Independence, VA 24348, (276) 773-3711, ‹grayson@ls.net›, ‹www.grayson.va.us›; or Fairview Ruritan Club, (276) 236-9474

✸ Festival by the New River

In the picturesque mill town of Fries, Virginia, there's a free festival on the third Saturday of each September. The Festival by the New River at Fries

BLUE RIDGE MUSIC CENTER

Ralph Stanley and band perform at the outdoor amphitheater at the Blue Ridge Music Center. (Photograph courtesy of the Blue Ridge Parkway, National Park Service)

The Blue Ridge Music Center, near milepost 213 on the Blue Ridge Parkway in Virginia just north of the North Carolina state line, is an interpretive site and natural area that was established to honor traditional music and music makers of the Southern Appalachians. The nearest town is Galax, Virginia, which lies some twelve miles northwest of the site. About two miles away is Fisher's Peak, a local landmark bisected by the state line and which overlooks the Round Peak community in Surry County, North Carolina. In addition to presenting traditional artists at the center, staff members will direct visitors to places in the Blue Ridge where they can hear and see fine examples of traditional music and dance.

The Blue Ridge Music Center is planned as a multifaceted interpretive complex. An amphitheater on the grounds is already in use as a venue for musical performances beginning in the spring and running through October. Construction of a visitors center has also commenced.

The Music Center's programs will eventually include museum-quality exhibits, an audiovisual interpretation of the region's musical legacy, outdoor performances, lectures and discussions, and other entertaining and educational offerings. A planned sales area will offer a selection of sound and video recordings and books on traditional music. The nearby headwaters of Chestnut Creek and the surrounding forests are accessible by walking trails, presenting opportunities for environmental studies.

A component of the Blue Ridge Parkway National Park, the Blue Ridge Music Center is operated by the National Council for the Traditional Arts (NCTA), a private, nonprofit corporation. The town of Galax donated the 1,045 acres of land on which the center is located.

CONTACT: Debbie Robinson, Director of Tourism, City of Galax, 111 E. Grayson St., Galax, VA 24333, (276) 238-8130, ‹drobinson@galaxcity.org›; or National Council for the Traditional Arts, (301) 565-0654, ‹info@ncta.net›

features old-time and bluegrass music, crafts, and food. It's held at the Fries Town Park, near the banks of the meandering New River. Festival hours are 10:00 A.M. to 6:00 P.M.

LOCATION: From Galax, take US 58/221 West toward Independence. When you come to VA 94, turn right and follow VA 94 to Fries. As you get into Fries, the New River will be on your right. Cross Eagle Bottom Creek and turn right toward the downtown. Turn again to the right and look for the park near the river. The park is also a terminus for the New River Trail.

CONTACT: Eva Vaughn, Festival by the New River, Fries Town Park, Fries, VA 24330, (276) 744-2709

Old-Time Fiddlers' and Bluegrass Convention in Fries

On the third Friday and Saturday of August, a week following the Old Fiddlers' Convention at Galax, the Fries Volunteer Fire Department hosts a competition at the town's ballpark for players of old-time fiddle, bluegrass fiddle, banjo, dobro, and other instruments. Musicians vie for cash awards and ribbons. An admission fee benefits the Fries Volunteer Fire Department and local merchants. There's free on-site parking and camping available on a first-come, first-served basis. The convention begins at 7:00 P.M. on Friday and runs through 5:00 P.M. on Saturday.

LOCATION: From Galax, take US 58/221 West toward Independence. When you come to VA 94, turn right and follow VA 94 to Fries. As you get into Fries, the New River will be on your right. Cross Eagle Bottom Creek and turn right toward the downtown. Follow this road through town. The ballpark is on the far side of town on the right next to the New River.

CONTACT: Betty Scott, Grayson County Tourist Information Center, PO Box 336, Independence, VA 24348, (276) 773-3711, ‹grayson@ls.net›, ‹www.grayson.va.us›

Grayson County Fiddlers' Convention

Another of the many fiddlers' conventions held each spring and summer in the central Blue Ridge is the Grayson County Fiddlers' Convention at Elk Creek on the last Friday and Saturday of June. The convention is a well-established event that includes a music competition, concessions, and free camping. It's said to be a favorite venue for many local musicians and was featured in the June 1999 edition of *National Geographic*. There are two

The dam on the New River at Fries, Virginia.

evenings of music beginning at 6:00 P.M. each day, and a nominal admission is charged.

LOCATION: From Independencé, Va., take US 21 North for approximately eight miles to SR 658 at Elk Creek. Turn left onto SR 658 and follow the signs to the Elk Creek School. The school will be on your left. Look for the ballfield.

CONTACT: Betty Scott, Grayson County Tourist Information Center, PO Box 336, Independence, VA 24348, (276) 773-3711, ‹grayson@ls.net›, ‹www.grayson.va.us›

✤ Grayson Highlands Fall Festival

This event, which is staged on the fourth Saturday in September, is held on the grounds of Grayson Highlands State Park, one of the most scenic spots in the state of Virginia. The Rescue Squad and Fire Department sponsors the Grayson Highlands Fall Festival. The festival features a variety of entertaining activities, including molasses and apple butter making, cider squeezing, a wild pony sale, crafts exhibitions and sales, barbecued chicken dinners, dancing, and old-time and bluegrass music. The festivities begin at 10:00 A.M. and conclude around 6:00 P.M. There is no admission charge for attending the festival, but there is a daily parking fee for all vehicles entering the state park.

LOCATION: From Independence, take US 58 West through Mouth of Wilson and Volney. Watch for the entrance sign to Grayson Highlands State Park on the right at VA 362. Turn right and follow the signs.
CONTACT: Betty Scott, Grayson County Tourist Information Center, PO Box 336, Independence, VA 24348, (276) 773-3711, ‹grayson@ls.net›, ‹www.grayson.va.us›

✵ Jam Sessions at Grayson Highlands State Park

On Sunday afternoons from Memorial Day through Labor Day, visitors can enjoy a weekly bluegrass jam session at the Grayson Highlands State Park visitors center, beginning at 1:30 P.M. This is an informal gathering of mostly local musicians that's open to anyone who wants to play or listen. There's a vehicle parking fee, but the jam session itself is free.

LOCATION: From Independence, take US 58 West through Mouth of Wilson and Volney. Watch for the entrance sign to Grayson Highlands State Park on the right at VA 362. Turn right and follow the signs. The visitors center is located at the extreme north end of the park's main roadway.
CONTACT: Betty Scott, Grayson County Tourist Information Center, PO Box 336, Independence, VA 24348, (276) 773-3711, ‹grayson@ls.net›, ‹www.grayson.va.us›

✵ Wayne C. Henderson Music Festival and Guitar Competition

The Wayne C. Henderson Music Festival and Guitar Competition is held annually on the third Saturday in June at Grayson Highlands State Park near Mouth of Wilson, Virginia. The entire event is broadcast live over radio station WBRF 98.1 FM in Galax. This is an outdoors music festival that features some of the region's best musicians. It is named for National Heritage Award recipient Wayne Henderson, who lives nearby. Henderson is a nationally acclaimed guitar maker, and the festival features a guitar-playing competition in recognition of his achievements as a musician and craftsperson. The winner of the top award receives a hand-built Wayne Henderson guitar. The festival begins at 10:00 A.M. and concludes around 6:00 P.M. The guitar com-

The Wayne C. Henderson Music Festival and Guitar Competition is presented at picturesque Grayson Highlands State Park. (Photograph by Sally Council; courtesy of the North Carolina Arts Council)

petition takes place in late morning. Wayne C. Henderson and many of his musical friends are featured performers at the festival. Admission fees are used in support of scholarships for local and regional music students.

LOCATION: From Independence, take US 58 West through Mouth of Wilson and Volney. Watch for the entrance sign to Grayson Highlands State Park on the right at VA 362. Turn right and drive uphill, following the signs.

CONTACT: Lenora Rose, Wayne C. Henderson Music Festival and Guitar Competition, 815 Grassy Knob Lane, Mouth of Wilson, VA 24363, (276) 579-7712, ‹greif@ls.net›, ‹www.waynehenderson.org›

❋ Independence Fourth of July Celebration

What better place to enjoy a Fourth of July celebration than in a place named Independence? Well, visitors have their chance every year. On July 4, the main street in front of the 1908 Grayson County Courthouse fills with local folk and visitors doing their part in observance of American independence. There's barbecue, games, country and bluegrass music, a festive parade, and lots of fireworks. The fun begins at 9:00 A.M. and continues through 3:00 P.M.

LOCATION: Independence is located fifteen miles west of Galax at the intersection of US 58/221 and US 21/221. The event is in town.

CONTACT: Betty Scott, Grayson County Tourist Information Center, PO Box 336, Independence, VA 24348, (276) 773-3711, ‹grayson@ls.net›, ‹www.grayson.va.us›

❄ Mountain Foliage Festival

On the second Saturday in October, starting at 9:00 in the morning, the streets surrounding the courthouse square in Independence, Virginia, come alive with a celebration of the leaves of autumn. Held at the height of the fall color season, the celebration includes a band festival, a parade, arts and crafts, and—best of all—the Grand Privy Race (yes, they race outhouses!). The Mountain Foliage Festival is a free event.

LOCATION: Independence is located fifteen miles west of Galax at the intersection of US 58/221 and US 21/221. The event is in town.

CONTACT: Betty Scott, Grayson County Tourist Information Center, PO Box 336, Independence, VA 24348, (276) 773-3711, ‹grayson@ls.net›, ‹www.grayson.va.us›

❄ Troutdale Fire Hall Monthly Bluegrass Show

Once a month during the winter, unless there's a fire, a bluegrass concert is presented at the Fire Hall in Troutdale, Virginia. Profits from a modest admission fee and concession sales support the community fire department. Call for dates and times.

LOCATION: From Independence, travel west on US 58 through Mouth of Wilson to Volney. Look for the sign at the Troutdale Fire Hall.

CONTACT: Big Country Bluegrass, c/o Tommy Sells, Troutdale Fire Hall, 3503 Troutdale Hwy., Mouth of Wilson, VA 24363, (276) 579-2265

WAYNE HENDERSON
I MAKE GUITARS

Wayne C. Henderson of Rugby, Virginia, is a rural-route postman in southwestern Virginia. In 1995 he was a recipient of the prestigious National Heritage Fellowship Award from the National Endowment for the Arts.

I was raised in the little community of Rugby, Virginia. I've lived right there in that same little community pretty much all my life. Both my grandpas were banjo players, my father played the fiddle, my brother plays, and all my cousins do, too. My dad played in a band called the Rugby Gully Jumpers, with E. C. Ball and a couple of other neighbors around there. E. C. Ball turned out to be a fairly well-known musician.

I started playing guitar when I was about five, actually playing a real guitar. You know, I make guitars, and as far back as I can remember I've done repair work on 'em. Once I started doing that, there was pretty much a constant stream of musicians coming to my house. And, always, we'd end up sitting around and picking for a while.

I remember one I made. My mom had a dresser drawer bottom that I'd seen in there for years, and it had walnut veneer on it, and it was loose on the edges. I thought, "Well, now, if could get that stuff off there, you know I might could make the sides of that guitar out of that." The only glue that I had was some old black rubber stuff that my father used to put weather stripping on his truck door with. Well, in August, the sun got hot enough that it melted that old rubber glue, and that thing just flew totally apart! That was horribly disappointing.

My dad kind of had a little sympathy for me. He took me to meet a man named Albert Hash. He was one of the best fiddlers in the country and a wonderful instrument
builder. Albert Hash gave me a piece of an old mahogany door and told me what kind
of glue to use, and he gave me an old catalog where you could order some spruce
wood to make a top. That first one I made was in 1964, and my mother still has it. I
took it and showed it to Albert. He bragged on it a sight, and said, "If I'd a known
you'd do that good, I'd have got you some good wood to use." I've been trying to
make 'em better ever since. I've made about two hundred and thirty-seven guitars
and seventy-two mandolins, fifteen banjos and two fiddles, one dobro, and one or
two dulcimers.

I developed sort of an unusual style of playing. Back in those days almost nobody
played fiddle tunes or flatpick tunes on a guitar. That's something you were not supposed to do. Guitar players were supposed to play rhythm for the fiddlers, you know,
and that's all. That was the guitar player's job. You weren't supposed to do anything
else. The style I play is not either bluegrass or old-time. Music's just music to me.

In the old-time fiddle playing, they usually use more bow work with the notes,
and in the bluegrass they use what they call long-bow—one stroke of the bow with a
lot of notes made on the fingerboard. The old-time music is what it is—old-time
music. What people have been playing here for hundreds of years. Old-time music is
really good for dancing. I guess that was the main form of entertainment. Every
weekend they'd go to somebody's house and they'd have a square dance. The fiddler
and the banjo player would sit in the doorway, and they'd dance in both rooms.

Now they're working on teaching it in school. People around here will work at
things like that, to keep their music going. There's one tiny little school up here at the
place where I live—the Mount Rogers School. It's a tiny high school band that doesn't
have trumpets or any horn instruments. The high school band consists of the fiddle,
banjo, guitar, and bass! Some good musicians have come out of that, and people
support that program. Just like my little festival I have over there at the Grayson
Highlands State Park. The money that we make from that goes to scholarships for
young folks in this region who want to learn music.

I'm very fortunate that I get to travel out to faraway places and promote our
music—to play for people who have never heard of it before. They see that generally
people here are a whole lot more calm and polite and honest than almost anywhere,
especially when they're compared to big cities. Probably the biggest promotion of
our music has been in things like the movie *Deliverance*, which makes everybody
think we're all hillbillies. On the other hand, such things as that have exposed more
people to our kind of music than would ever possibly have happened otherwise.

❧ Troutdale Old-Time and Bluegrass Music Festival

The Troutdale Fire Hall is also the scene of an annual festival celebrating the traditional music of the region, held the second Saturday in September. The music is presented "concert" style by the Big Country Bluegrass Band and other popular local and regional groups. The event takes place rain or shine. There is a small admission fee, and food is available. Call for updated information.

LOCATION: From Independence, travel west on US 58 through Mouth of Wilson to Volney. Look for the sign at the Troutdale Fire Hall.
CONTACT: Big Country Bluegrass, c/o Tommy Sells, Troutdale Fire Hall, 3503 Troutdale Hwy., Mouth of Wilson, VA 24363, (276) 579-2265

❧ White Top Mountain Maple Festival

The Grayson County community in the White Top Mountain–Mount Rogers area hosts a series of annual events that feature traditional music as a principal component. On the last Saturday of March, at the Mount Rogers School, there's a civic fair that celebrates the local maple syrup–making tradition. Starting at 8:00 A.M., visitors can enjoy music, crafts, storytelling, tours of a maple-tapping area and a sugarhouse, and pancakes with freshly made maple syrup. The event is free; proceeds from the sale of pancakes and syrup support activities at the Mount Rogers School.

LOCATION: From Independence, travel west on US 58 through Mouth of Wilson toward the Grayson Highlands State Park. Once you've passed the entrance to the park, continue on US 58 for approximately ten more miles and the Mount Rogers School will be on your left. Watch for the signs.
CONTACT: Betty Scott, Grayson County Tourist Information Center, PO Box 336, Independence, VA 24348, (276) 773-3711, ‹grayson@ls.net›, ‹www.grayson.va.us›

❧ White Top Mountain Molasses Festival

The Mount Rogers Fire Hall is the site for the annual White Top Mountain Molasses Festival, held on the second Sunday in October. This event is the fall counterpart to the White Top Mountain Maple Festival and features music, crafts, and demonstrations of apple butter and sorghum molasses making. The activities begin at 11:00 A.M. and conclude around 7:00 P.M. A small admission fee is charged.

Some Blue Ridge residents still make molasses in the fall. Here Gary Poe and Larry Pennington feed sorghum cane into a press to extract the juice for cooking.

LOCATION: From Independence, travel west on US 58 through Mouth of Wilson toward the Grayson Highlands State Park. Once you've passed the entrance to the park, continue on US 58 for approximately fifteen more miles and the Mount Rogers Fire Hall will be on your left. Watch for the signs.

CONTACT: Betty Scott, Grayson County Tourist Information Center, PO Box 336, Independence, VA 24348, (276) 773-3711, ‹grayson@ls.net›, ‹www.grayson.va.us›

❀ White Top Mountain Ramp Festival

Ramps are a type of wild onion that grows in the eastern highlands from North Carolina to Canada. They resemble scallions with broad leaves. Also known as wild leek, ramps have an assertive, garlicky-onion flavor that is exceptionally strong. They are sometimes jokingly referred to as "wild leeks with a reek" because of their pungent odor. Their trademark scent is really quite overwhelming—the "fragrance" may linger for days on the breath of

Ramps are referred to as "wild leeks with a reek." (Photograph by Roger Haile)

a person who has eaten them, and the judicious and considerate consumer of ramps will withdraw from society until the stench has subsided. Sautéed ramps, pickled ramps, ramps and eggs, potatoes and ramps, ramp soup, and ramp casserole are just a few of the ways in which this wild herb is prepared and served.

The Mount Rogers Fire Hall is the locale for the White Top Mountain Ramp Festival, celebrated on the third Sunday in May. This event includes music by local musicians, crafts, games, dancing, a ramp-eating contest, and barbecued chicken made with ramps. Festivities, including the ramp-eating components, begin at 11:00 A.M. The day ends around 7:00 P.M.

LOCATION: Follow directions above for the White Top Mountain Molasses Festival.
CONTACT: Betty Scott, Grayson County Tourist Information Center,
PO Box 336, Independence, VA 24348, (276) 773-3711, ‹grayson@ls.net›,
‹www.grayson.va.us›

❄ Baywood Fall Festival

The Baywood Fall Festival is held each year at the Baywood School on the first Saturday in October. It's sponsored by the local Ruritan Club and features a parade, crafts, a horse pull, an antique car show, and a variety of traditional music. The festivities begin at 9:00 A.M. A nominal admission fee is charged.

LOCATION: From Galax, take US 58 West toward Independence. Baywood is five miles west of Galax.
CONTACT: Betty Scott, Grayson County Tourist Information Center,
PO Box 336, Independence, VA 24348, (276) 773-3711, ‹grayson@ls.net›,
‹www.grayson.va.us›

WILL THE CIRCLE BE UNBROKEN?

Will the circle be unbroken
By and by, Lord, by and by?
There's a better home awaiting
In the sky, Lord, in the sky.

The Carter Family of
Maces Springs, Virginia
(Photograph courtesy of the
Country Music Foundation)

The Carter Family of southwestern
Virginia was one of the first country
music groups to achieve real show-
business stardom. The group's memo-
rable songs, first recorded in the 1920s,
have influenced and guided the course
and development of country music ever
since. To this day, the early recordings
of the Carter Family remain touchstones
in the country music recording and
entertainment industry.

Hiltons, Virginia, is the home of the
legendary Carter Family. Some consider
it the originating point of American
country music. Hiltons is the location
of the Carter Family Music Center, also
called the Carter Family Fold.

According to a Carter Family Fold
Internet site (‹www.fmp.com/orthey/
carter.html›), the Carter Family Music Center has presented programs of
old-time and bluegrass music every weekend since 1974. Formally estab-
lished in 1979, the center's objective is to promote old-time music and to
pay tribute to the original Carter Family—A. P. Carter, Sara Carter, and
Maybelle Carter. The Saturday concerts highlight the musical style that
was made popular by the Carter Family nearly a century ago. Both the
weekly concerts and an annual festival were begun by Jeannette Carter,
A. P. and Sara's daughter. Jeannette promised her father before he died
that she would try to carry on his music. In keeping with the traditional
music style of the Carter Family, no electrical instruments are allowed
onstage at the Carter Family Music Center.

Once each year, on the first weekend of August, a two-day festival at
the Carter Family Music Center features a variety of bluegrass and old-
time music, along with plenty of mountain dancing. Showtimes are 2:00
P.M. to 11:00 P.M. each day. It's a grand event.

Call or visit the website listed below for further information about upcoming programming.

LOCATION: From I-81 South, take exit 1 (Bristol/Gate City) onto VA 58. Stay in the right lane to Gate City and follow VA 58 to Hiltons, about twenty-five miles. Turn right onto VA 709 at the store in Hiltons and follow it over the railroad tracks, then bear right onto VA 614. It's about three miles to the Carter Family Fold.
CONTACT: (540) 386-6054, ‹www.scarlet.org/carter/index.html›, ‹www.fmp.com/orthey/carter.html›

✵ Bridle Creek Fall Festival

Two weeks after the Baywood Fall Festival, on the third Saturday in October, there's another fall festival, this one near the town of Independence, Virginia. The Bridle Creek Fall Festival is staged at the Bridle Creek School. It begins at 11:00 A.M. and lasts until around 3:30 P.M. and features old-time music, dance, crafts, and food. Proceeds from the festival benefit the school.

LOCATION: From Independence, take US 58 West and go approximately five miles. Turn left on Bridle Creek Rd. (SR 681) and follow the directional signs to the school.
CONTACT: Betty Scott, Grayson County Tourist Information Center, PO Box 336, Independence, VA 24348, (276) 773-3711, ‹grayson@ls.net›, ‹www.grayson.va.us›

CARROLL COUNTY

✵ Community Dance in Hillsville

The Grover King VFW Post 1115 in Hillsville, Virginia, sponsors a traditional mountain dance every Saturday evening, April through September, at its meeting hall. This event usually draws between 150 and 300 dancers and listeners. Local bands provide music for the event. The Grover King VFW hall is a large building with ample room for dancing and enjoying the music. The dance begins around 8:00 P.M. and ends at midnight. An admission fee is charged.

A LEGENDARY SHOOTOUT AT THE CARROLL COUNTY COURTHOUSE

The Carroll County Courthouse in Hillsville, Virginia, is a two-story, red brick structure. Four massive white-washed masonry columns support its front portico, and its roof is crowned with a six-sided, wood-frame dome. It's a handsome building that appears to be a pretty typical southern county courthouse.

A reenactment of the shootout at the Hillsville Courthouse (Photograph courtesy of the Blue Ridge Institute, Ferrum, Va.)

But on March 12, 1912, an incident occurred within its walls that would forever change the way that old courthouse is viewed, at least by those who know the story. "The Ballad of Sidna Allen" tells it this way:

In the state of Old Virginny,
In the year Nineteen and Twelve;
Was the famous Allen gangsters,
We all remember well.

Claude Allen was on trial,
And Sidna, too, was there,
When a shot rang out in the courtroom,
And the judge fell from his chair.

The sheriff, too, was murdered,
An attorney of the state,
The blame was laid on Sydna,
And no one knew his fate.

Till the jury found him guilty
And the judge his sentence read,
Then the court pronounced his sentence,
It was twenty years, they said.

Elements of the shocking incident that took place in the courtroom at Hillsville that day would include the deaths of the presiding judge, Thornton L. Massie, Carroll County sheriff Lewis Webb, prosecuting attorney William Foster, juror Augustus Fowler, and witness Betty Ayers;

Floyd Allen (Photograph courtesy of the Blue Ridge Institute, Ferrum, Va.)

the firing of as many as seventy-five gunshots inside the courtroom; the wounding of Floyd Allen, the defendant; the wounding of a number of bystanders and other shooters; and the flight from law by several relatives of Floyd Allen, including Sidna Allen, Claude Allen, Freel Allen, Wesley Edwards, and Sydney Edwards.

The whole affair had begun almost a year earlier, when Wesley Edwards, a nephew of Floyd Allen, had a Sunday morning altercation with several other young men outside a church service. When Wesley and his cousin Sidna Allen, who had come to his aid in the fight, were indicted for "disturbing religious worship and fighting," they quickly departed Hillsville and went into hiding in North Carolina. Before their uncle, Floyd Allen, could arrange bond for the pair, Carroll County deputy sheriffs Pink Samuels and Peter Easter located the fugitives. The lawmen arrested them and brought them back into Hillsville bound in ropes and manacles.

Floyd Allen encountered the arriving party just as he returned from posting bond. A quick-tempered man, he angrily demanded that the deputies immediately remove the boys' restraints and release them. The officers refused to do so, and in the heated discussion that followed, one of them pointed his pistol at Floyd Allen. Allen then grabbed the weapon from the deputy, smashed it with a rock, and turned his nephews loose. Subsequently, Floyd Allen was charged with assault and battery and with interfering with an officer in pursuit of his duty. It has been said he swore then that he'd never serve a single day in jail.

Allen was freed on bond, and nearly a year passed before he was brought to court. After a short trial, the jury announced a verdict. The word "guilty" was barely out of the foreman's mouth before gunfire erupted. Floyd Allen, who was quoted as saying, "Boys, I won't be taken," reached into his pocket, reportedly for a pistol. Many others, including several court officers, began firing.

Five people were killed and seven others wounded, including Floyd Allen and the clerk of the court, Dexter Goad. All of the Allen kin, except Floyd, made their escape from the melee on horseback, but all were subsequently caught. Wesley Edwards and Sidna Allen were the last two to be arrested, months later, in Des Moines, Iowa, where they were working as carpenters. Floyd Allen and his son, Claude, who had come to his assistance in the courtroom shooting, were sentenced to die in the electric chair and were later executed. The other Allens were all given lengthy jail terms. Another ballad, the "Ballad of Claude Allen," gives the moral of the story:

> Now, young people, all take warning,
> Pay heed to what your parents say.
> Else you may end like poor Claude Allen,
> And have some awful debt to pay

LOCATION: The Grover King VFW Post 1115 complex is located in Hillsville. From the center of downtown, where US 52 and US 58 intersect, take US 58 (W. Stuart Dr.) South. The VFW complex will be on your left within a half-mile. Please enter through the side gate near the Veterans Monument.

CONTACT: Hillsville Round and Square Dancing, Grover King VFW No. 1115, Hillsville, VA 24343, (276) 728-2911

❧ Heritage Shoppe and Heritage Records

Bobby Patterson, an excellent musician from a family of outstanding singers and instrumentalists, created the Heritage Shoppe and Heritage Records in Woodlawn in Carroll County. Heritage Records specializes in recordings of local musicians. The label also features CDs and tapes made from selected performances at the Galax Old Fiddlers' Conventions.

LOCATION: From I-77, take exit 14 and turn west onto US 58/221 toward Galax. Travel approximately three-and-a-half miles to Woodlawn (Harmon's Discount Center) and turn right onto Coulson Church Rd. (VA 620). As soon as you turn, the shop is within sight on the left.

Owner Bobby Patterson has documented many of southwestern Virginia's outstanding traditional artists on his record label. (Courtesy of Heritage Records)

JIM MARSHALL
THE BALLAD OF FANCY GAP

I was born on the mountain, where the windy breezes blow,
I remember experiences of many years ago.
I've seen the twisted wreckage, heard of many a widowed wife,
When old Fancy Gap took another trucker's life.

Fancy Gap, Fancy Gap,
They named it Killer Mountain,
That old Fancy Gap.
    From "The Ballad of Fancy Gap," by Jim Marshall

Jim Marshall is a retired businessman who lives near the town of Hillsville, Virginia. He and his wife, Artie, performed as a duo in the region for many years.

"The Ballad of Fancy Gap" is more or less the story of my life. I was raised out there about ten miles from Fancy Gap, up on the mountain. I started hauling livestock down from the mountain in 1946. That's where that song comes from. There's been so many wrecks on that mountain. It's dangerous. I'd have to go down it and with not too much brakes on that old truck. This was cattle country, and my dad bought the packing house down in Hillsborough, North Carolina. He bought livestock—hogs and cattle—and I hauled them down there, down the mountain.

I was born in Galax in 1929. My wife, Artie, was born in Mount Airy. Artie and I played music together for over fifty years. We started playing together in the 1940s. We both went to Hillsville High School up here, and we had a little band there at the school. The janitor played the fiddle, Artie was the guitar player, and I played the banjo. Artie learned her style of guitar picking from the Carter Family and from Charlie Monroe. She could play note-for-note anything that Charlie Monroe ever done. She was one of the best guitar players in southwest Virginia.

My dad was a good musician. He played fiddle and old-time banjo. People would come over to our house and play music on Saturday nights. I learned to play, more or less, from the people who would play there, you know? It was just a natural thing to do. I started out on guitar, and then I picked up the five-string banjo. Then we got a radio. So they'd come to our house and listen to the *Grand Old Opry*. Didn't many people have radios then. Mama got one though, and everybody would come to listen to it.

I think the music in the Blue Ridge right now is real good. There's lots of fiddlers' conventions, festivals, and so on. I don't think it's dying out. I think it's going good. There's lots of jam sessions in this area. On Monday night there's one in Sparta, and on Tuesday night there's another one in Sparta, except at a different place. We play out here at my place on Wednesday nights, and on Thursdays they play at the Andy Griffith Playhouse, down in Mount Airy. On Friday nights, they have music at the Floyd Country Store over in Floyd, Virginia.

At our jam sessions, we give everybody a chance to play whatever they want to play. In this area, in southwest Virginia, east Tennessee, and western North Carolina, we've still got a big supply of old-time musicians. And a lot of young people are learning it. Every time I go out to anything, I see a lot of young people that's coming in on the old-time style. I'd like to see it continue on. We've got an awful lot of talent.

I don't think there's anybody around who's known as many old-time and bluegrass musicians as I have, at least anybody that's living now. I've thought about doing a little biography on each one, on the style of music they played, the songs that they done, what they played, and all that stuff. Most of the oldest are dead. Just me and my brother's about all that's left living now.

CONTACT: Bobby F. Patterson, Heritage Shoppe and Heritage Records, 4729 Coal Creek Rd., Galax, VA 24333, (276) 236-9249, (276) 236-9079, ‹heritage@naxs.net›

WYTHE COUNTY

✿ Chautauqua Festival in Wytheville

In 1985 the first Chautauqua Festival was staged in the southwest Virginia community of Wytheville. The annual celebration includes children's activities, arts and crafts, hot-air ballooning, magic shows, music, drama, dance, and special exhibits. It's held the third weekend in June at Wytheville's Elizabeth Brown Memorial Park and is cosponsored by the Wythe Arts Council, the Town of Wytheville, and Wythe County. The music begins in the early afternoon. An admission fee is charged.

LOCATION: From I-81, take exit 73 onto Main St. Follow it to the fifth traffic light (they are numbered). At this light, take a left onto First St. Continue on First St. until you come to Spring St. Take a right onto Spring St. and proceed until you come to Fourth St. Take a left on Fourth St. and look for the signs to the festival.
CONTACT: Wytheville Arts Council, Chautauqua Festival, Elizabeth Brown Memorial Park, PO Drawer 533, Wytheville, VA 24382, (276) 228-6855

REGION THREE

THEY FEED ME ON CORNBREAD AND BEANS

In Southern Appalachia, traditional food and traditional music are close friends. They're seen together all the time. In fact, they're practically inseparable. Mountain musicians will sometimes stop playing long enough to eat; they sure don't stop very long for anything else! The combination of good homemade food and good homemade music can be found at dozens of music venues in Southern Appalachia. Almost without exception, every folk festival, fiddlers' convention, hometown opry, and every other music and dance venue in the Blue Ridge provides a greater or lesser bounty of food to go with the music, often paying deference to regional specialties. Festival organizers sometimes contract with commercial vendors and community service organizations to prepare and serve special traditional foods at hometown celebrations.

As the lyrics to "Lonesome Road Blues" imply ("Oh, they feed me on cornbread and beans / Lord, I ain't a-gonna be treated this-a way"), pinto beans are a longtime favorite food in Southern Appalachia. In the past, during hard times, they served, and were served, as the basic staple for many mountain families. Traditionally eaten with a big square piece of corn bread and a thick circle of sliced raw onion, pinto beans may be the most frequently served of all the regional favorites in the Blue Ridge. They're prepared nowadays at festivals, at fiddlers' conventions, at street fairs, in restaurants, and at home.

While you're looking for truly regional cuisine, with or without music, drop in on one or two of the local cafés and restaurants scattered here and there in the smaller cities and towns of the Blue Ridge. Harold's Restaurant, located on US 15 in Wilkesboro, North Carolina, is one of many local eateries that have a full range of Appalachian regional favorites from which to choose. For example, Harold's breakfast menu lists homemade biscuits with

Fried apple pies are a specialty of O'Henry's Restaurant.

your choice of bacon, bologna, chicken fillet, country ham, eggs, grilled chicken, hog jowls, jelly, livermush, sausage, steak, tenderloin, bacon, bacon and egg, boiled ham and egg, bologna and egg, country ham and egg, hog jowls and egg, livermush and egg, sausage and egg, or steak and egg. Breakfast sandwich combinations at Harold's include egg with your choice of bacon, boiled ham, livermush, sausage, steak, bologna, brains, bacon, lettuce and tomato, or country ham, as well as other favorites such as egg salad, grilled chicken, grilled chicken and cheese, or tenderloin.

Seafood restaurants are surprisingly numerous in the Blue Ridge, and even though the mountains are several hundred miles from the Atlantic coast, many eating establishments specialize in fresh seafoods that are regularly shipped into the high country. Fresh flounder, redfish, shrimp, and crabs are listed on menus side by side with such locally supplied and traditionally prepared delicacies as pepper catfish and pan-fried mountain trout. In Deep Gap, North Carolina, in Watauga County, there's one such restaurant called Thompson Seafood. Doc Watson and several of his musician friends sometimes gather at Thompson's to eat and, on occasion, present an impromptu set of traditional music.

Other traditional foods prepared with a regional flair and often served with music include barbecued pork and chicken and all of the related side dishes, homemade ice cream, roasted corn on the cob, chili, and a great variety of home-baked cakes, pastries, and cookies. Most of the larger community festivals in the region also feature at least several of such nearly universally sold street fair foods as funnel cakes, Polish sausages, hot dogs, hamburgers, soft-serve ice cream, lemonade, gyros, fried pork skins, cotton candy, candy apples, popcorn, and snow cones.

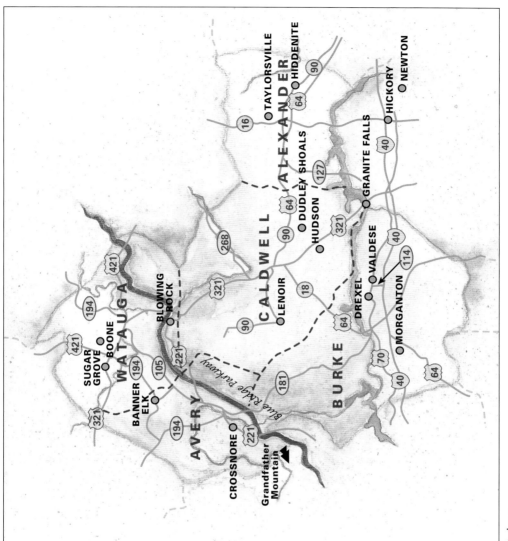

✿ Sims Country Bar-B-Que Inc.

Sims Country Bar-B-Que Inc. located on the Charlie Little Road in Dudley Shoals, North Carolina, advertises itself as being "centrally located in the middle of nowhere." So before you try to find your way there without knowing exactly where you're going, save yourself some trouble—get good directions from someone who knows. You *can* get there. It *is* possible. Lots of people have done it. It's easy—if you know how.

Hidden from view until you've driven up, down, and around a half-mile of dirt driveway, Sims Country Bar-B-Que Inc. is suddenly revealed as you crest a gentle open ridge. Situated beneath a grove of huge trees that stand clustered on the edge of a broad, grassy slope sits a large, rustic, meandering building that can accommodate up to a thousand people. That's the restaurant. It's essentially one big room divided into two parts by a massive, double-sided stone fireplace. The enormous dining area is furnished with lines of simple tables and wooden benches set up in long end-to-end rows, boarding-house style.

There are many things to do at this place, which is part restaurant, part park, part music stage, and part dance center. Some folks enjoy a leisurely walk around the edge of a nearby pond before dining, or a stroll out onto the earthen walkway that runs a short distance into the water. The grassy banks of the pond are neatly kept and mowed. A few crumbs of bread tossed onto the surface of the water will often attract surprisingly large fish.

Between the pond and the main building, near a small creek, are several spots for tossing horseshoes. Horseshoe pitching is a popular pastime at Sims, especially for the men and boys, and during the early evening hours

the courts are very busy. Inevitably some of the players are rank novices, so a word of caution is in order. The accuracy of the aim of some of the players can't be relied on. Meanwhile, inside the place, the food is ready when you are. It's a bountiful buffet that's continuously replenished, as needed, throughout the evening.

The main dish at Sims Country Bar-B-Que Inc. is, as you might guess, barbecue—specifically, pit-cooked barbecue.

A heaping platter of Sims barbecue

THAT GOOD OLD MOUNTAIN DEW: FACTS AND FICTION

A widely held public stereotype about mountain culture is one that associates the region's residents, and particularly its music, with moonshine whiskey. Some writers and filmmakers more attracted to myth than to reality have perpetuated this image. It is true, however, that older generations of musicians throughout the Blue Ridge still tell stories, some humorous and some tragic, of times when music was playing, dancers were dancing, and the moonshine was flowing.

Sign at Young's Mountain Music

For early mountain settlers, liquor was a part of everyday life. It has long been an essential ingredient in many folk medicines, and the distilling of liquor was a legal activity during the nineteenth and early twentieth centuries.

Bessie Eldreth, a ballad singer who lives in the Meat Camp community near where Watauga and Ashe Counties meet, learned ballads and love songs while posted as a lookout on a hill near her father's still. She was supposed to give a signal if revenue agents approached. Heralded Surry County musicians Tommy Jarrell and Fred Cockerham played a unique version of "John Henry," which they learned from an uncle who picked it up from other musicians while making moonshine in a nearby county.

Nowadays most public music venues—fiddlers' conventions, festivals, square dances, concerts, and community jam sessions—are alcohol free. Open public consumption of alcohol at such events is illegal in most places and met with general disapproval all around. It's typical to see large notices posted inside and outside public music venues declaring in no uncertain terms that the public consumption of alcohol will not be tolerated.

Now, there are many things in this nation that are termed barbecue. Too many. As a matter of fact, in some precincts (mostly outside the traditional South) any kind of meat cooked out-of-doors and over (or even near) a burning flame is considered to be—and is thus entitled—barbecue. It's not so! Honest-to-god, traditionally prepared, authentic, real southern barbecue has to be cooked over a pit. *Pit-cooked* is the operative term here. If it ain't pit cooked, it ain't barbecue.

And don't worry about how to spell barbecue correctly. There's no univer-

Visitors compete in a game of horseshoes.

sally accepted spelling of the word in the South and, with luck, there never will be. It can be *bar-b-cue, barbecue, barbeque, B-B-Q, bar-b-que,* and more.

Keith Sims, along with his wife, Shirley, and other family members including Susan Sims Bumgardner and Joe Sims, owns and operates Sims Country Bar-B-Que Inc. Three generations of the Sims family are involved in the management and operation of this colorful place. The image of a family operation and a family-oriented spot to enjoy good food accompanied by traditional music and dance is exactly what Keith Sims strives to portray. His menu board reads "Coffee, Soft Drinks, and the Best Iced Tea Around! (No alcohol is served or permitted.)"

For a set price (one price for adults, a lesser one for children), patrons get the all-you-can-eat buffet, served cafeteria style. The buffet is the only choice offered at Sims, but it's a good one. It includes pit-barbecued beef, pork, and chicken, baked beans, coleslaw, cornbread fritters (fried cornbread patties), pickles, potato chips, and loaf bread. Pitchers of iced tea or lemonade, coffee, and soft drinks, along with desserts, are extra. Each table is furnished with several jars of homemade strawberry jam to accompany the fried cornbread—an unusual and unexpectedly tasty treat! And don't forget, it's all-you-can-eat!

Once you've loaded your tray with that enormous plate of food and something to drink, look around and select a table that's as close as possible to the dance floor and music stage. Then settle in. You have a full evening ahead of you—eating more tasty barbecue than you should, drinking lots of iced tea, meeting and socializing with nice people, listening to hours of fine bluegrass and old-time music, and watching—and perhaps participating in—lively mountain dancing.

The restaurant is open to the public year-round on Thursday evenings from 5:30 to 8:30, Friday evenings from 5:00 to 9:00, and Saturday evenings from 5:00 until the band quits playing. Music is on Friday and Saturday evenings only. A campground is located adjacent to the restaurant.

LOCATION: From Lenoir, take US 321 South to Granite Falls, N.C. At the traffic light near the Valley Chevrolet dealership, turn left onto Pinewood Extension. Proceed on Pinewood Extension to the stop sign and turn left onto Dudley Shoals Rd. Follow Dudley Shoals Rd. for approximately six miles. Turn right onto Charley Little Rd. just past the Gateway School (on your right) and the Dudley Shoals Baptist Church (on your left). At the stop sign on Charley Little Rd., turn left onto Petra Mill Rd. Sim's Bar-B-Que will be approximately 100 yards ahead on the right.

From Hickory, take US 321 North to Granite Falls. At the traffic light near the Valley Chevrolet dealership, turn right onto Pinewood Extension and pick back up with the directions above.

CONTACT: Joseph D. Sims, 3339 Bowman Rd., Granite Falls, NC 28630, (828) 396-5811, (828) 396-6136; or Caldwell County Chamber of Commerce, 1909 Hickory Blvd. SE, Lenoir, NC 28645, (800) 737-0782, (828) 726-0616, ‹visitors@caldwellcochamber.org›, ‹www.caldwellcochamber.org›

✤ Sunday Afternoons at the Bolick Pottery

In northern Caldwell County, not far from the popular tourist mecca of Blowing Rock, North Carolina, an outdoor summer concert series takes place at the Bolick Pottery and Traditions Pottery shops, which are located side by side on Blackberry Road about three miles south of Blowing Rock, off US 321.

The Sunday afternoon picking and singing sessions feature old-time, bluegrass, and country music, occasional storytelling, and clogging and buck dance demonstrations. Shop owner and potter Glenn Bolick serves as host, emcee, and leader of the jam session. Musicians sit on old chairs and stools in and around a small, open-fronted wooden shed that Bolick constructed himself just for this purpose. The music is all acoustic. A concrete-floored stage provides a space for dancing, and Bolick's granddaughter, a champion clog dancer, gives occasional demonstrations. Listeners sit informally in the shade offered by a grove of hardwood trees—some on rough plank benches, others on one of several large boulders that are scattered here and there under the trees, and still others in folding chairs they've

Glenn Bolick helps his son-in-law, Mike Calhoun, fire the pottery kiln.

brought along for the occasion. Soft drinks and light snacks are provided free of charge, but donations are welcome. A bumper sticker on a nearby pickup truck reads, "I'm a potter, that's why my eyes are glazed," and a sign tacked high up on the music shed declares, "This is a work free, smokin', pickin', chewin' area."

The woodlands, fields, and pastures surrounding the Bolick complex are nestled within a beautiful mountain hollow forested with hardwood trees and thickets of mountain laurel. It's a picturesque and relaxing place to go on a Sunday to hear some good traditional mountain music. The Sunday afternoon music sessions begin on the second Sunday in July and continue through the last Sunday in September. The fun starts at 2:00 P.M.

LOCATION: From Blowing Rock, N.C., take US 321 South for approximately three miles. At St. Mark's Lutheran Church (on left), turn left onto Blackberry Rd. (SR 1500). Follow the unpaved road downhill for about a half-mile and turn right onto Bolick Rd. Bolick Pottery is the first drive on the left and Traditions Pottery is the second drive on the left. The pottery shops are identified by signs.

GLENN BOLICK
SAWMILL MAN

A visit to Glenn Bolick's shop on Blackberry Road in Caldwell County, North Carolina, treats visitors to a rare look at an operating antique sawmill, a lesson on contemporary stoneware pottery making, or a performance of old-time music.

I'll just start with my grandfather and this old house here that I live in. This house is a hundred and twelve years old. I grew up just across the way over there, and I spent a lot of time here with my grandparents. My grandfather, grandmother, and aunt would sing together—gospel hymns—using the *Christian Harmony* songbook. They sang three-part harmony. They didn't have a guitar, or a banjo, or nothing playing with 'em. That's the first remembrance that I have of any kind of music.

I was born in 1939, June the thirtieth. I was the sixth child of ten. My parents sang shape-notes at the Baptist church. They'd teach the shaped notes to us, the do-re-mi. I didn't really learn it like I should have. But I've always loved singing. As I grew older, we had a battery-powered radio at our house. And we had one of those crank-up record players—a talking machine, we called it—that we listened to different artists on. We listened to the *Grand Old Opry* on the radio sometimes on Saturday night when I was a child.

We're part of that same family of Bolicks that came from Germany in 1753. They didn't get out anywhere much then, and nobody much came in here from somewhere else. It was mostly just the local folks, so that's who they married—each other. It's like Jeff Foxworthy says, "Our family tree don't fork all that much." My great-grand-fathers were brothers, so I think that would make Mama and Papa second cousins.

We didn't get to go to dances until we got grown and left home. When I was a teenager in the fifties, they had some dances at Blowing Rock with live bands that would play all kinds of music. Rock and roll was going strong then, and I liked it pretty good. But I got over it. I got back to the old traditional stuff. I had always had a guitar and banjo, you know, just messing around with them. I had my banjo in my car one day when we had come home here for the weekend. We stopped to visit my grandmother. She saw that banjo in the car, in the back seat, and she said, "Lord, there's an old banjer! Let me see that thing." So I got it out and handed it to her. She went to tuning on that thing, and she tuned it up in one of the older styles of tuning. Then she played "Fly Around My Pretty Little Miss" and she sung it. After I saw her do that, I just had to play in her style. That's the way I learned it, after I saw her do it that way.

My wife is Lula Owens, and her folks were in pottery. I married into the pottery business. We worked for her dad, M. L. Owens, at his pottery for ten years before we come back here. I got a chance to buy this old farm and we started our pottery business here in 1973. My family just done sawmilling and farming and digging roots and herbs. That's the way we grew up. I wrote a song about my dad, and his dad and granddad, about them all being sawmillers. I call it "The Sawmill Man." Each generation used a different power system to run the sawmill with, from a water wheel to a steam engine to a kerosene burner to a diesel, which I now use myself.

My daughter Janet and my son-in-law Michael have a shop of their own here. They call it the Traditions Pottery. My daughter started making pottery when she was very young. They both wanted to do pottery. They opened a shop at Blowing Rock and after a couple of years up there, they built their own shop down here. So they have their own business. We fix our clay together. We dig it and process it together. We work together a lot. I think the two shops complement one another.

The musicians who play here do it just for the enjoyment of it. They're not paid. People come to enjoy the music, but once they're here, they can go in the shops and look around, buy pottery. Our Heritage Day was started very small, with mostly family and friends. The first year we had some quilts, a fellow brought his oxen and wagon, his wife churned butter, and we had just all different kinds of old-timey things—blacksmithing, log skidding with mules, the sawmill going, and so on. We cooked pinto beans in there on the wood cookstove—about thirty pounds of beans—and we baked cornbread. Last year my sister-in-law made fried pies. A niece made homemade ice cream. The whole family is involved in it. People like it 'cause it's so laid back. I don't have a lot of rules and regulations. We just ask that they don't have any alcohol or use any bad language. It's a family event and we want to keep it that way.

From Lenoir, N.C., take US 321 North for approximately fourteen miles. At St. Mark's Lutheran Church (on right), turn right onto Blackberry Rd. (SR 1500) and pick back up with the directions above.

CONTACT: Janet Calhoun, 4443 Bolick Rd., Lenoir, NC 28645, (828) 295-5099, ‹www.traditionspottery.com›; or Caldwell County Chamber of Commerce, 1909 Hickory Blvd. SE, Lenoir, NC 28645, (800) 737-0782, (828) 726-0616, ‹visitors@caldwellcochamber.org›, ‹www.caldwellcochamber.org›

A steam-driven sawmill is often cranked up on Heritage Day.

✤ Heritage Day and Kiln Opening at the Bolick Pottery

A special expression of Glenn Bolick's love of history and traditional cus-
toms is the annual Heritage Day that the Bolick family stages on the last
Saturday in June. The festivities include old-time and bluegrass music, clogging, flatfooting, and buck dancing, displays of mountain crafts, and "heritage" demonstrations—blacksmithing, ox handling, lumbering, quilting,
colonial knotting, children's games, and pottery making; an important
event is the opening of a wood-fired pottery kiln that Bolick patterned after
a style used by the pottery-making Owens family, his wife's forebears.

LOCATION: Follow directions above for Sunday afternoon jam sessions at Bolick's.
CONTACT: Janet Calhoun, 4443 Bolick Rd., Lenoir, NC 28645, (828) 295-5099,
‹www.traditionspottery.com›; or Caldwell County Chamber of Commerce,
1909 Hickory Blvd. SE, Lenoir, NC 28645, (800) 737-0782, (828) 726-0616,
‹visitors@caldwellcochamber.org›, ‹www.caldwellcochamber.org›

❄ Jam Session at Lenoir Mall

Down the mountain from Blowing Rock, at the Lenoir Mall on Morganton Boulevard SW in Lenoir, North Carolina, there's a jam session every Thursday night featuring bluegrass, country, and gospel music. The jam gets underway at 7:00 P.M. in the center court of the mall. During the course of the evening, smaller groups of musicians frequently break away from the main jam and form other sessions throughout the complex. The mall remains open, and the music continues, until 9:00 P.M.

LOCATION: When traveling north or south, take US 321 to downtown Lenoir. At the intersection with US 64/NC 18, turn southwest onto 64/18 Bypass (Morganton Blvd.). (Do not take 64/18 Business.) Follow 64/18 Bypass southwest for approximately one mile and the Lenoir Mall will be on your left.

From Taylorsville, follow US 64/NC 90 West toward Lenoir. Just outside of downtown, 64/90 will merge with NC 18. When NC 90 splits off, follow US 64/NC 18 Bypass (Morganton Blvd.) southwest for approximately one mile and the Lenoir Mall will be on your left.

From Morganton, take US 64/NC 18 East toward Lenoir. When the road splits into business and bypass routes, stay on 64/18 Bypass (Morganton Blvd.). The Lenoir Mall will be on your right in approximately one mile.

CONTACT: Lenoir Mall Management Offices, 1031 Morganton Blvd. SW, Lenoir, NC 28645, (828) 754-2481; or Caldwell County Chamber of Commerce, 1909 Hickory Blvd. SE, Lenoir, NC 28645, (800) 737-0782, (828) 726-0616, ‹visitors@caldwellcochamber.org›, ‹www.caldwellcochamber.org›

❄ Hudson Railroad Depot Museum and Picking in the Park

On the first Friday of each month, June through September, between two and three hundred folks show up to jam, listen, and dance at the Hickman Windmill Park and Hudson Railroad Depot Museum in Hudson, North Carolina. The depot was built around the turn of the twentieth century and went out of use as a train station in the 1970s. It has since been renovated to serve as a museum of railroad and local history. The sessions are called Picking in the Park because they take place in an open park area in front of the museum. There's a stage for clogging and for the occasional performance that requires a sound system; the musicians typically play acoustic instruments. Fixed seating is limited, so many listeners bring their own folding chairs. This event runs from 7:00 to 9:00 P.M. on first Fridays, and it is free and open to the public.

LOCATION: From Hickory, take US 321 North. When US 321 splits with US 321-ALT, continue following US 321 northbound. Take the exit for Hudson. Turn left onto Pine Mountain Rd. and follow it into downtown Hudson. Continue through the first traffic light. Pass through the intersection with US 321-ALT and turn right onto Central St. Proceed one block and the depot will be on the left.

From Blowing Rock, take US 321 South. When US 321 splits with US 321-ALT, continue following US 321 southbound through Lenoir. Take the exit for Hudson. Turn right onto Pine Mountain Rd. and pick back up with the directions above.

CONTACT: Bill Warren, 3336 Clarks Chapel Rd., Hudson, NC 28638, (828) 726-1009, ‹6084@polygon.net›; or Caldwell County Chamber of Commerce, 1909 Hickory Blvd. SE, Lenoir, NC 28645, (800) 737-0782, (828) 726-0616, ‹visitors@caldwellcochamber.org›, ‹www.caldwellcochamber.org›

ALEXANDER COUNTY

�֎ First Sunday Singing Convention

The First Sunday Singings are monthly gatherings of the shape-note choirs of three Alexander County African American churches. These three choirs, plus a guest gospel choir, convene at one of the three churches to sing and to worship. This trio of churches is the last remnant of a group that goes back more than fifty years.

Shape-note singing is "a traditional style of unaccompanied group singing using a notation in which the shape of the note indicates its pitch" (*American Heritage Dictionary of the English Language*, 4th ed.). While the practice of shape-note singing is not uncommon among white congregations in the Southern Appalachian region, the Alexander County First Sunday Singing Convention is one of the few known examples of African American churches in the Blue Ridge that continue the tradition.

According to folklorist Lucy Allen, good singing and harmonizing were especially important in the days before these churches had instrumental accompaniments. "The choirs helped the members of the church to become closer to one another and strengthened the sense of community and pride within the church and the convention. For most of the members, the note singing provides a real sense of achievement because so much effort goes into it. The notes are fairly easy to learn, but the challenge is to sing them correctly—with the right pitch, tone and conveyed meaning in each note and word. That takes years."

At one time, up to eleven different churches participated as member organizations of the convention, the purpose of which is to promote fellow-

Participants in the singing at
Mount Carmel Baptist Church

ship, harmony, and better singing in the county. In those days, when the choirs gathered in the singers' homes for their practice sessions, family members—both adults and children—were exposed to the music on a frequent basis. Many of them developed an interest and later joined choirs themselves. As a result, some individual members have been involved for thirty or more years. As Everette Dula, a local convention leader, says, "I can do notes better than I can talk."

The singings, which are open to the public, take place on the first Sunday of each month, December through June, at 2:30 P.M. The First Sunday Singing Convention rotates from month to month among the Third Creek Baptist Church, the Mount Carmel Baptist Church, and the Liberty Grove Baptist Church. Please call or e-mail in advance to inquire about locations for specific dates.

LOCATION: Directions to each of the three churches are as follows:

Third Creek Baptist Church, Stony Point, N.C. From Lenoir, take US 64/ NC 90 East for approximately seventeen miles. When US 64 and NC 90 split, take US 64, continuing east. In approximately six miles, take the exit for Hiddenite. After exiting, turn right onto Old Mountain Rd. and travel southeast for approximately three miles. Turn right onto Third Creek Rd. and begin looking for the church.

From the east, follow US 64 West and take the exit for Hiddenite. Upon exiting, turn left onto Old Mountain Rd. and pick back up with the directions above.

Mount Carmel Baptist Church, Taylorsville, N.C. From Lenoir, take US 64 East to the Taylorsville exit. Turn left onto Liledoun Rd. (also called NC 16), traveling north. Within a half-mile, veer right onto 7th St. You should pass the Senior Center on your left. Mount Carmel Baptist Church is located on the right within one block. Parking is available in rear.

Gethsemane Baptist Church, Newton, N.C. From I-40, take exit 131 (approximately five miles east of Hickory) to NC 16 South. Follow NC 16 to downtown Newton. Upon entering the city limits, continue to the second traffic light and turn left. Proceed to the next traffic light and turn right onto College Ave. Go approximately three blocks to the church.

CONTACT: Everette Dula, 131 Dula Loop, Taylorsville, NC 28681, (828) 632-6503, ‹Judgedula@Charter.Net›; or Alexander County Chamber of Commerce, 104 W. Main Ave., Taylorsville, NC 28681, (828) 632-8141, ‹alexnc@twave.net›, ‹www.alexandercountychamber.com›

❀ Hiddenite Celebration of the Arts

At first glance, one might think that "Hiddenite" was the name of a religious sect—similar to, say, Mennonite. But, in actuality, Hiddenite is a small town in Alexander County, North Carolina. The name of the town is taken from a type of gem mineral found in abundance (or at least it once was) in the nearby earth. Until recent finds in Madagascar and Brazil, Hiddenite was mined exclusively in Alexander County. Hiddenite and emeralds were first discovered there in the latter part of the nineteenth century, and, as a result, the county experienced an "emerald rush" of prospectors looking for quick wealth.

Among these prospectors was "Diamond Jim" Lucas, an eccentric traveler and businessman who built a three-story, twenty-two-room Victorian house in Hiddenite. In 1981 Eileen Lackey Sharpe founded the Hiddenite Center in the old Lucas mansion and established a festival called the Hiddenite Celebration of the Arts, which has been held annually except in 1989, when Hurricane Hugo wreaked havoc on the community the day before the event was to open.

The Hiddenite Celebration of the Arts takes place on the grounds of the Hiddenite Center and all along Hiddenite's Church Street, which is blocked off for the occasion. Festival week begins each year on a Saturday with a community square dance hosted by the Emerald Squares, a local dance team. On Sunday afternoon there's a gospel sing and on Thursday a Family Night, and the festival concludes with the main events on the following Saturday, when as many as five thousand people descend upon the little town to enjoy musical presentations on four stages.

Performances run the gamut from brass bands, steel drum bands, and mariachi groups to bluegrass, blues, and old-time mountain music. A favorite area at the celebration is the nearby ballfield, where three tents define the folklife area. One tent houses a music stage, and the other two allocate space to regional craftspeople who both demonstrate traditional arts and sell their creations. This festival is very much *of* the community, from performers to volunteers to vendors to festival attendees.

The culmination of the Hiddenite Celebration of the Arts occurs on the second Saturday in September, from 10:00 A.M. to 5:00 P.M. Festival events are free and open to the public. There's an admission charge, however, to enter and view the exhibits inside the Lucas mansion and for an associated gem and mineral show in the nearby Education Building.

LOCATION: From I-40, take exit 148 (just west of Statesville) onto US 64 West. Follow US 64 for approximately twelve miles toward Taylorsville, then take the exit for Hiddenite. Turn right onto Old Mountain Rd. and follow the signs for Hiddenite. Go one mile on Old Mountain Rd. to the flashing light. At this point, look for parking. The festival stretches directly ahead for three blocks.

From Wilkesboro, take NC 16 South to Taylorsville. Continue straight through the first traffic light in Taylorsville. At the next traffic light, turn left onto US 64 East. In approximately four miles, take the Hiddenite exit. Turn left onto Old Mountain Rd. and pick up with the directions above.

CONTACT: The Hiddenite Center, PO Box 311, Hiddenite, NC 28636, (828) 632-6966, ‹HidNight@aol.com›, ‹www.Hiddenite.appstate.edu›; or Alexander County Chamber of Commerce, 104 W. Main Ave., Taylorsville, NC 28681, (828) 632-8141, ‹alexnc@twave.net›, ‹www.alexandercountychamber.com›

BURKE COUNTY

❀ Drexel Barber Shop Jam Session

One of the more quaint music venues in the Blue Ridge region is the tiny Drexel Barber Shop, located on South Main Street in the little town of Drexel in Burke County, North Carolina. The shop features a very informal jam session most every Thursday, Friday, and Saturday afternoon, year-round. Around noon, Lawrence Anthony and the other guys at the barber shop generally put aside their scissors, shears, and combs to sample the fare that's been simmering away in a crock pot they keep in the back of the shop. After eating, they grab their instruments for a few hours of picking. They favor old-time, bluegrass, country, and western swing tunes. This event occurs on most—though not all—Thursday, Friday, and Saturday afternoons from 1:00 to around 5:00 P.M.; the stew from the crock pot is generally all gone by 2:00. The sessions are free and open to the public, but the space is very small, so call ahead before you go.

LOCATION: From I-40, take exit 107 (approximately two miles east of Morganton). Turn north onto NC 114 and go approximately three miles to downtown Drexel. (Once you've crossed US 64/70, NC 114 becomes Main St.) The barber shop, located at 100 S. Main St., will be on the left just before the railroad tracks. Look for a red stripe down the middle of the building.

The inner sanctum at Drexel Barber Shop

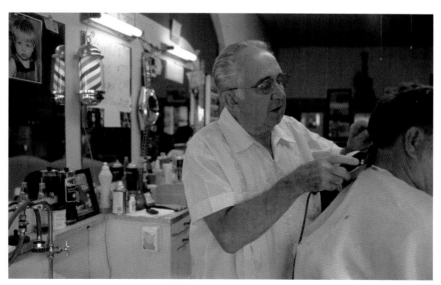

Owner Lawrence Anthony excels at cutting hair and playing bluegrass.

OLD-TIME FIDDLERS' AND BLUEGRASS FESTIVAL
AT FIDDLER'S GROVE

Cover of program book
from 1999 festival

The tradition of organizing fiddlers' contests goes back to 1924 in the small rural community of Union Grove, North Carolina. In that year, H. P. Van Hoy needed money to buy supplies for the school where he taught. Realizing that the local community was full of good stringband musicians, he and his wife, Ada, held a fiddlers' convention on the school grounds the Saturday before Easter. Half of the proceeds were used for prize money for competitors and half for the school. The contest caught on and became an annual affair.

During the 1960s and early 1970s, the fiddlers' convention changed from a local to a national event. Outsiders from across the country, some interested in traditional music and others who saw the festival as an opportunity to participate in a large, open-air party, were attracted to Union Grove. The audience expanded more than tenfold, prompting one of Van Hoy's sons to move the convention to his nearby farm. Crowds continued to grow, however, and eventually overwhelmed security and support services. Disruptive behavior by attendees caused Van Hoy to discontinue the event.

Harper Van Hoy, another of H. P.'s sons, created the festival at Fiddler's Grove campground in 1970 as an alternative to the larger convention down the road. Harper chose Memorial Day weekend as the date, instituted strict rules against drug and alcohol usage, and made the festival accessible to musicians by invitation only.

The Fiddler's Grove festival is held among the rolling hills of Harper and Wanona Van Hoy's farm. A main stage at the bottom of a shaded hillside is the site of most of the competitions and concerts. Other smaller stages and performing areas can be found near outbuildings on the property. Festival participants camp on the grounds, and jam sessions can be heard at all times of the day and night. The pleasant surroundings, good music, and hospitality of the Van Hoys have created devoted fans. Many people bring their children and return year after year.

The event draws stringband and bluegrass musicians from throughout the region to vie for prizes. Competitions and performances are held beginning on Friday night and run throughout the next day and evening. Saturday night's program usually concludes with three fiddlers competing for the title of "Fiddler of the Festival." Concerts by well-known traditional musicians are presented onstage throughout the weekend, and instructional workshops on instrumental and singing styles are also offered.

For many musicians, the Van Hoys' festival is a reunion where friendships are renewed through music. The event also marks the unofficial start of the summer festival season. Beginning with Fiddler's Grove, stringband musicians can attend conventions and contests in western North Carolina and Virginia on almost every weekend through Labor Day.

LOCATION: Fiddler's Grove campground is located in the community of Union Grove in Iredell County, North Carolina. Take I-77 to US 901 at exit 65. Travel west approximately two miles until you come to the community of Union Grove. Look for the signs to Fiddler's Grove campground.

CONTACT: Harper and Wanona Van Hoy, 235 Warren Bridge Rd., PO Box 11, Union Grove, NC 28689, (704) 539-4417, ‹fiddlersgrove@yadtel.net›, ‹www.fiddlersgrove.com›

CONTACT: Lawrence Anthony, PO Box 391, Drexel, NC 28619, (828) 432-7255, (828) 874-2490, ‹grampop41@hci.net›; or Burke County Travel and Tourism Commission, 102 East Union St., Courthouse Square, Morganton, NC 28655, (888) 462-2921, (828) 433-6793, ‹bcttc@hci.net›, ‹www.hci.net/~bcttc›

✳ Smoky Creek Barbecue and Music Barn

Located just outside Lenoir, North Carolina, the Smokey Creek Barbecue and Music Barn is an establishment that features music along with pork barbecue, seafood, and beef ribs. The restaurant is open for dinner Thursday through Saturday nights from 5:00 to 9:00 P.M. Music is presented on Fridays and Saturdays only, from 6:30 until around 9:30. The bands usually play several forty-five-minute sets of bluegrass, country, old-time, gospel, and, occasionally, beach music. On the second weekend of each month, the Music Barn features old-time music by Roger Hicks and the Homestead Band.

LOCATION: From Blowing Rock, take US 321 South to Lenoir, N.C. When US 321 splits with US 321-ALT, continue on US 321. Turn right onto Southwest Blvd., traveling west. At the second traffic light, turn left onto Connelly Springs Rd. Follow Connelly Springs Rd. south for approximately two miles and turn right onto Union Grove Rd. Travel around three-and-a-half miles on Union Grove Rd. When the road forks, bear right onto Burke Smokey Creek Rd. Continue three-fourths of a mile, and Smokey Creek Barbecue will be ahead on the right, approximately a mile past the Burke County line.

From Hickory, take US 321 North to Lenoir. When US 321 splits with US 321-ALT, continue on US 321. Turn right onto Southwest Blvd., traveling west, and pick up with the directions above.

CONTACT: Bill Viggers Jr., 2821 Burke Smokey Creek Rd., Lenoir, NC 28645, (828) 728-5398; or Burke County Travel and Tourism Commission, 102 East Union St., Courthouse Square, Morganton, NC 28655, (888) 462-2921, (828) 433-6793, ‹bcttc@hci.net›, ‹www.hci.net/~bcttc›

❧ Bluegrass at the Old Rock School in Valdese

The Old Rock School in downtown Valdese, North Carolina, is a renovated school building constructed of local rock in the distinctive "Waldensian" style. The Waldenses in western North Carolina are descendants of French religious dissenters who settled in the valleys of the Cottian Alps of Italy. In 1892 a group of Waldenses immigrated to North Carolina and created the community of Valdese. They brought their language, distinctive

The Old Rock School was constructed in the 1930s.

cultural traditions, and occupational skills, including masonry, with them. Waldensian masons use a technique whereby roughly cut stones are carefully fitted together into thick, solid walls using little or no mortar.

The refurbished Old Rock School serves as a community cultural center for the Valdese area and features a 473-seat auditorium, an art gallery, a town meeting space, and offices. On one Saturday each month, from September through April, there's a bluegrass concert there that features both locally and nationally known musicians. The doors open at 6:30 P.M., and the shows begin at 7:30. There is an admission charge. Call for performance dates, ticket prices, and other information.

LOCATION: From I-40, take exit 112 (approximately five miles east of Morganton). Turn north on NC 350 (Eldred St.) and follow until it intersects with Main St. in downtown Valdese. Turn left onto Main St. and follow for a distance of about seven city blocks. The Old Rock School will be on your right.

CONTACT: Russ Jordan, 923 McEntire Rd., Tryon, NC 28782, (828) 863-2917, ‹russ52@earthlink.net›; or Burke County Travel and Tourism Commission, 102 East Union St., Courthouse Square, Morganton, NC 28655, (888) 462-2921, (828) 433-6793, ‹bcttc@hci.net›, ‹www.hci.net/~bcttc›

WATAUGA COUNTY

✵ Woodlands Barbecue and Pickin' Parlor

In Blowing Rock, North Carolina, there's a barbecue place called Woodlands Barbecue and Pickin' Parlor. Woodlands offers a menu that features a variety of sandwiches, Mexican food, and your choice of really delicious and distinctive barbecued beef, pork, ribs, or chicken. The food comes with entertainment by local musicians, presented in the entry-level dining room every night of the week except Mondays, when the restaurant is closed. Sometimes the music is bluegrass or old-time; other times it is nontraditional. Call before you visit or check the free *Mountain Times* weekly newspaper to see who's playing at Woodland's that evening.

Woodland's is a popular dining spot for local high-country residents, and the atmosphere there is friendly and informal. The music starts around 6:30 P.M. and lasts all evening.

LOCATION: From I-40, take exit 123 in Hickory to US 321 North. Follow US 321 North for approximately thirty-six miles to Blowing Rock. US 321 will split just south of Blowing Rock into a business and bypass route. Continue north on

ETTA BAKER
A WONDERFUL LIFE

Etta Baker of Morganton, North Carolina, was born in 1913. Her father had taught her to play guitar by the time she was only three years old. Now considered to be one of North Carolina's living treasures, Etta Baker is admired by thousands for her finger-picked style of blues guitar playing.

I was born in Caldwell County, west of Lenoir. That was in nineteen and thirteen. My daddy was Madison Boone. He was Indian and Irish. Cherokee. My mother was Sarah Sally Wilson. I've had people ask me, "What nationality are you?" I say, "I'm so mixed up, if I ever find out, I'll let you know."

When I was almost three, my daddy decided he'd move to east Virginia. So we went down there. Then when I was fourteen my dad moved back to his father's place on Johns River in Caldwell County. And there is where I spent the most of my time, until I was twenty-three years old. It was a community that seemed like one big family. Back then, they'd dance, play music, have a good time. They'd break long enough for dinner and then they'd go right back into playing again. It would be at my daddy's house one night, and then the next night it would be at one of his friends. It was a wonderful, wonderful life.

I got married to Lee H. Baker at the age of twenty-three, and we raised a family, a family of nine children. I lost one son in the Vietnam War. But the good Lord blessed me with raising eight of my children. Now they're scattered all about. But they all remember me, and they all come home as often as they can. They still find time to come visit with me. The good Lord has blessed me with a lot of merry chatter.

When I was three, coming onto three years old, I would hear my dad tuning up the guitar or the banjo. That tuning got me out of the bed! I would get up and go over to my dad, go through under his knee, and stand up between him and the guitar so I could peep over and see what he was doing. I learned where he was putting his fingers. He'd set me up in the middle of the bed, and I'd lay the guitar across and put my fingers right where I had seen him put his. Finally he bought me a little Stella guitar, a little tiny one, and I began to make chords. I could do my three basic chords when I was three.

Daddy and his brothers, they all learned guitar. My mother played the harmonica. They played mostly what they call country music, but when we moved to Virginia Dad started hearing those blues musicians down there. They taught blues to my daddy, then my Daddy taught me. That's the way the blues got into the family. A lot of people nowadays hear records and different music and learn from that, but my family had their own way of playing and their own sounds. I think the kind of music I play has a lot to do with the race that we are.

I worked at the Buster Brown plant here in Morganton when I was raising my family. I stayed there for twenty-five years. When I was working, I would play my guitar at home. I'd sleep a little while and then I'd get up and play a little while. You know, when you're working at night, daytime sleep don't do you no good no way, so I just stayed up and played.

While I was working there at Buster Brown, a man came through here from Portland, Oregon. He heard me play my music and he said, "Etta, why do you punch the clock and work a hard eight hours?" I said, "That's all I *can* do." And he said, "No, pick up your guitar and make it that way, that'll be so much easier." I'd gotten disgusted with my job. Everybody was nice to me and all, but I had stayed there till I was just tired of it. Well, that was on a Wednesday, and I went to the office and told them, "I'm quitting on Friday." They were *so* surprised. They said, "You're what?" I said, "I'm quitting on Friday!" But I went on and I quit on Friday. I never *did* go back. I was seventy-three years old when I quit. I think it was high time.

The first little music trip I made was to Winston-Salem, down at the Reynolda Building. And from there I went to Wolf Trap, and I played there. Different people, you know, would come by and they would hear me play. Then it wouldn't be long before I'd hear from somebody else. Mr. Joe Wilson was one. And I've loved doing it ever since the first day. I have really been blessed.

I made some records that turned out real good, I think. It's just mostly the type of music that was in my father's family. I love other people's music, but I don't think it's fair to take other people's music. Let their way be theirs and I'll do mine. Mine is fully homemade! The first pieces I played was "Goodbye Booze," "Railroad Bill," "Looking for the Bully of the Town," and "Never Let Your Deal Go Down." I love that one. In fact, I played it yesterday.

I have to say it — I have really enjoyed my life. I've tried to make the very best of it that I could. It's been a very, very happy life.

US 321 Bypass (Valley Blvd.). Woodland's Barbecue is at 8332 Valley Blvd., on the left immediately following the Days Inn.

CONTACT: Gina and Butch Triplett, PO Box 1043, Blowing Rock, NC 28605, (828) 295-3651, ‹www.woodlandsbbq.com›; or Watauga/Boone Convention and Visitors Bureau, 208 Howard St., Boone, NC 28607, (800) 852-9506, (828) 262-3516, ‹chamber@boone.net›, ‹www.boonechamber.com›

❁ Mountainhome Music

While in Boone, be sure to catch a live show on the Mountainhome Music stage. The Mountainhome Music program features concert performances by Appalachian musicians, dancers, storytellers, and poets. The concerts are staged on Saturday nights at St. Luke's Church in downtown Boone during the summer and at the Blowing Rock Stage Company in Blowing Rock in the fall.

In recent years, the Mountainhome Music program has varied its venues, including excursions into other mountain communities in North Carolina and Tennessee, so be sure to call ahead or check the website to learn the location of the show you're interested in attending before you show up. Schedules are updated regularly on the website. The live shows begin at 8:00 P.M. There is an admission fee. Tickets to the concerts are available on-line, at the performance site door, and at Farmers Hardware or the Curiosity Shop in Boone and at Greenhouse Crafts in Glendale Springs.

LOCATIONS: Directions to the two main venues are as follows:

St. Luke's Episcopal Church: From the east, take US 421 North to downtown Boone. At the traffic light where US 421 intersects with US 321 (catty-corner from the Dan'l Boone Inn), turn right onto Councill St./Edgewood Dr. Within a few hundred feet, follow Councill St. left as it splits off from Edgewood Dr. St. Luke's Episcopal Church will be on your right, directly behind the Harris-Teeter.

From Blowing Rock, take US 321 North (Blowing Rock Rd.) into Boone. You will pass the campus of Appalachian State University and the Dan'l Boone Inn on your left. At the intersection of US 321 and US 421, continue straight through the traffic light onto Councill St./Edgewood Dr. Follow the directions given above.

Blowing Rock Stage Company: From Boone, take US 321 South to Blowing Rock. At the Shoppes on the Parkway, US 321 will split into a business and a bypass route. Stay straight on US 321 Bypass. At the third traffic light, turn right onto Sunset Dr., and the Blowing Rock Stage Company will be immediately on your left.

From Lenoir, take US 321 North to Blowing Rock. When US 321 splits into business and bypass routes, stay straight on US 321 Bypass. At the first traffic light, turn left onto Sunset Dr., and the Blowing Rock Stage Company will be immediately on the left.

CONTACT: Joe Shannon, Mountainhome Music, PO Box 572, Boone, NC 28607, (828) 264-8118, ‹www.mountainhomemusic.com›, ‹info@mountainhomemusic.com›; or Watauga/Boone Convention and Visitors Bureau, 208 Howard St., Boone, NC 28607, (800) 852-9506, (828) 262-3516, ‹chamber@boone.net›, ‹www.boonechamber.com›

❧ Gospel Singing at the High Country Fairgrounds

The Gospel Singing Jubilee at the High Country Fairgrounds is a four-day gospel music event held during the second week of August in Boone, North Carolina. The jubilee features gospel groups from all around the southern circuit, including some from western North Carolina. A local gospel group called the Singing Greenes is the host presenter at this event. There is an admission fee. Camping is available at the site.

LOCATION: From Boone, take US 421 South for four miles. Just past Mack Brown's Chevrolet dealership (on the right), turn left onto Roby Greene Rd. and continue approximately a half-mile. The fairgrounds will be on your left.

CONTACT: Everette R. Greene, PO Box 446, Boone, NC 28607, (828) 297-3030, ‹timgreene@boone.net›; or Watauga/Boone Convention and Visitors Bureau, 208 Howard St., Boone, NC 28607, (800) 852-9506, (828) 262-3516, ‹chamber@boone.net›, ‹www.boonechamber.com›

❧ Clogging at Tweetsie

A two-day clogging competition is held on the third or fourth weekend of June each year at Tweetsie Railroad near Boone. There is an admission charge. Call ahead for details and information on event dates.

LOCATION: Tweetsie Railroad is located on US 321 between Boone and Blowing Rock. From the Blue Ridge Parkway, take the Boone exit at milepost 291.

CONTACT: Chris Robbins, Clogging Jamboree at Tweetsie Railroad, PO Box 388,

Jingle taps worn on their shoes enable cloggers to create a more percussive sound during performances.

Blowing Rock, NC 28605, (800) 526-5740, (828) 264-9061, ‹info@tweetsie.com›, ‹www.tweetsie.com›; or Watauga/Boone Convention and Visitors Bureau, 208 Howard St., Boone, NC 28607, (800) 852-9506, (828) 262-3516, ‹chamber@boone.net›, ‹www.boonechamber.com›

✿ Appalachian Cultural Museum

The Appalachian Cultural Museum in Boone, North Carolina, includes exhibits on regional musicians, musical instruments, and regional story-telling traditions. The museum gift shop sells a nice variety of tapes and CDs of mountain music. To begin your tour, watch the interesting introductory film on the traditional life and cultural history of the region. There's also a unique exhibit featuring salvaged items from a defunct Watauga County tourist attraction called the Land of Oz.

Opening hours at the Appalachian Cultural Museum are 10:00 A.M. to 5:00 P.M. Tuesday through Saturday and 1:00 to 5:00 P.M. on Sunday. There is an admission charge, but admission is free on Tuesdays. Call for details on exhibits and programming.

LOCATION: From downtown Boone, N.C., take US 321 South toward Blowing Rock. Approximately a half-mile south of the NC 105 intersection, turn left onto University Hall Dr. (between Staples and Greene's Motel). The museum is located on the first floor of University Hall, the second (and last) building on University Hall Dr.

CONTACT: Charles A. Watkins, Appalachian Cultural Museum, Appalachian State University, Boone, NC 28608, (828) 262-3117, ‹watkinsca@appstate.edu›, ‹www.museum.appstate.edu›; or Watauga/Boone Convention and Visitors Bureau, 208 Howard St., Boone, NC 28607, (800) 852-9506, (828) 262-3516, ‹chamber@boone.net›, ‹www.boonechamber.com›

✿ Doc Watson MusicFest

The Doc Watson MusicFest, also known as Doc Watson Appreciation Day and locally known simply as DocFest, is a relative newcomer among the major traditional music events in the high country—and it's a good one. DocFest usually happens on the second Saturday in July on the spacious grounds of Watauga County's old Cove Creek School in the mountain community of Sugar Grove. Attractions at the event include a handful of local craft and CD vendors, festival T-shirts, barbecue and other festival foods, and lots of mountain music of the highest order.

Doc Watson himself is the center of attention and the main attraction at

Doc Watson tunes up.

this event. The venerable blind guitarist and vocalist seems virtually un-aware of his ever-increasing celebrity as he mixes easily with the crowd of fans and admirers who are there to greet him in this informal and friendly setting. They're also there to hear his music and the music of his best musi-cal friends. They won't be disappointed.

The music starts at 10:00 A.M., goes all day, and lasts well into the night. Free shuttles are provided to transport visitors from several parking areas to the festival gate. An admission fee is charged; proceeds from admission fees and sales help to fund the newly established Doc and Merle Watson Mu-seum, which is housed inside the nearby old Cove Creek School. Dates for the event are subject to change, so call in advance for a schedule or check on-line at ‹www.covecreek.net/docfest.htm›.

LOCATION: From Boone, take US 421/321 North toward Tennessee for approximately five miles. When US 421 and US 321 split, turn left and follow US 321. Proceed west for about one mile to Sugar Grove. The Cove Creek Grocery is on the right; the Sugar Grove Post Office is on the left. Turn right on Old US 421 just past the Cove Creek Grocery. Follow signs for parking for the events.

To get to the historic old Cove Creek School building, after turning on Old US 421, turn left at George's Gap Rd. Follow it around the bends, past Skyline Telephone, to Dale Adams Rd. on the right. Turn right on Dale Adams Rd. The school building is on the left.

CONTACT: Cove Creek Preservation and Development, Inc., PO Box 344, Sugar Grove, NC 28679, (828) 297-2200, ‹ccp&d@boone.net›, ‹www.covecreek.net›; or Watauga/Boone Convention and Visitors Bureau, 208 Howard St., Boone, NC 28607, (800) 852-9506, (828) 262-3516, ‹chamber@boone.net›, ‹www.boonechamber.com›

AVERY COUNTY

❄ Jim and Jennie's High Country Music Barn

Situated near the end of a long dirt road outside of Crossnore is Jim and Jennie's High Country Music Barn. In contrast to the tightly constructed performance hall at the Maggie Valley Opry House and the freshly restored Marshall railroad depot, Jim and Jennie's High Country Music Barn is just that—a barn. It's also a campground. Every Saturday night at Jim and Jennie's, there's an open performance that features Jim and Jennie Vance and other local musicians.

The High Country Music Barn is a huge, weathered wood structure positioned on a sloping hillside. It's constructed in such a way that the natural slope of the hill creates a raked floor for the auditorium. At the rear of the room, uphill, is a concession area where soft drinks, snack foods, and bowls of pinto beans with cornbread and onions are sold to appease hunger and quench thirsts. Downhill, at the other end, is a performance area split into two parts—two stages placed side by side. On the right side is a bandstand, and on the left, separated from the bandstand by a low board fence, is a dance floor. Between the uphill concession area and the downhill performance stage is seating for six hundred or more visitors. It's a big place.

The show at Jim and Jennie's High Country Music Barn is hosted by Jennie Vance, a veteran mountain musician who introduces each selection and does most of the singing. She's backed up by a band of musicians playing guitar, fiddle, mandolin, harmonica, bass, and banjo, all with a great deal of

Outside Jim and Jennie's High Country Music Barn

gusto. From time to time, Jennie will tell a joke or two. She often invites other local musicians who are in the audience to come down front and perform. Jennie also calls square dances for anyone in the audience who's interested in dancing. The High Country Music Barn shows run from Memorial Day through Labor Day. Children and teenagers from nearby summer camps often attend in sizable groups, and Jennie always encourages them to sing the camp songs that they've learned.

In addition to the Saturday evening show, Jim and Jennie's Music Barn is the site for a series of annual music events. On Memorial Day weekend, the Music Barn hosts an annual Ramp Festival; on the first Friday and Saturday in July, the annual Crossnore Bluegrass Festival and Clogging Competition takes place there; on the Friday and Saturday nights of Labor Day weekend, it's the Western North Carolina Championship Fiddlers' Convention; and on the second weekend in October, the Fire on the Mountain Festival is staged at Jim and Jennie's.

LOCATION: The community of Crossnore is located off US 221 between Linville Falls and Pineola. At the flashing caution light, turn onto Crossnore Dr. toward town. Pass through Crossnore and travel approximately one to two miles. Look for Johnson's Cemetery on your right. Just beyond the cemetery, turn right onto

Hawshaw Fire Tower Rd., which is marked by a hand-painted sign for Jim and Jennie's. Follow the signs to the Music Barn. The address is 43 Hawshaw Fire Tower Rd.

CONTACT: Jim and Jennie Vance, PO Box 132, Crossnore, NC 28616, (828) 733-2807, (828) 733-0682; or Avery/Banner Elk Chamber of Commerce, Shoppes of Tynecastle No. 2, PO Box 335, Banner Elk, NC 28604, (828) 898-5605, (888) 972-2183, (800) 972-2183, ‹chamber@averycounty.com›, ‹www.banner-elk.com›

❀ Singing on the Mountain at MacRae Meadows

For more than three-quarters of a century now, since 1924, there's been an annual gospel singing at MacRae Meadows near the base of Grandfather Mountain near Linville, North Carolina. The event, titled Singing on the Mountain, is the oldest ongoing old-time gospel convention in the Southern Appalachians. The event's motto has remained the same from the beginning to the present: "Whosoever will may come." Founded in 1924 by Joe Hartley Sr. as a family reunion, the singing is always held on the fourth Sunday in June. It features a dozen or more of the most popular of the southern gospel groups. Musicians perform on an outdoor stage throughout the day, breaking only around mid-day for a sermon. Admission to the Singing on the Mountain is free, and camping (no hookups) is available on the grounds on a first-come basis. It's a good idea to call ahead for details.

LOCATION: From Blowing Rock, take the Blue Ridge Parkway South for approximately fourteen miles to the US 221 intersection at milepost 305. Take US 221 South one mile to the entrance of Grandfather Mountain.
From the south, take US 221 North to the entrance of Grandfather Mountain.
CONTACT: Harris Prevost, Grandfather Mountain, PO Box 129, Linville, NC 28646, (828) 733-2013, (800) 468-7325, ‹nature@grandfather.com›, ‹www.grandfather.com›; or Avery/Banner Elk Chamber of Commerce, Shoppes of Tynecastle No. 2, PO Box 335, Banner Elk, NC 28604, (828) 898-5605, (888) 972-2183, (800) 972-2183, ‹chamber@averycounty.com›, ‹www.banner-elk.com›

REGION FOUR

FOLK FESTIVALS, GOSPEL SINGINGS, AND A FLEA MARKET

FRANKLIN COUNTY

✿ Blue Ridge Folklife Festival

It's midday at the annual Blue Ridge Folklife Festival at Ferrum College in
Ferrum, Virginia. The deep-voiced baying of coon hounds—Treeing Walk-
ers, Mountain Curs, Redbones, Plotts, and Blueticks—can be heard in the
distance as a half-dozen of the rangy animals enthusiastically swim across a
lake, chasing furiously after the raccoon skin that's being pulled before
them by a rope. The braying of jumping coon mules (coon hunters sometimes ride on muleback in the Blue Ridge) scaling fences nearly as tall as
themselves mixes strangely with the rhythmic sounds of the bluegrass banjos and old-time fiddles that waft across the hillside from three music stages.
These and myriad other distinctive sounds all mix together and reverberate
through the mountain air in a wild cacophony of noises. It's quite an experience for the ear.

Since 1973 the staff, students, faculty, and volunteers at Ferrum College's
Blue Ridge Institute have joined together to organize and stage a wonderful
and hugely popular one-day extravaganza that enacts, interprets, and celebrates the folklife and living cultural traditions of the Blue Ridge mountains.
Here, at the Blue Ridge Institute, they do it right!

Every year on the fourth Saturday in October, rain or wind or snow or
shine, fifteen thousand or more people flock to one of the largest presentations of bona fide regional traditional culture in the United States for a day
of fun, crafts, food, and music. The assortment of activities literally covering
the college campus relate to the lifeways and cultural heritage of Appalachia. The fun includes sheepherding, heirloom apple tasting, a quilt show,

123

The Virginia State Championship Coon Dog Water Race

molasses making, log skidding, folk art exhibits, tours of a steam-powered shingle mill, coon dog water races, the Virginia state championship coon mule jumping contest, children's games, marbles and checkers, pear butter making, apple butter making, antique gas engine and vintage tractor demonstrations, a petting zoo, a display of antique automobiles and street jalopies, draft horse log-stacking demonstrations, horse pulling contests, coon dog treeing contests, and traditional music presented on three stages.

The music runs continuously from 10:00 A.M. until after 5:00 P.M. One stage is for presentations of sacred music, another for Blue Ridge string bands, and a third is the Blue Ridge Heritage stage, where a wide variety of musicians playing country blues, rockabilly, old-time traditional, and country hold forth all day long. It's an impressive gathering of the region's finest traditional players, and the music is presented in an even and informative way without any of the unnecessary and intrusive banter that's so often encountered at commercial music events.

Food available at this festival throughout the day includes Brunswick stew, fried pies (get in line early for these), chili beans, fried chicken, fresh

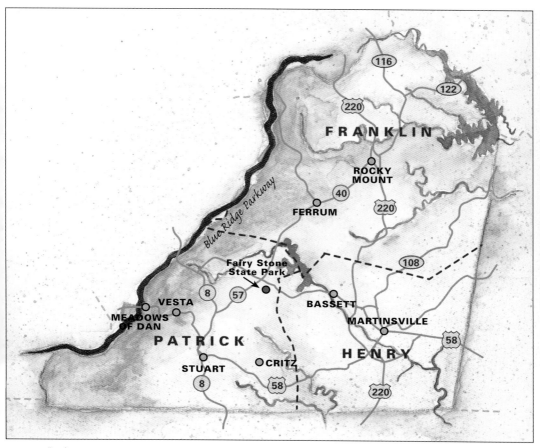

Region 4

vegetables, fried fish, hardtack candy, pinto beans and hoecakes, fried pork skins, candy apples, chitterlings (that's *chittlins* to those in the know), barbecued pork, black-pot chicken, pancakes and sausage, strawberry shortcake, homemade bread and rolls, cakes and pies, apples, and—that old festival standby—funnel cakes.

The crafts demonstrations and exhibits are just as numerous as the food items—and as interesting. They range from mandolin making and a wide range of other handicrafts—walking sticks, bowls and wooden rakes, dough trays, split-oak baskets, and animal carvings—to tobacco curing and twisting, rag doll making, chair caning, canning and food preservation, beekeeping and honey production, herbal medicine, and a variety of textile arts that includes tatting, knitting, crocheting, weaving, quilting, and general

The Folklife Festival presents many aspects of Blue Ridge culture, including foodways.

stitchery. Guitar making, knife making, and model making round out the incredible selection of craft demonstrations.

If there's a problem with the Blue Ridge Folklife Festival, it's that there's just too dang much to see. There's also too much to hear and too much to eat—more than you can possibly deal with in a single day, even if you get there first thing in the morning and stay until the end. The only solution is to attend the festival year after year, and that's what many people do. But even that plan is only partially successful, because the festival organizers are continuously adding new items to their menu of festival activities. It's a problem, though, that thousands of devoted festivalgoers have decided they can live with, and quite happily so.

The Blue Ridge Institute and Museum, founded and directed by historian Roddy Moore, is a multicomponent interpretive center focusing on the cultural history and contemporary folklife of the southeastern Virginia Blue Ridge region and beyond. The institute, which is located on the Ferrum College campus, has gallery spaces in which a year-round variety of rotating, in-depth exhibitions on Blue Ridge folklife and cultural history are mounted; an archive (visits by appointment) housing extensive collections of vintage photographs, audio recordings, video recordings, books, manuscripts, documents, and other materials that relate to Virginia folkways; and a seasonally active living history farm where Blue Ridge life as it was once lived is re-created.

The Blue Ridge Folklife Festival occurs annually on the fourth Saturday in October. The gates open at 10:00 A.M. and the final rounds of music and other activities begin at 5:00 P.M. An admission fee is charged.

LOCATION: From Rocky Mount, take VA 40 West to Ferrum and follow the signs to Ferrum College and the parking areas.
CONTACT: The Blue Ridge Institute, Ferrum College, PO Box 1000, Ferrum, VA 24088-9000, (540) 365-4416, ‹www.blueridgeinstitute.org›

Music traditions are showcased on several stages located on the campus.

Price Pugh fashioned this banjo from the aluminum brake drum of a 1961 Buick. The instrument is part of an exhibit mounted by staff of the Blue Ridge Institute and Museum.

When residents of the region hear stringband music, they often respond by flatfooting, clogging, or finding a partner and two-stepping.

❋ Dairy Queen in Rocky Mount

One of the truly remarkable things about the Blue Ridge region of the Southern Appalachians is the sheer number of traditional musicians who live there and who play music in public places. Maybe because there are so many of them, they literally spill over into spaces where they seemingly were never intended to fit. One such place is in Rocky Mount, Virginia.

At first glance, there's nothing unusual about the Dairy Queen in Rocky Mount. It's pretty much a typical Dairy Queen, as Dairy Queens go. Maybe its dining area is a bit larger than those at other Dairy Queens, but nevertheless it serves Peanut Buster Parfait and Blizzard Treats the same as any other. You can order the usual Dairy Queen fare for breakfast, or for lunch. The official Dairy Queen theme, "The spirit of endless summer in hometown America," seems to fit just fine there.

In fact, unless you happen to be at the Rocky Mount Dairy Queen at the right time, there's nothing at all unusual about the place. But if you are there on a Thursday morning from September to the end of May, you're in for a treat—and one that's not very likely to be served at any of the other 5,200

Dairy Queen locations here or abroad. Because on Thursdays there's mountain music—mainly bluegrass—at the Rocky Mount Dairy Queen.

Every Thursday a free concert and jam session starts at 9:00 in the morning! You'd better get there early, too, or you'll be left standing out by the coffee dispenser. The Dairy Queen's dining area, which seats fifty or sixty people (once extra chairs are brought in), quickly fills up with the regular attendees who are there week after week. They're mostly senior citizens who come to play and to hear the music, maybe to dance a bit, to savor a cup of coffee or two, and, perhaps, to eat a sausage biscuit. It's an important social event for the musicians and for the community of retirees who support it by attending. They dress up for it.

Jam sessions, including the one at the Rocky Mount Dairy Queen, are definitely one of the most popular sorts of social gatherings that happen among the many mountain musicians and music lovers around the Blue Ridge region. The jam at the Dairy Queen lasts about an hour and a half or perhaps a little longer if the musicians and their listeners are feeling especially perky that morning.

LOCATION: The Dairy Queen in Rocky Mount is located a short distance south of downtown on VA 40; the address is 995 Franklin St. From US 220, take the VA 40 exit going west. Remain on VA 40 through Rocky Mount. On the western side of town, the Dairy Queen will be on your left.

CONTACT: Debra Russell, Arrington Enterprises, 1035 Franklin St., Suite 100, Rocky Mount, VA 24151, (540) 483-7754, ‹drussell@arrington.com›

HENRY COUNTY

❀ Billy's Flea Market

One of the music places in southwestern Virginia where visitors can mix with the "homefolks" in a unique environment is Billy's Flea Market near the little town of Bassett. A jam session and dance called the Jamboree happens there every Sunday afternoon year-round (weather permitting).

Billy's Flea Market is housed in a rambling, ramshackle conglomeration of weatherworn rooms, booths, passageways, sheds, and porches, located three miles or so west of Bassett, Virginia. Owned and operated by musician and flea-marketeer Billy Sheldon, Billy's Flea Market appears at first glance to be a fairly typical mountain roadside stand, except, perhaps, for the giant eight-foot-long banjo that's mounted high up on its front.

Most people show up at Billy's Flea Market early enough before the music

Billy's Flea Market

Owner Billy Shelton with his pet
snakes Francis, Juanita, and Betty

starts to swallow down a homemade sausage biscuit, a cup of coffee, or
some other bit of local fare cooked up right there in Billy's kitchen. Waiting
for the music to begin, visitors wander all around the meandering flea market. They may watch a NASCAR race or a ballgame on television; read and
discuss the many articles, notices, and photographs on music-related topics
that Billy has found and stapled up on the interior walls of the porch and
passageways; or just sit quietly out on one of the porches and talk. They may

also take turns peering into a large plexiglass exhibit case on a makeshift stand at one end of the front porch. This coffin-sized box houses Billy's pet timber rattlesnake, his copperhead moccasin, and occasionally other (more short-lived) occupants.

The music and dance session at Billy's begins around 2:00 P.M. in a spacious interior room that's been furnished with a small stage and a large dance floor. The dance floor is surrounded by an amazing array of old, worn-out, overstuffed sofas and chairs and various stools and benches, including plywood platforms that, some time in the past, must have held flea-market merchandise. While the music is playing inside the main indoor space, other musicians gather to jam and joke around with one another at various additional spots inside the building, outside in the yard, and around the flea-market parking lot. There's no admission charge for the jam at Billy's, but now and again someone will "pass the hat" around, hoping for small contributions to help cover the expenses of heating and lighting the place.

LOCATION: From US 220 in Martinsville, take VA 57 West. Billy's Flea Market is approximately three miles past the Bassett Middle School in Bassett. Look for the big banjo on your right.

CONTACT: Billy Shelton, 6766 Fairystone Park Hwy., Bassett, VA 24055, (276) 629-4114, ‹billys@kimbanet.com›

PATRICK COUNTY

✤ Easter Brothers' Homecoming Gospel Sing

Every year, on the last Saturday in July, the Easter Brothers' Homecoming Gospel Sing is held at Dominion Valley Park in Stuart, Virginia. This all-day event celebrates the success of a favorite hometown gospel group and its contributions to the music of the region and beyond. The Easter Brothers are a trio of men—and they are actually brothers—who were pioneers in developing and popularizing bluegrass and country gospel music nearly four decades ago. They've recorded numerous albums and have appeared on stages including that of the Grand Old Opry. The music starts in the morning and lasts all day.

LOCATION: From Stuart, take US 58 East toward Martinsville. One mile past the sign for Critz, turn right onto VA 700. Proceed approximately three miles and turn right onto Dominion Valley Lane. The park will be on your right.

From the Blue Ridge Parkway at milepost 176, take US 58 East to Stuart and then follow directions above.

CONTACT: Dominion Valley Park, 481 Dominion Valley Lane, Stuart, VA 24171, (276) 694-7009

✤ Singings at Dominion Valley Park

Dominion Valley Park is also the location of several other gospel singings, including one held annually on Labor Day weekend and another on the weekend of Memorial Day.

For more than a decade now, people have gathered at the park amphitheater on the Saturday before Labor Day to enjoy singing and hearing sacred music. The music starts in the morning and lasts all day. There is an admission fee, and campsites are available. Concessions are provided by the local volunteer fire department.

The Memorial Day gospel singing is similar to the Labor Day gathering; it is held on the Saturday of Memorial Day weekend, the fourth weekend in May.

LOCATION: From Stuart, take US 58 East toward Martinsville. One mile past the sign for Critz, turn right onto VA 700. Proceed approximately three miles and turn right onto Dominion Valley Lane. The park will be on your right.

From the Blue Ridge Parkway at milepost 176, take US 58 East to Stuart and follow the directions above.

CONTACT: Dominion Valley Park, 481 Dominion Valley Lane, Stuart, VA 24171, (276) 694-7009

✤ Poor Farmer's Farm

The Poor Farmer's Farm in Vesta, Virginia, is a country store that features a whole slate of annual and weekly music events, including the Fire on the Mountain Fourth of July Celebration, the Poor Farmer's Farm Sunday Bluegrass Concert and Dance, the Poor Farmer's Farm Cabbage Festival, and others.

Beginning at noon on July 4 each year, there's a celebration with music, dancing, and food to commemorate Independence Day. On the fourth Saturday in August, the country store sponsors the Poor Farmer's Farm Cabbage Festival. This event features cabbage cooking and eating and a selection of traditional mountain music in celebration of the annual cabbage harvest. From May through September, the Poor Farmer's Farm hosts a bluegrass concert and dance every Sunday afternoon from 2:00 P.M. until 5:00 P.M.

A gazebo near the store serves as a stage for the various musical presentations. The field surrounding the gazebo allows space for audience seating and a festival environment. Food is served at the store. There is no admission fee for any of the events.

LOCATION: From the Blue Ridge Parkway or from Meadows of Dan, take US 58 East toward Stuart. The farm is about five miles down US 58 on your right.

CONTACT: Ronnie or Joyce Greene, 7958 Jeb Stuart Hwy., Vesta, VA 24177, (276) 952-2560

REGION FIVE

IT STRIKES WITH TERROR IN MY HEART

MITCHELL COUNTY

❧ Kona

The tiny community of Kona in Mitchell County, North Carolina, is an exceptional place. The racing waters of a mountain river, the wet, dark shadows of temperate rainforests, the lofty heights of a dizzying overlook, and the shimmering light of dramatic vistas can all be experienced in the landscapes surrounding this mountain hamlet. Yet it is not just the natural beauty of the spot that makes it special. Kona is a place that has witnessed dramatic human conflicts and tragic deeds. When we know those stories, their special, mysterious quality permeates the landscape.

The century-old Kona Baptist Church, at the center of the community, is a small, neatly painted, white wood-frame chapel poised just above the curving paved surface of NC 80. It sits just below the summit of a round, sodcovered peak. In front it overlooks the broad, lush valley of the Toe River and peeks westward over the treetops toward the lofty blue hills of Yancey County. The dual tracks of the Clinchfield and Yancey Railroads run in parallel along the margin of the riverbank below. For several miles, the twin tracks hug the low river bluff, traveling from northwest to southeast. Then both they and the river split apart, each railway following its own chosen branch of the river—the Yancey sticking with the westerly flow and the Clinchfield the more southeasterly branch.

On a grassy knoll immediately behind and uphill from the Kona Baptist Church, a small graveyard overlooks the ancestral mountain homeplace of the Silver family. An old log dogtrot house, the Silver family's pioneer homestead, sits several hundred yards away from the graveyard, down the hill

Charlie Silver's gravesite in Kona

and under a slope, almost hidden from view. Several generations of the Silver family and their kin are entombed here in this isolated, high-country burial ground. Among them, side by side and close together, are three graves for one man, a man named Charles Silver.

To the north of the cemetery, down a steep hill through a quarter-mile or more of nearly impenetrable forested slope, lie a number of flat stones scattered about here and there, hidden among the trees and the bushes. Those stones are the only surviving remnants of a now infamous hewn-log mountain cabin that was once the home of the young Charles Silver and his wife, Frankie.

Charles Silver, or Charlie as he was often called, was born October 7, 1812. On December 22, 1831, Charlie was murdered by Frankie, who struck his head with an ax as he napped on a pallet on the cabin floor. Their little child, a toddler named Nancy, was asleep in his arms, apparently the only witness to the murder—or so the story sometimes goes.

Lana A. Whited's concise summary of the saga of Frankie Silver describes in absolute terms the generally accepted facts of an early nineteenth-century incident that has sustained both popular and academic interest among North Carolinians for nearly two centuries now:

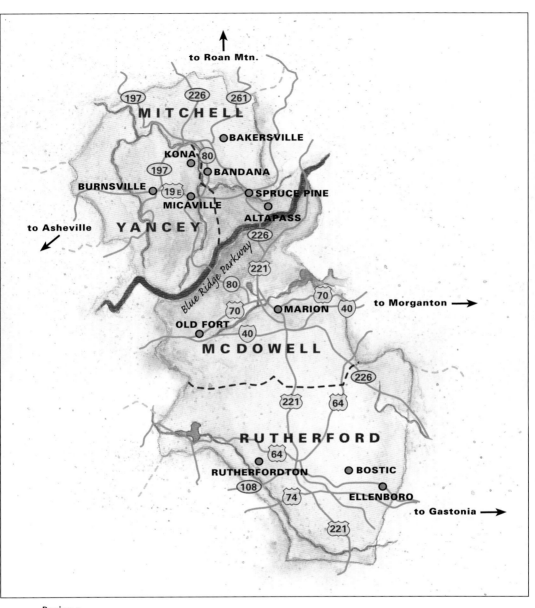

Region 5

The Kona Baptist Church and Silver Family Museum

On Dec. 22, 1831, Charles Silver was murdered at his cabin in Burke County, N.C. His body was dismembered and parts subsequently found at various locations in and around the cabin. On Jan. 10, 1832, his wife, Frances ("Frankie") Stewart Silver, her mother Barbara Stewart, and brother Blackstone Stewart were taken to Morganton, N.C., and charged with the crime. Barbara and Blackstone Stewart were released on Jan. 17 due to insufficient evidence, but Frankie was indicted by the grand jury in March 1832 and tried later that month. She was convicted on April 2, and sentenced to be hanged on July 27 of the same year. Documents were sent to the N.C. Supreme Court for appeal, but oral arguments were not made on her behalf. The verdict was upheld, and Frankie Stewart Silver was hanged in Morganton on July 12, 1833. Charlie Silver is buried behind the Kona Baptist Church in Mitchell County, N.C., in three separate graves. Frankie Silver is buried about nine miles west of Morganton. (‹www.ferrum.edu/lwhited/silver.htm›, 09/15/2000)

At the time of the murder, Frankie Silver was only eighteen years old. Her husband, Charlie, was nineteen.

Why? Why did this young mountain wife, the mother of an infant, slay her young husband? Well, it seems that nobody knows for sure, but it's been said by some that Charlie was a popular dancer who may have been more than just a sociable companion to some of the other young ladies around the isolated community. It's been said that he had a roving eye, and that jealousy was the motivation for the killing. Others think that he was mean to Frankie, even abusive, and that Frankie acted to defend herself. Still another notion holds that Frankie wanted to leave the remote Blue Ridge hilltops and Toe River backwoods and move westward to Kentucky—to search for greener pastures. But such a move would have necessitated Charlie's selling his house and land, which he refused to do. If he were dead, then Frankie would inherit the place and be free to sell it. Then she could head west. Or so they say. Among certain related mountain families and in certain related mountain communities, all these possibilities and many more are tossed around, discussed back and forth, and argued over, as they have been since 1832. They're argued as if the murder of Charlie Silver happened just last week, and not nearly two centuries ago.

Frankie Silver was charged with violently murdering her husband. When she was brought to trial, according to the custom of the times, she was not allowed to speak up in court in her own defense. She was found guilty, was condemned to die, somehow escaped from jail while she awaited her death, was recaptured, and finally was executed by hanging—an execution that caused a great controversy at the time, especially since the victim was female. A ballad composed shortly after her execution has Frankie expressing remorse for the crime and trepidation over the fate that waits her in the afterlife.

In actuality, many of the facts and circumstances surrounding these events remain obscure, and successive generations have interpreted Frankie's motives differently. In the 1990s, some North Carolina public school students petitioned the governor to pardon Frankie Silver on the basis that Charlie had abused her and therefore she had acted in self-defense. Today, even after more than 175 years of supposition, investigation, gossip, and scholarly research, the murder of Charlie Silver and the subsequent condemnation and execution of Frankie Silver continue to intrigue residents of western North Carolina and beyond. Numerous articles and television stories, a pair of full-length books, a play, and a ballet based on Frankie's story have appeared in recent years. And, of course, the ballad continues to be sung by traditional musicians in the region.

The Kona Baptist Church is no longer used for worship services and de-

THE BALLAD OF FRANKIE SILVER

This dreadful, dark and dismal
   day
Has swept my glories all away;
My sun goes down, my days are
   past,
And I must leave this world at last.

Oh! Lord, what will become of me?
I am condemned, you all now see;
To heaven or hell my soul must fly,
All in a moment when I die.

Judge Daniels has my sentence
   passed;
These prison walls I leave at last;
Nothing to cheer my drooping
   head,
Until I'm numbered with the dead.

But, oh, that zealous judge I fear;
Shall I that awful sentence hear?
"Depart, ye cursed, down to hell,
And forever there to dwell."

There shall I meet that mournful
   face,
Whose blood I spilled upon this
   place;
With flaming eyes to me he'll say,
"Why did you take my life away?"

I know that frightful ghost I'll see,
Gnawing its flesh in misery,
And then and there attended be,
For murder in the first degree.

The jealous thought that first gave
   strife
To make me take my husband's
   life;
For days and months I spent my
   time,

Thinking how to commit this
   crime.

And on a dark and doleful night;
I put his body out of sight;
To see his soul and body part,
It strikes with terror in my heart.

I took his blooming days away,
Left him no time to God to pray;
And if sins fall on his head,
Must I not bear them in his stead?

My mind on solemn subjects roll,
My little child, God bless its soul,
All ye that are of Adam's race,
Let not my faults this child
   disgrace.

You all see me and on me gaze,
Be careful how you spend your
   days;
And ne'er commit this awful
   crime,
But try and serve your God in
   time.

Awful indeed to think of death,
In perfect health to lose my breath;
Farewell my friends, I bid adieu,
Vengeance on me you must now
   pursue.

Great God! How shall I be
   forgiven?
Not fit for earth, not fit for
   Heaven;
But little time to pray to God,
For now I try that awful road.

—Sung by Bobby McMillon,
   December 1, 1999

Wayne Silver, a descendant of Charlie Silver, and singer Bobby McMillon discuss motives for the murder. (Photograph by Sally Council; courtesy of the North Carolina Arts Council)

scendants of Charlie Silver have turned it into the Silver Family Museum. Newspaper articles on the murder and genealogical documents are mounted on the church walls. The building is not opened unless visitors are expected, so please call Mr. and Mrs. George Silver in advance at (828) 688-4959 to schedule an appointment.

LOCATION: From I-40 near Marion, take exit 85 for US 221 North. US 221 will merge with NC 226 north of Marion. Follow US 221/NC 226 North for approximately seven miles. When the two highways split, take NC 226 North to Spruce Pine. At the subsequent split between NC 226 North and NC 226-ALT, stay straight on NC 226 going north. At the traffic light in Spruce Pine, turn left onto US 19-E, going west. Follow 19-E West for approximately six miles. Turn right onto NC 80 North. Continue on NC 80 for approximately five miles, and the Kona Baptist Church will be on the right.

From the Blue Ridge Parkway, take the exit for Spruce Pine (between mileposts 330 and 340). Travel north on NC 226 into Spruce Pines and pick up with the directions above.

BOBBY McMILLON
IN AN UNBROKEN TRADITION

As a child, Bobby McMillon of Lenoir, North Carolina, was intrigued by
the songs and stories he heard from family members. That interest led him
to learn more about the folklore of the Southern Appalachians. Today he
is an authority on the subject of traditional mountain music.

My father, Gordon McMillon, was born in eastern Tennessee, in the McMillon settlement near Cosby. My grandfather was called to preach here in Caldwell County, so he brought the members of his family and they settled here. About three years later, my mother's mom and dad moved here from Mitchell County to run a grocery store. It was at that little store where my mother met my father.

I was born here in Lenoir in December of 1951. As a child, I listened to the stories that the family told. I grew up listening to the scary stories and the witch tales and things like that that our family knew about. I just loved to listen to 'em. My grandfather had a Victrola talking machine and he had a lot of old records. About the time I was twelve I began to realize that some of the songs that my granddaddy had on records were similar to the songs that were being sung out and about in the community. When I was between twelve and fourteen, I started learning the songs that people I knew were singing. I was thirteen or fourteen when I became aware of the recorded and written folklore collections, and I began to read everything I could about them. I slowly began to learn what all this was about.

Toward the end of the 1960s my father went up to an electronic store and bought me a tape recorder. That summer I began to record everything that was being said or sung. It was about that time, also, that I met a man from Watauga County named Rolf Ellison. Rolf, he had a banjo and he got to playing a few songs. He started out with one called "Down Yonder" and then he took the picks off his fingers and started playing in a different style. He kept the picks off his fingers and just hooked his forefinger up on the second string and went to playing in a modal key. He started out:

> Oh, the first came down was dressed in red,
> And the next come down in green;
> And the next come down was Daniel's wife,
> Dressed fine as any queen, queen;
> Dressed fine as any queen

and he proceeded to sing "Lord Daniel." I knew I had hit the jackpot then! That was just exactly what I was looking for. The hair was standing up on my arms 'cause he played the banjo real well and it was in a minor key. Then he did

Well met, well met my own true love,
Well met, well met said he;
I've just returned from the salt, salt sea
And it's all for the love of thee.
I've just returned from the salt, salt sea,
And it's all for the love of thee.

We began a friendship that night that lasted the rest of his life.

One of my best friends in school had an uncle who was a doctor in North Wilkesboro who just loved old-time music. We had become close friends, so I called him up and asked him was he going to the Fiddlers' Convention at Union Grove. He said, yeah, come on down. So we went down to Union Grove. There was this couple from Tennessee that were there singing named Jean and Lee Schilling. Lee Schilling played the recorder and Jean played the autoharp. The songs they were singing were familiar to me, so I went and introduced myself to them after one of their performances. They told me that if I would come to their festival, which was called the Folk Festival of the Smokies, that they would introduce me to Jeannette Carter.

Jeanette is the daughter of A. P. and Sara Carter, and Maybelle Carter's first cousin. They had composed the original Carter Family, and Jeannette was singing their music and carrying on the tradition. One night during the festival the Schillings asked me to perform. So they set me up a time to sing, and I did a couple of songs. The last one I did, I did a Carter Family song. I didn't know that Jeannette Carter was in the crowd. After it was over, she came backstage there and introduced herself to me and we became fast friends after that. That was my first real public performance.

My friend here in Lenoir named Cody Lowe was a student at UNC in Chapel Hill. During the years that he was in college, I used to go down there every so often and spend a few days with him. He'd take me to the library, because I was an avid fan of books. It was just like putting Alice in Wonderland for me to go to Chapel Hill. I mean, that was just like being in the Treasure House of Captain Kangaroo!

From the perspective of having visited the United Kingdom this summer, I've found a great resurgence of interest in all kinds of old songs and singing. It's revivalist in nature, but still, it's keeping it on. If it wasn't for the revivalists, and if it wasn't for the Yankees [laughs], I think we would have lost four-fifths of all this music. I have to put that on the record.

I'm not sure about the future of folk music. There's probably very few people left now that have it strictly from the traditional culture which they grew up in. But there's some people today whose families, in an unbroken tradition, have had a song like "Barbara Allen" for three or four centuries. Maybe, someday, when people become enlightened to the point that they can accept something besides their own narrow view of what the world should be like, they'll reaccept the traditions that they have left behind.

❄ Saturday Night Jams at Five Oaks Campground

The jam sessions held at this site in the Glen Ayre community take place under an open-sided shelter with a concrete floor. They feature regional musicians playing bluegrass, old-time, and gospel music. Visitors are welcome to join in. The jams start at 7:00 P.M. each Saturday night from mid-May through October, though the season may be cut short if the weather gets too cold to play outdoors. The event is free and open to the public.

The campground is also the site of various gospel sings, family reunions, and other community events in which traditional music may be a component.

LOCATION: From I-40 near Marion, take exit 85 for US 221 North. US 221 will merge with NC 226 north of Marion. Follow US 221/NC 226 North for approximately seven miles. When the two highways split, take NC 226 North to Spruce Pine (approximately eight more miles). At the subsequent split between NC 226 and NC 226-ALT, stay straight on NC 226 going north. Continue through Spruce Pine to Bakersville (about ten miles north of Spruce Pine). In Bakersville, follow signs to NC 261 North. Follow NC 261 North for approximately six miles toward Roan Mountain. Look for the "old rock school building" on the left. The Five Oaks Campground is on the school grounds.

From the Blue Ridge Parkway, take the exit for Spruce Pine (between mileposts 330 and 340). Travel north on NC 226 through Spruce Pine to Bakersville. Pick back up with the directions above.

For additional details, call one of the numbers below.

CONTACT: Berlin Ledford or Charles E. McKinney, 100 Evergreen Rd., Bakersville, NC 28705, (828) 688-3572, ‹evergreen@m-y.net›; or Mitchell County Chamber of Commerce Visitor Center, 79 Parkway Rd., Spruce Pine, NC 28777, (800) 227-3912, (828) 765-9483, ‹info@mitchell-county.com›, ‹www.mitchell-county.com›

YANCEY COUNTY

❄ Music in the Mountains Festival

This one-day celebration of regional music takes place on the third Saturday in September at the Patience Park/Toe River Campground in Yancey County, North Carolina. Patience Park is a beautiful county-owned property on the banks of the South Toe River. The Music in the Mountains Festival is centered around a rustic log pavilion and dance hall. The music presented includes mostly bluegrass, old-time, and gospel, but there's also ballad singing, storytelling, and mountain dancing. Local civic clubs offer festival foods and other refreshments, while the nearby river is popular for rafting and swimming. A modest admission fee is charged.

LOCATION: From I-40 near Marion, take exit 85 for US 221 North. US 221 will merge with NC 226 north of Marion. Follow US 221/NC 226 North for approximately seven miles. When the two highways split, take NC 226 North to Spruce Pine (about eight more miles). At the subsequent split between NC 226

Local old-time musician Red Wilson is a favorite of audiences attending the Music in the Mountains Festival. (Photograph by Sally Council; courtesy of the North Carolina Arts Council)

and NC 226-ALT, stay straight on NC 226 going north. In Spruce Pine, take US 19-E for approximately seven miles. At Micaville, take NC 80 South. Four miles south of Micaville, turn left onto Blue Rock Rd. and follow the signs to the festival.

From Asheville, take US 19/23 North. In about eighteen miles US 19 and US 23 will split. Follow US 19 east (it will become US 19-E) for approximately twenty miles to Burnsville. Once you've passed through Burnsville, go around four miles to Micaville and turn right onto NC 80 South. Four miles south of Micaville, turn left onto Blue Rock Rd. and follow the signs to the festival.

CONTACT: Denise Cook, Toe River Arts Council, PO Box 882, Burnsville, NC 28714-0882, (828) 682-7215 or (828) 765-0520, ‹TRAC@yancey.main.nc.us›, ‹main.nc.us/TRAC›; or Yancey County Chamber of Commerce, 106 W. Main St., Burnsville, NC 28714, (800) 948-1632, (828) 682-7413, ‹info@yanceychamber.com›, ‹www.yanceychamber.com›

❄ Young's Mountain Music

As soon as visitors to Young's Mountain Music find a spot to park and open their car doors, they are greeted by the sounds of live music. Along the

Stage performance at Young's Mountain Music

driveway that leads to Young's Mountain Music and in the parking areas behind the building, musicians gather to jam and to form bands for the coming evening's shows. Inside, additional groups of players get together in the hallways, in the practice rooms, and in the designated smoking areas to rehearse.

Every Saturday night, Young's Mountain Music, located between Burnsville and Spruce Pine, North Carolina, welcomes a crowd of two hundred or more music and dance lovers into its warm, hand-hewn interior to enjoy stage performances by regional musicians who play country, bluegrass, and gospel music. Visitors enter a spacious lobby and concession area where volunteers sell hot dogs, popcorn, and homemade desserts. The performance hall, with its raised stage, dance floor, and theater-style seating, is adjacent to the lobby. There, bands play and dancers enjoy clogging, buck dancing, and the mountain two-step. Another room nearby is reserved for socializing, jamming, and smoking. This room leads backstage to a series of rooms in which the bands warm up before going onstage.

Meanwhile, owner Bill Young and Alice Hyatt Powers act as emcees. They introduce eight to ten bands, each of which plays a twenty- to thirty-minute set, much to the delight of an appreciative audience. All musicians perform without payment. Dedicated volunteers called the Golden Eagles stock and man the concession area, organize appreciation events for the musicians, and raise funds for utilities, equipment, and repairs. They also occupy a special section near the dance floor, from where they encourage and lead the dancing. The tradition at Young's Mountain Music is for the audience to stand during the performance of a gospel selection or other religious number.

This venue draws a crowd of Saturday night regulars who come from as far as seventy-five miles away. A modest admission fee is charged.

LOCATION: Young's Mountain Music is located on US 19-E between Spruce Pine and Burnsville on the Yancey/Mitchell County line. From Spruce Pine, take US 19-E west for approximately four miles; Young's Mountain Music will be on the right.

From Burnsville, take US 19-E east for approximately nine miles, and Young's will be on the left.

Visitors choose from a wide assortment of cakes and pies.

CONTACT: Bill and Shirley Young, Young's Tractor, Route 2, Box 636, Burnsville, NC 28714, (828) 765-4060; or Yancey County Chamber of Commerce, 106 W. Main St., Burnsville, NC 28714, (800) 948-1632, (828) 682-7413, ‹info@yanceychamber.com›, ‹www.yanceychamber.com›

MCDOWELL COUNTY

❀ Old Fort Mountain Music

Every Friday evening, folks in western North Carolina gather to hear and play traditional music at one of the region's most successful "hometown oprys," Old Fort Mountain Music. The building that's home to Old Fort Mountain Music is a former auto dealership that has undergone a succession of renovations and expansions over the years, all of them accomplished with the labor of the small group of music enthusiasts who coordinate and present the weekly music program. The place currently seats an audience of up to four hundred people. Master of Ceremonies Gene Padgett keeps a running tally of the number of consecutive Friday nights traditional music has been presented there (well over six hundred at the time of this writing).

During the evening, bluegrass and old-time musicians gather in groups outside the building to jam and to form bands that will later perform inside. Each group plays for twenty minutes. None of the participating musicians are paid. The attending dancers, who clog, flatfoot, and buck dance, all wear taps on their shoes. When they're not dancing in front of the performance stage, they sit around the room and pat their feet on the floor to the beat of the music. Snacks, soft drinks, and coffee are sold in the concession area.

LOCATION: The Old Fort Mountain Music Friday night concert and dance is located in the Rockett Building on Main St. in downtown Old Fort.

From Asheville, take I-40 East for approximately eighteen miles. Take the Old Fort exit (exit 72) and veer right. At the first traffic light, go straight onto Main St. and the Rockett Building will be on the left, across from the fire station.

From Marion, take I-40 West for approximately eight miles. Take exit 73 for Old Fort and stay right. At the second traffic light, turn right onto Main St. and the Rockett Building will be on the left.

CONTACT: Gene Padgett, Old Fort Mountain Music, 851 Airport Rd., Marion, NC 28752, (828) 652-3330, (828) 652-2838; or Traci Ross, McDowell Arts and Crafts Association, PO Box 1387 (50 S. Main St.), Marion, NC 28752, (828) 652-8610

Banjo player Bobby Briton and friends wait for a
chance to perform at Old Fort Mountain Music.

❈ Orchard at Altapass

On Saturday and Sunday afternoons beginning in late May and running
through October, the Orchard at Altapass features mountain music, dancing, and storytelling in the packing house. This historic apple orchard
stretches over a mile along the Blue Ridge Parkway near Spruce Pine, North
Carolina. Most of the trees are at least eighty years old. Apples from the orchard are picked and sorted by hand, an operation that is open for visitors to
view. Hayrides are also offered for the kids. Visitors are welcome to bring an
instrument or to sing along with the resident musicians. The music starts at
1:30 P.M. and goes until around 4:00.

LOCATION: The Orchard at Altapass is located between mileposts 328 and 329 on
the Blue Ridge Parkway.

From the north, turn south on NC 226 at Spruce Pine and travel about five
miles to the entrance to the Blue Ridge Parkway (across from the N.C. Minerals

Picking apples in the Orchard at Alta Pass

Museum). Take the Parkway north and go three miles to Orchard Rd. on the downhill side. Orchard Rd. leads you to the orchard and the red packing house.

From the south, take exit 86 off I-40. Follow NC 226/US 221 past Marion and the Wal-Mart. In approximately nine miles, turn left, following NC 226 as it separates from US 221. In another mile, NC 226 turns right and heads up the mountain. At the top (where the road comes to a T-intersection), turn right to the entrance to the Blue Ridge Parkway. Take the Parkway north and go three miles to Orchard Rd. on the downhill side. Orchard Rd. leads you to the orchard and the red packing house.

CONTACT: Bill and Judy Carson, The Orchard at Altapass, PO Box 245, Little Switzerland, NC 28749, (888) 765-9531, ‹bcarson@mitchell.main.nc.us›, ‹www.altapassorchard.com›; or Traci Ross, McDowell Arts and Crafts Association, PO Box 1387 (50 S. Main St.), Marion, NC 28752, (828) 652-8610

❧ Mountain Gateway Museum

Displays at this state-operated museum showcase the lifestyles and cultural history of Southern Appalachian mountain residents, from the earliest original inhabitants through the settlement period to the present. Museum highlights include an introductory video presentation, self-guided tours, living history exhibits, collections of photographs, regional musical instruments, songbooks, tools, and housewares, two 1800s log cabins, an outdoor amphitheater, and a picnic area. The Mountain Gateway Museum complex is situated on the banks of historic Mill Creek. It's open daily except for official state holidays.

LOCATION: The museum is located in downtown Old Fort. From I-40, take exit 73 onto Catawba Ave. Travel north on Catawba Ave. for approximately a quarter of a mile. The museum is a large stone building on the right.

CONTACT: Sam Gray, Director, Mountain Gateway Museum Service Center, PO Box 1286, Old Fort, NC 28762-1286, (828) 668-9259, ‹gateway@wnclink.com›, ‹nchistory.dcr.state.nc.us›; or Traci Ross, McDowell Arts and Crafts Association, PO Box 1387 (50 S. Main St.), Marion, NC 28752, (828) 652-8610

RUTHERFORD COUNTY

❀ Ellenboro Fiddlers' and Bluegrass Convention

The annual Ellenboro Fiddlers' and Bluegrass Convention is a daylong competition held the Saturday before Thanksgiving in the Ellenboro School auditorium in Ellenboro, North Carolina. The music begins at 6:30 P.M. There is an admission fee. Call for details.

LOCATION: The school is located between the towns of Rutherfordton and Shelby. From Gastonia, North Carolina, take US 74 West. In Mooresboro, US 74 splits into a business and a bypass route. Follow US 74 Business West toward Ellenboro. Within a couple of miles, take the Ellenboro exit. Turn left at the top of the exit ramp. Proceed one half-mile to a stop sign and turn right. Continue two blocks to a traffic light and turn left. Travel two more blocks to the next light and turn right. Go one block and then turn left. The Ellenboro School is two blocks down on the right.

From I-40, take exit 103 in Morganton and follow US 64 West toward Rutherfordton. In Rutherfordton, follow the signs to US 74 Business going east toward Forest City. Approximately five miles past Forest City, take the Ellenboro exit. Pick back up with the directions above.

CONTACT: Frances Bailey, Annual Ellenboro Fiddlers' and Bluegrass Convention, PO Box 154, Ellenboro, NC 28040, (828) 453-7457, ‹cwillis@rutherford.k12.mc.us›; or Rutherford County Tourism Development Authority, 162 N. Main St., Rutherfordton, NC 28139, (800) 849-5998, (828) 286-1110, ‹rctda@blueridge.net›, ‹www.rutherfordtourism.com›

Before the crowds arrive

✻ Bluegrass at the Golden Valley Music Park

At the Golden Valley Music Park in Rutherford County, there's a weekly concert and dance featuring regional bluegrass and country musicians. The park is a complex of buildings located off the Bostic-Sunshine Road north of Forest City, North Carolina. The main building is a five-thousand-square-foot structure whose rustic construction features a raised stage, a dance floor, and tables, chairs, and pews adequate to seat an audience of 280 people. There's also a sit-down restaurant offering a full-service menu six days a week. The Music Park bluegrass concerts occur year-round on Friday nights from 8:00 to 11:00 P.M. There is an admission charge.

LOCATION: From I-40 at Marion, take exit 86 onto NC 226 South. Travel south on NC 226 for approximately twenty miles until it intersects with the Bostic-

Sunshine Hwy., which is marked by a caution light. Turn right onto the Bostic-Sunshine Hwy. and the Golden Valley Music Park will be two miles ahead on the left.

From the intersection of I-85 and US 74 West, take US 74 West toward Shelby. Just west of Shelby, US 74 will intersect with NC 226 North. Turn right (north) onto NC 226 and follow for approximately twenty miles until it intersects with the Bostic-Sunshine Hwy., which is marked by a caution light. Turn left onto the Bostic-Sunshine Hwy. and the Golden Valley Music Park will be two miles ahead on the left.

CONTACT: Vern Berry, Golden Valley Music Park, Box 666, Polkville, NC 28136, (704) 538-8797, ‹berryjv1@earthlink.net›; or Rutherford County Tourism Development Authority, 162 N. Main St., Rutherfordton, NC 28139, (800) 849-5998, (828) 286-1110, ‹rctda@blueridge.net›, ‹www.rutherfordtourism.com›

REGION SIX

FIDDLES, BANJOS, AND BLACK COFFEE

ROANOKE

❦ Roanoke Fiddle and Banjo Club

Up the road and down the mountain, the Roanoke Fiddle and Banjo Club hosts a "jam" on the first Saturday evening of every month in the city of Roanoke. This event is actually a musical bonanza staged in a comfortable, climate-controlled, modern facility, the Roanoke Civic Center—and it's free. The civic center auditorium is an enormous, multilevel hall that seats up to five thousand people. While they may call this event a jam, it's actually a concert and a stage show. The average monthly attendance is around fifteen hundred folks, but because the place is so big there's almost always very good seating available close to the stage. Actually, in this facility all the seats are good, including those in the large balcony that wraps around the upper level in the rear of the auditorium.

Each monthly session of the Roanoke Fiddle and Banjo Club features twelve bluegrass bands and a team of precision clog dancers. The club does not allow electrical instruments or drums to be used in performances. Bands are allotted twenty minutes each for their sets, which are typically well rehearsed, lively, and well played. A longtime veteran announcer presents each act in an informative and entertaining way. While the band of the moment is performing onstage, the other musicians gather to play and talk in the front lobby of the auditorium and in a series of small "dressing rooms" located behind the stage. This backstage area is easily accessed, and the musicians, their friends, and many others freely come and go during the course of the evening. No one seems to mind this at all. Some of the best music at this event is played behind the stage and in the lobby of the auditorium, and

Stage performance at the Roanoke Fiddle and Banjo Club

many of the music fans who regularly attend divide their time between these two areas and the more formal stage presentation inside.

The Roanoke Fiddle and Banjo Club was founded in 1969 in an effort to preserve old-time and bluegrass music in the Roanoke area. Over the years, the members have met at several different places, but as the crowds grew and more bands began to play at the monthly gatherings, the group finally settled on the Roanoke Civic Center as its regular venue.

Membership in the Roanoke Fiddle and Banjo Club numbers around five thousand. It's a nonprofit organization and there's no charge to join. No one who has anything to do with the Fiddle and Banjo Club production gets paid. The setup work, the scheduling and printing, the announcing and stage management, the operation of the sound and light systems, the music playing, and the dancing are all done by volunteers. They do a great job.

Drinking, eating, and smoking are prohibited in the Roanoke Civic Center auditorium, although soft drinks, snacks, and freshly made popcorn are available for purchase in the front lobby. The stage show begins precisely at 6:00 in the evening and lasts until around 10:00.

LOCATION: From the north or west, take I-81 to Roanoke. Merge onto I-581 South and travel approximately five miles to US 460-E/Orange Ave. at exit 4E. Exit and

Backstage in the dressing rooms

travel east for less than a mile. Turn right onto US 11/221 South. The civic center will be on the right.

From the south, travel on US 220 North to Roanoke. As you come into Roanoke, US 220 merges with I-581. Travel to US 460-E/Orange Ave. at exit 4E and pick up with directions above.

CONTACT: Roanoke Civic Center, 710 Williamson Rd. NE, Roanoke, VA 24016, (276) 386-2241

❀ Mill Mountain Coffee Shop Jam

Fiddler and washboard player Jay Griffin leads the old-time jam at the Mill Mountain Coffee Shop in downtown Roanoke, where the musicians meet every Thursday beginning around 7:00 P.M. Most of the participants are youngish "revivalist" players, but several old-timers enjoy playing there, too.

The jam begins when three or four players gather in a small circle at the back of the coffee shop. Before sitting down to play, the musicians collect a number of the small metal tables that are scattered around the rear of the coffee shop and move them to one side to create an open floor space. Then they form a large circle using fifteen or twenty of the shop's iron-bodied café chairs. The ironwork on the back of each of chair is fashioned to read "Mill Mountain Coffee and Tea Co." The circle of musicians, all crowded into the back end of the storefront coffee shop, grows larger and larger as the nine

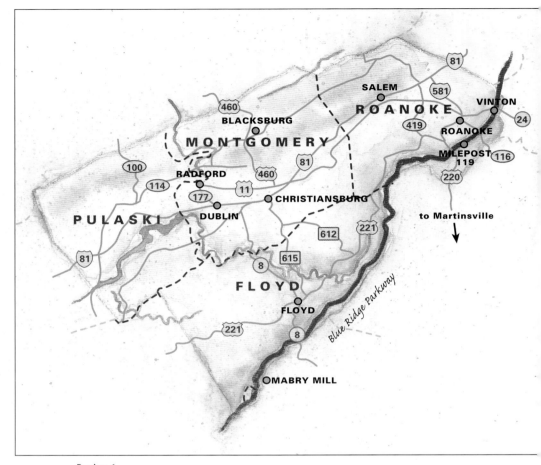

Region 6

o'clock hour approaches. Then, by 10:00, the number dwindles again to just four or five players, and shortly thereafter everyone usually calls it quits and goes home.

At the height of the evening, there may be as many as twenty-five players using fiddles, banjos, washboards, guitars, spoons, hammered dulcimers, mandolins, and assorted other instruments deemed proper for the rendering of old-time mountain music. The musicians range in age from teenagers to seniors. Men hold a very slight majority over women among the players.

Most tunes are played without singing, but every once in a while Jay Griffin or one of the other male players, usually one of the fiddlers, will sing out an old favorite with great fervor and at considerable volume. At the Mill Mountain Coffee Shop, everyone plays in unison, typically at the prompting

A typical Thursday night at the Mill Mountain Coffee and Tea Shop

of Jay Griffin's fiddle or that of another of the veteran musicians who take turns at the lead. The others fall in as they are able. It's a lively session, and everyone there seems welcoming, agreeable, and enthusiastic. The freshly roasted and brewed coffee of the Mill Mountain Coffee Shop goes very well with the music.

An interesting counterpoint to the traditional music scene at the coffee shop is the frequent appearance there of a small group of teenagers sporting baggy clothing, numerous body piercings, multicolored spiked hairdos, and other fanciful cosmetic devices. The teens try their best to appear altogether unaware of the presence of the mountain musicians in the back part of the shop, but the location of the coffee shop's restrooms and its water fountain, situated behind the circle of musicians, inevitably causes the kids and the musicians to be drawn into close proximity to one another. The resulting en-counters are polite and cordial, if not completely joyful.

JAM SESSION PROTOCOL

Jam session at Mill Mountain
Coffee and Tea Shop

The majority of jam sessions in the Blue Ridge are friendly affairs where people gather to play and to listen to traditional music in an informal setting. The seating, or standing, arrangement of the participants varies from place to place and from time to time. However, there seems to be a general custom that the most experienced and skilled musicians will occupy the most central positions of the group. Generally, but not always, mountain jam sessions are circular in form, and the veteran musicians sit or stand right in the middle of the assembled players.

The other musicians often place themselves closer to or more distant from the center in accordance with their particular skill levels. Rank beginners will occasionally select a spot entirely removed from the main group, a few chairs or steps away, sometimes even to the point of retreating into an adjacent room, if one is available. But, as with many aspects of mountain music, there are no hard-and-fast rules. Sometimes a master player will sit or stand quietly off to the side, intentionally choosing not to be positioned at the center of things.

According to fiddler Jay Griffin, visiting musicians who want to join in on an open jam session such as the one at the Mill Mountain Coffee Shop in Roanoke, Virginia, are welcome to show up with their instruments. But every jam session is different, so musicians who have an interest in joining in should be observant and respectful of local procedures. Generally, you should wait until you've been offered that unmistakable cue to participate before barging in.

There are certain parameters to be considered before unpacking your banjo or guitar. Some jams, such as the one at Mill Mountain Coffee Shop, are strictly focused on old-time music. Others are entirely bluegrass. There are a number of open jams at which the tunes played are restricted entirely to those deemed by the regular participants to be truly traditional to the region. At others, the selection of what's to be played is wide open, and the music may range from centuries-old pieces to contemporary country hits or even occasional Beatles tunes.

*The following set of tongue-in-cheek guidelines for participating
in jam sessions has been circulated through e-mail among revivialist
old-time musicians:*

THE TEN COMMANDMENTS OF JAMMING

I. *Thou shalt not ever forsake the beat.*

II. *Thou shalt arrange thyselves in a small circle so that thou mayest
hear and see the other musicians. Thou shalt listen with thine ears
to the songs and attempt to play in accord with the group; also,
open thine eyes betimes to look about thee, lest there be some visual
sign someone is endeavoring to send thee. Thou shalt play softly
when someone lifteth his voice in song, when playing harmony,
and when thou knowest not what thou is doing.*

III. *Thou shalt play in tune. Tune thine instument well, and tune it
often with thine electric tuner, lest the sounds emanating from
thine instrument be unclean.*

IV. *Thou shalt commence and cease playing each tune together as
one, so that the noise ye make be a joyful noise, and not a heinous
tinkling that goeth in fits and starts, for that is unclean, and is an
abomination. Whensoever a musician sticketh forth his foot as
though he were afflicted with a cramp in the fatted calf, thou must
complete the rest of that verse, and then cease.*

V. *Thou shalt stick out thine own foot or else lift up thy voice crying
"This is it!" or "Last time!" if thou hast been the one to begin the
song, and it has been played sufficient times over. If the one who
began a tune endeth it not by one of these signs, then the tune will
just go on and on, like the Old Testament, until the listeners say,
"Hark! It all soundeth the same."*

VI. *Thou shalt concentrate and thou shalt not confound the music by
mixing up the A part and the B part. Most songs, but not all, pro-
ceedeth according to the ancient law "AABB." But if thou sinneth in
this regard, or make any mistake that is unclean, thou may atone
not by ceasing to play—but by reentering the tune in the proper
place and playing on.*

VII. *Thou shalt be ever mindful of the key the banjo is tuned in, and
play many tunes in that key, For the banjo is but a lowly instrument, which must be retuned each time there is a key change.*

VIII. *Thou shalt not speed up or slow down accidentally when playing a
tune, for it is an abomination. (see Commandment I)*

ix. *Thou shalt not, by thine own self, commence noodling off on a tune the other musicians know not, unless asked or unless thou art teaching that tune, for it is an abomination, and the other musicians will not hold thee guiltless, and shall take thee off their computer lists, yea, even unto the third and the fourth generation.*

x. *Thou shalt not come to the jammeth session to impresseth others with thine amazing talents, for this also is an abomination. The song shalt be the center aroundeth which all musicians shall rotateth, not viceth-versaeth. "Attempts to make thine own star shine shall lead thee into darkness."*

LOCATION: From the north or west, take I-81 to Roanoke. Merge onto I-581 South at exit 143. Take I-581 South to exit 5. Exit and stay left at the fork in the ramp, onto US 11/220. US 11/220 becomes Williamson Rd. Take Williamson Rd. south to Salem Ave. Turn right on Salem and go to the second left, which is Market St. Go one block and turn left again onto Campbell. Mill Mountain Coffee House is in the next block on the left.

From the south, travel on US 220 North to Roanoke. As you come into Roanoke, US 220 merges with I-581. Take I-581 North to exit 5 and follow directions listed above.

CONTACT: Jay Griffin, 511 Bethel Rd., Fincastle, VA 24090, ‹newroanokejugband@yahoo.com›; or Mill Mountain Coffee and Tea Co., 112 Campbell Ave., Roanoke, VA 24011, (540) 342-9404

❊ Roanoke Mountain Music Series

Every Sunday afternoon from the end of June to mid-October, there's an informal concert at the Roanoke Mountain Campground on the Blue Ridge Parkway. The audience at this event is a mix of campers who are staying in the park and local people who come especially for the music. The concert takes place in a beautiful natural setting that's a great place for sitting and listening. The music starts around sunset.

LOCATION: From downtown Roanoke, follow the signs to Mill Mountain Star, the large star on Mill Mountain that is the landmark most associated with Roanoke. You will travel out of town on Walnut Ave. for approximately three miles. At the entrance to Mill Mountain, Walnut Ave. turns into a spur road of the Blue Ridge Parkway. The campground is one mile beyond Mill Mountain Park on your right.

JAY GRIFFIN
COME SEE FOR YOURSELF

Jay Griffin of Roanoke, Virginia, describes himself as a "revivalist" musician. He learned his music from records and other mass media as well as from older traditional musicians around the Blue Ridge.

I grew up with these mountains all around me. My earliest memories are of always having these mountains in place. There's no direct family connection to the style of music I play. When I was sixteen years old, I saw Jean Ritchie play an Appalachian dulcimer on TV, and I just had to have one of those things for myself. It took off from there. I have to blame Jean Ritchie, I guess.

I attended the University of Virginia for two years. My junior and senior years were spent there, and there was an old-time circle in Charlottesville. When I first started, my friends and I were learning fiddle tunes fourth- or fifth-hand from recordings of friends. But then I started listening to the Skillet Lickers and stuff like that, and I developed a different concept of what the music should sound like.

When I was about nineteen or twenty, I started playing the washboard. Shortly after that, all on the same afternoon, I discovered both the blues of Robert Johnson and the fiddling of Hobart Smith. I just happened to play those two records on that one day, the same day—Robert Johnson and Hobart Smith! I've been addicted to both blues and to old-time music ever since. I didn't take up the fiddle until I was about twenty-five. I'd go to fiddlers' conventions and to festivals, but I played the washboard. Now fiddle playing has turned into a twenty-year obsession of its own.

I'm constantly learning something. There's a young fellow named Jim Barnhill playing banjo with us now. He just took up banjo like two years ago. Well, after he'd been at it for several months, he asked me if I would play fiddle tunes with him—slowly, you know, if I had the time—and I said "sure." So we started playing once a week, and we still do. Much to my amazement, he now goes around to other people, spends time with them, and then brings me new tunes to learn! I thought I was going to do all the teaching, but I've learned as much from him as from anybody.

There is more and more personal exchange of music going on these days—thank goodness! Musicians that are about my age learned a lot from the people that were three or four generations ahead of us, and when they passed on, we really started to feel the weight on our shoulders. We feel obliged to pass along what the old guys had taken the time and trouble to show to us. The main reason for doing this jam that we do here at Mill Mountain Coffee Shop is that there are kids in their twenties coming in here wanting to learn the old style.

In Charlottesville, back when I started to school at the University of Virginia, there was a coffee house near the campus called the Prism. In the early sixties it was a pretty hot place. Bob Dylan even came and played there. But by the time I got there in 1975, it had deteriorated because of the various hippie dynasties that went through the place. We decided that it would be a shame to let the Prism just fall apart. We decided we were gonna do something! We went to the Presbyterian Church, and they said, "Well, if you can prove to us that there's a community interest in this thing, we'll see what we can do." So we put on a benefit concert with seven or eight different local acts playing various kinds of music, and one thousand people showed up! It's been going continuously now since 1975.

If you are a musician, and you want to sit in with us and play, then I'd say just walk up with your instrument in your hand—and if somebody doesn't say "Hey, get it out and play," then you're at the wrong jam. Everyone is welcome here. Just find a seat, if you can, and soak it up. It's a wonderful old place. We encourage people to bring their tape recorders to our sessions. We try to think of this place as a beacon, you know? We say, "Come on, and share the light a little bit." My idea here is to try and get my fellow musicians to just come out and show other people how much fun this stuff really is. People like Russ Harbaugh, Glenn Reed, and Charlie Henderson are faithful participants who show up regularly. If you come to our jam, be ready to open your instrument case—and your mind—and enjoy the evening. We just try to let the music do the talking.

Make the trip and see for yourself.

Small farms and pastures can be viewed from the
Blue Ridge Parkway in southwestern Virginia.

From the Blue Ridge Parkway, travel north approximately one mile from the intersection of the Parkway and US 220. Turn left onto the spur road leading to the campground and look for signs.

CONTACT: Ranger Station at Roanoke Mountain, Roanoke Mountain Campground (campsite #10), MP 119 on the Blue Ridge Parkway, (540) 767-2491, ‹www.nps.gov/blri›

❄ Vinton Old-Time Bluegrass Festival and Competition

The Vinton Farmer's Market in Vinton, Virginia, is the setting for an annual music event called the Vinton Old-Time Bluegrass Festival and Competition, which features a contest for amateur musicians during the day and band performances in the evening. This festival is held on the third Thursday, Friday, Saturday, and Sunday in August. The music begins at 6:00 P.M. on Thursday and continues through Sunday afternoon.

LOCATION: From the Blue Ridge Parkway, take US 24 toward Roanoke. In approximately two miles, US 24 turns sharply to the left. Stay straight ahead on East Washington Ave. and come into Vinton. Take a left on Pollard St., then a right on Lee Ave. The farmer's market will be on your right within one block, at 204 Lee Ave.

From I-81, take I-581 South in Roanoke. Take exit 4E and turn east onto US 460 (Orange Ave.). At the fifth stoplight, turn right onto Gus W. Nicks Blvd. Go approximately one mile and turn right on Pollard St., then right again onto Lee Ave. Pick up with directions above.

CONTACT: Donnie and Rhonda Ray, Vinton Farmer's Market, Vinton Bluegrass Festival, PO Box 422, Vinton, VA 24179, (540) 345-8548, ‹DRMUSIC1@aol.com›

SALEM

❀ Olde Salem Days

Every year, on the second Saturday in September, there's music, arts and crafts, and even an antique car show in downtown Salem, Virginia. Olde Salem Days, which extends over several blocks on Main Street, starts at 10:00 A.M., continues through the day, and ends around 5:00 P.M. It's free.

LOCATION: The city of Salem is located adjacent to the northwestern edge of Roanoke. From Roanoke, take either US 11 North or US 460 West. Either will take you into Salem.

From I-81, take exit 140 into downtown Salem.

CONTACT: Roanoke County Jaycees, PO Box 782, Salem, VA 24153, (276) 228-6855

RADFORD CITY

❀ Appalachian Folk Arts Festival

The Appalachian Folk Arts Festival is held annually at Radford University in Radford, Virginia, on the fourth weekend in September. That's also parents' weekend at Radford. The focus of this free event is a celebration of Appalachian heritage. The festival, which is staged on Heath Lawn on the university campus, begins at 9:00 in the morning and features regional bands playing bluegrass and old-time mountain music.

LOCATION: From I-81, take exit 109 and follow VA 177 West (Tyler Ave.). This road will take you right into the campus. The event will be well marked.

CONTACT: Dr. Grace Toney Edwards, Appalachian Folk Arts Festival, Heath Lawn of Radford University, PO Box 7014, Radford, VA 24142, (540) 831-5366, ‹gedwards@radford.edu›, ‹www.runet.edu/~arsc›

✤ Hillbilly Opry

The Hillbilly Opry takes place every Saturday evening year-round at Mc-Guire's Family Campground in Dublin, Virginia. This event features local bluegrass and old-time bands that play for an audience of both listeners and dancers. The music starts at 7:00 P.M. and lasts until around 10:30. A small admission fee is charged. There's a café on the grounds, and camping with hookups is available.

LOCATION: From I-81, take exit 101 (State Park Rd. or VA 660) and turn south toward Claytor Lake State Park. McGuire's Family Campground will be on the right in approximately one-and-a-half miles.
CONTACT: Mike McGuire, Hillbilly Opry, McGuire's Family Campground, 4925 State Park Rd., Dublin, VA 24084, (540) 674-5561, ‹jenilyn17@hotmail.com›

✤ Bluegrass and Old-Time Music at New River Community College

Bluegrass and old-time bands play on the second Saturday evening of every month at the New River Community College in Dublin, Virginia. This monthly event features one bluegrass and one old-time band at each gathering. The music is played at Edwards Hall in a space that affords ample room for the musicians and an audience and for dancing. No admission fee is charged, but the hat is passed for donations to cover expenses. The music starts at 7:00 P.M.

LOCATION: From I-81, take exit 98 onto VA 100 North. Go approximately two miles to New River Community College, which will be on your left. Turn into the college. Edwards Hall is the first building on your right.
CONTACT: Charlie White, Bluegrass and Old-Time Music Event, New River Community College, Dublin, VA 24084, (540) 673-3631, ‹nrwhite@nr.vccs.edu›

✤ Floyd Country Store Jam Sessions and Concerts

Weekly jam sessions—the Friday Night Jamborees—are held every week at the Floyd Country Store in Floyd, Virginia, and bluegrass concerts are

Local residents socialize in front of the Floyd Country Store before the concert starts.

staged there every Saturday night. The main floor of the rustic and pictur-esque old two-story store, built in 1913 (formerly Cockram's Store), is cleared every weekend and large audiences fill the building by the begin-ning hours of 6:30 P.M. on Fridays and 7:30 P.M. on Saturdays. The Friday and Saturday night events at the Floyd Country Store are worthy tributes to old-time and bluegrass music and to mountain dance. Many of those who attend the Friday Night Jamboree are regulars, but the jamboree also at-tracts visitors from all across the country. Articles about the jamboree have appeared in *Bluegrass Unlimited*, *Country Living*, and the *Roanoke Times*, and the event has been featured on National Public Radio's *Morning Edition*.

The Friday evening jam sessions begin with an hour of gospel music per-formed by a group of local old-timers. Following that, various bands take turns playing onstage for the rest of the evening. A large open area in front of the bandstand is reserved for friendly and enthusiastic dancers. During the warmer months, musicians gather informally to play outside on the sidewalk in front of the store and in nearby driveways and parking lots. When the weather is too cold to be outside (and for these mountain musi-cians, it has to be pretty cold), the impromptu groups can usually be found playing together in one of the upstairs rooms above the main store space. On

Saturday nights, the Floyd Country Store presents a concert series that features the best of the region's bluegrass bands.

There's an admission charge both nights. Snacks, soft drinks, and ice cream are available at the store, and there's a very good hometown restaurant right around the corner on East Main Street. Call the store for details on the Friday Night Jamboree or check the website for a schedule of upcoming Saturday night concerts.

LOCATION: The Floyd Country Store is located at 206 S. Locust St., one block south of the only stoplight in town. Floyd is accessible from I-81 (exit 114), Stuart, and Christiansburg via VA 8 and from Roanoke and Hillsville on US 221.

From the Blue Ridge Parkway, exit near milepost 166. Then turn onto VA 8 and continue north into Floyd.

CONTACT: William Morgan, Floyd Country Store, S. Locust St., Floyd, VA 24091, (540) 745-4563, (828) 693-0868, ‹wcmorganjr@yahoo.com›, ‹www.floydcountrystore.com›

❄ County Sales

Dave Freeman created the label County Records in 1965 to issue recordings of mountain bluegrass and old-time music. County Sales, the mail-order business that arose to distribute County Records and similar offerings from other small labels, is an amazing business that's located around the corner and about a block away from the Floyd Country Store. County Sales lists an impressive selection of vintage and contemporary traditional American music in its catalog, much of which has been remastered on CD from the original 78-rpm and LP recordings. The main shop is located in two basement-level, warehouse-sized rooms crammed full of row after row and shelf after shelf of CDs, videos, and books that feature traditional southern music and musicians. Even though the vast majority of County Sales business is through mail order, browsers are welcome to look around and to purchase directly from the local store. The sales area is open from 9:30 A.M. to 4:00 P.M. Monday through Friday, and from 9:00 A.M. to 1:00 P.M. on Saturday.

LOCATION: County Sales is located at 117 Main St. in Floyd. Coming from the north, turn right at the one stoplight in town. Go one block and you will see Talley's Alley on your left. Walk down this alley and look for the building on your left. County Sales is located in the basement of this building.

Floyd is accessible from I-81 (exit 114), Stuart, and Christiansburg via VA 8 and from Roanoke and Hillsville on US 221. From the Blue Ridge Parkway, exit near milepost 166. Then turn onto VA 8 and continue north into Floyd.

Mabry Mill at milepost 176 on the Blue Ridge Parkway in Virginia

CONTACT: Call (540) 745-2001 for details or to request a catalog, or visit the website at ‹www.countysales.com›.

❀ Mabry Mill

Operated by the National Park Service, Mabry Mill is one of the Blue Ridge Parkway's most popular sites. It features a restored gristmill and a water-powered sawmill that was in local use for many years in the early part of the twentieth century. An interpretive walking trail with outdoor exhibits is located at nearby Rocky Knob.

Mabry Mill has been a popular gathering spot for local musicians for many years. On Sunday afternoons from Memorial Day through Labor Day, they assemble for impromptu music sessions at an outdoor space near the re-created blacksmith shop. The musicians play beneath and around a small, open-sided shed that shelters the complex's syrup-making apparatus. Several sheets of heavy plywood for dancing are placed together side by side on a grassy lawn in front of the shed, and the musicians sit around in chairs or on the edge of the stone syrup furnace housed beneath the shelter. The music at Mabry Mill is primarily of the old-time instrumental variety. Visitors bring their own folding chairs or blankets and sit scattered around on the shady, spacious lawn. There is no admission fee. The music starts around 1:00 P.M. and lasts for several hours.

LOCATION: From Stuart or Hillsville, take US 58 to the Blue Ridge Parkway entrance at Meadows of Dan. You'll find Mabry Mill near milepost 176.1. on the Parkway just north of Meadows of Dan.

CONTACT: For general Parkway information, call (828) 298-0398 or (828) 271-4779 or visit the Parkway's website at ‹www.nps.gov/blri›.

❧ WGFC Radio Bluegrass Programs

There is a daily program of bluegrass music every Monday through Friday from 7:00 A.M. to 8:00 A.M. on radio station WGFC 1030 AM in Floyd County. Gospel music is also played on the station every Monday through Sunday, all day following the bluegrass show.

Call the station for additional programming details.

CONTACT: Harold Mitchell or Tony Gallimore, WGFC Radio Bluegrass and Gospel Programming, 401 Shooting Creek Rd., PO Box 495, Floyd, VA 24091, (540) 745-9811

MONTGOMERY COUNTY

❧ Tuesday Night Jam in Blacksburg

The town of Blacksburg is home to Virginia Tech University. Members of the Virginia Tech faculty manage the Tuesday Night OldTime Jam of the New River OldTime Community, staged in Baylee's Restaurant at 117 South Main Street. The principal organizer, founder, and energetic proponent of the jam is Bill Richardson. Richardson is also the creator and master of a comprehensive Internet website called New River Valley OldTime (address below), which describes in detail the history and characteristics of this jam and of the traditional music scene in southwestern Virginia. The site also contains announcements of the dates and locations of many of the numer-

Flatfooting is a style of mountain dance in which the feet are kept close to the floor.

ous jam sessions, concerts, dances, and other mountain music–related events that occur in the Blacksburg area all year round.

The Tuesday Night OldTime Jam of the New River OldTime Community is one of the few traditional music venues in the Blue Ridge at which beer and other alcoholic beverages are sold and openly consumed. In addition, the 9:00 P.M. starting time for this jam is a bit later than that of most other such gatherings in the region, but as Richardson explains it, "It's a college town—and it's a party!" Sure enough, on Tuesday nights by 10:00 P.M., the jam session and the dance party are both going strong.

Fiddlers take the lead here, joined by bluegrass and old-time banjo players, bassists, guitarists, mandolin players, and occasional spoon players, all of whom offer an entertaining fare of breakdowns, hornpipes, reels, and slower tunes, including waltzes and two-steps. Dancers respond by performing in a variety of styles that may include reels, square dances, circle dances, couples dancing, two-steps, waltzes, and individual clog dancing or flatfooting. The area set aside for dancing isn't all that big, so things can get pretty crowded as the evening progresses. It's a fun event that's made all the more interesting by the unusual mix of young and older players, the variety and enthusiasm of the energetic dancers who show up, and the generous smattering of students and faculty from the nearby university who are there to participate in the festivity.

The music starts at 9:00 P.M. and seldom ends before midnight. There is no admission fee. Food and drink are available at the site.

LOCATION: From I-81, take exit 118C and turn north on US 460 West. As you approach Blacksburg, US 460 Business will veer off to your right. Take Business 460 toward downtown Blacksburg. Through downtown, US 460 is called Main St. Take a left off Main St. onto College Ave. and look for the sign on the left that says "Top of the Stairs."

CONTACT: Baylee's Restaurant, (540) 961-7611; or Bill Richardson, (540) 951-1061, ‹billrich@vt.edu›, ‹www.vektors.com/oldtime/nrothome›

✸ Traditional Mountain Square Dance in Blacksburg

On the first Saturday evening of every month, the Traditional Mountain Square Dance gets under way at the Gilbert Linkous School gymnasium in Blacksburg. This well-attended and popular event, which has been sponsored by the Old-Time Music and Dance Group since 1981, is a dance that features live traditional music and a skilled dance caller, one who really gets the dancers moving. An admission fee is charged. The music starts at 8:00 P.M.

LOCATION: From I-81, take exit 118c and turn north on US 460 West. Stay on US 460 Bypass around Blacksburg. From US 460 Bypass, take the exit for Tom's Creek Rd. and turn south toward downtown. Continue on Tom's Creek Rd. for less than a mile, and you will see the school on the left.
CONTACT: Bill Richardson, (540) 951-1061, ‹billrich@vt.edu›, ‹www.vektors.com/oldtime/index.html›

✸ WKEX Bluegrass and Gospel Programs

Station WKEX 1430 AM in Blacksburg, Virginia, features recorded bluegrass music twenty-four hours a day, seven days a week, except for the special gospel bluegrass programming that it carries on Sundays.

CONTACT: WKEX 1430 AM, 150 Lark Lane, Blacksburg, VA 24060, (540) 951-9531

✸ Wilderness Trail Festival

The Wilderness Trail Festival is an annual family oriented event that includes arts, crafts, food, a children's area, sidewalk art sales, an antique car exhibit, a race car display, and live music—particularly a stage show featuring local dancers and musicians playing bluegrass, country, and gospel. It is staged in downtown Christiansburg, Virginia, on the third Saturday in September. The Christianburg Chamber of Commerce sponsors the event. There is no admission fee. Food and other concessions are available. The music goes all day, from 9:00 A.M. to 9:00 P.M.

LOCATION: From I-81, take exit 114 and head north on VA 8, which will take you onto Main St. and into the middle of Christianburg. Follow Main St. downtown to the festival.
CONTACT: Kathy Mantz, Executive Director, Christianburg Chamber of Commerce, 205 West Main St., Suite 4, Christianburg, VA 24073, (540) 382-4251, ‹cmcc@cmcc.org›

REGION SEVEN

THE ORANGE BLOSSOM SPECIAL

MADISON COUNTY

❦ Marshall Railroad Depot Friday Night Music and Dance

Driving down North Carolina Highway 213 from the college town of Mars Hill to the little town of Marshall is just plain fun. The last several miles are a twisty, curvy trail of a mountain road that brings you slowly down to the floodplain of the historic French Broad River and, just before you get to town, to an intersection with NC 25. It's a beautiful drive. As you turn right onto Main Street, the wide river is revealed on your left and a mountainside shoots nearly straight up beside you on the right. In between the river and the bluff, on an almost ridiculously narrow spit of flat land, lies Marshall, the seat of government for Madison County.

This seems like a funny place to put a town. Maybe it is, but Marshall is so picturesque that the questionable logic of building on such a narrow expanse of level land situated so very close to a wide river doesn't seem to matter all that much.

The old railroad depot, located at the southern end of town, sits directly beside the river. Its front door faces the narrow lane that is Marshall's main business street and, for several blocks, its only street—at least the only street that's not perpendicular to the river. Near the depot, attached to a wire fence that separates a row of streetside parking spaces from the river bank, is a sign the reads, "WARNING—WATER MAY RISE WITHOUT WARNING."

In fact, during the years since the old Norfolk-Southern Railroad depot was first constructed in the late 1800s, the rising floodwaters of the French Broad River have washed it off its foundations at least twice. After more than one hundred years as a center of activity, the old depot finally went out of use as a train station. In 1995, however, the abandoned building was renovated, and the weekly picking sessions that had filled the back room of

Freight trains still use the tracks adjacent to the Marshall Railroad Depot.

Jerry Adams's pharmacy near Marshall moved there—to a larger, more publicly accessible venue. The newly refurbished facility provided the weekly jam sessions with a stage, a sound system, and, for the first time, adequate space for a sizable audience. The new location also allowed for expanded performance elements and dancing. The people of Marshall and surrounding Madison County communities have responded to their new musical venue with enthusiasm.

After you climb up the steps from the street and enter the depot's front door (a handicapped-access ramp is located on the back of the building, overlooking the river), you'll find yourself in a lobby area where several volunteers stand behind a small counter selling tickets. Don't worry, though, they're not selling admission tickets. The music and dance event is free. Instead, they're selling tickets for a raffle to be conducted later on in the evening—a so-called half-and-half drawing, in which the lucky winner splits the proceeds half-and-half with the sponsoring organization. Hanging on the wall behind the volunteer counter, a little higher than head level, is a framed, high-resolution satellite photograph of Marshall. A close look at the photo confirms what you've already suspected. Marshall hasn't anyplace to

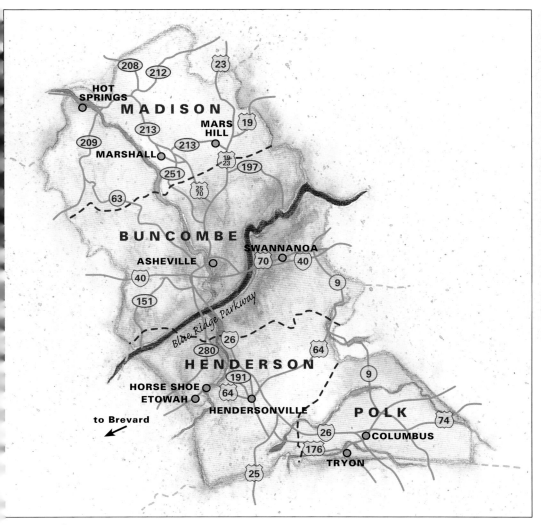

Region 7

grow. In fact, when a new school was built there a number of years ago, it was constructed on an island that sits right out in the middle of the French Broad River. There just wasn't anywhere else to put it.

Beneath the main roof of the depot is an auditorium with a seating capacity of about 150 people. Rows of theater seats run through the center of the room, and around the back, and along the side walls. The interior walls and ceiling have been finished with a clear varnish to show off the natural beauty of the unpainted vintage pine timbers and wallboards. Several large

Town of Marshall

floor-to-ceiling sliding-glass doors open onto a spacious elevated deck that overlooks the French Broad River. From there, you can see a huge, seemingly abandoned mill building and dam. The dam stretches across the river at such an acute angle that its length is probably twice the river's width.

The first part of the evening's program is sometimes reminiscent of the old jam sessions at Jerry Adams's store. Groups of local fiddlers, guitarists, and banjo pickers, including Adams, Josh Goforth, Everett Boone, and five or six others who have played together many times before, command the stage and play a set of old-time and bluegrass favorites. Out beside the depot, in two tiny metal sheds, more groups of musicians, some of whom are slated to go onstage later in the evening, tune up, get their acts together, or just enjoy small private jam sessions. The arrangement here is informal. Some of the groups play mostly old-time, some play exclusively bluegrass, and others play everything from country standards to the latest country pop hits. Meanwhile, inside the depot, fifteen or twenty dancers are energeti-

The Marshall Railroad Depot

cally doing their very best to stomp holes in the depot's old hardwood floor-boards.

Dancing is an integral part of the Friday night scene at the Marshall depot. The dancing styles range from individual (and sometimes hilariously individualistic) buck dancing and flatfooting to cakewalks and conga lines that spill out into the aisles and circle all around and among the seated audience members. The rousing finale of each Friday evening at the Marshall Depot is a "dance-off"—a full half-hour of continuous old-time or bluegrass music during which each of the dancers on the floor will try to outlast, and out-stomp, all the others. It's a pretty wild scene.

The tracks of the Norfolk-Southern Railroad—still an active line—lie directly between the depot and the French Broad River, within thirty feet of the building and the party inside. A long freight train storms by there every Friday night, passing like fury alongside the depot, speeding by in a thundering blur. The train's passing takes nearly four full minutes—and for nearly four minutes it tries its dead-level best to drown out the sounds of the musicians and the dancers inside. It fails.

The Marshall Railroad Depot Friday Night Music and Dance gets going every Friday night between 6:00 and 7:00 P.M., except for one week out of the year—the event is closed on the Friday night of the Old Fiddlers' Convention in Galax, Virginia. But on every other Friday evening year-round, the depot opens at 6:00 P.M. So does the little kitchen and grill located just inside the front door. Marshall Depot Committee volunteers cook

One of the prizes awarded during the cakewalk

hamburgers and hot dogs there and sell them—along with chips, soft drinks, and candy—throughout the evening. An adjacent dining area is furnished with several school lunchroom tables and folding metal chairs for the convenience of those who prefer to eat there.

LOCATION: From Asheville, take US 25/70 North toward Hot Springs. When US 25/70 splits into a business and bypass route, take US 25/70 Business (which becomes S. Main St.) to Marshall. Continue approximately one mile to a T-intersection and turn right. The Marshall Railroad Depot will be the first building on the left after you enter downtown Marshall. Look for the red caboose.

CONTACT: Darlyne Rhinehart, Marshall Railroad Depot, PO Box 548, Marshall, NC 28753, (828) 649-3031, ‹Darhine@main.nc.us›; or Madison County Visitors Center, Inc., 72 S. Main St., PO Box 1527, Mars Hill, NC 28754, (828) 680-9031, (877) 262-3476, (828) 689-9351, ‹MadisonTourism@main.nc.us›, ‹www.madisoncounty-nc.com›

Bluff Mountain Music Festival

The Bluff Mountain Music Festival is a daylong outdoor festival that features traditional, old-time, and bluegrass musicians from in and around Madison County. The festival usually takes place on the Saturday following the second Friday in June and is held on the grounds of the Hot Springs Spa and Campground in Hot Springs, North Carolina.

The Hot Springs resort was one of many built at the turn of the twentieth century in response to an influx of visitors seeking the healing powers of mountain mineral waters. Over time, as the attraction of the hot springs faded, the numbers of people who visited dwindled, and the resort fell into disuse. In 1990, however, the hot springs of Madison County came into new ownership and the facility was revived. The mineral waters of the Hot Springs Spa maintain a 100°F temperature all year round. Jacuzzis filled with curative waters are available at the spa, and the campground there features full hookups and hot showers.

The Bluff Mountain Music Festival features many of the best old-time and

Stranger Malone, who made records in the 1920s with members of the famous north Georgia string band, the Skillet Lickers, accompanies six-year-old Clay Sutton at Bluff Mountain.

bluegrass performers in the region, including several local ballad singers. Bring your folding chair or a blanket for a full day of music under the trees beside the French Broad River. The concert is followed by an evening square dance. Proceeds from the festival benefit the Madison County Arts Council. Call for a festival schedule.

LOCATION: The Hot Springs Spa and Campground is located at 1 Bridge St. in Hot Springs, N.C. From Asheville, take US 25/70 North to Hot Springs. After you cross the French Broad River, the festival will be on your right before you get to the railroad tracks.

CONTACT: Rodney Sutton, Madison County Arts Council, PO Box 32, Marshall, NC 28753, (828) 689-5507, ‹rsutton@buncombe.main.nc.us›, ‹www.main.nc.us/bluff/›; or Madison County Visitors Center, Inc., 72 S. Main St., PO Box 1527, Mars Hill, NC 28754, (828) 680-9031, (877) 262-3476, (828) 689-9351, ‹MadisonTourism@main.nc.us›, ‹www.madisoncounty-nc.com›

JERRY ADAMS
A GOOD PLACE TO BE

*Jerry Adams of Marshall,
North Carolina, says that
he's a banjo player who
just happens to work for a
living as a pharmacist.*

I was born and raised here, born in 1947. All my folks are from the Laurel section of Madison County, which is across the mountain here. Walnut Mountain sort of cuts the county in two, and that has a lot to do with the history of the county. Everything on the north side over there was connected to east Tennessee. They were Union during the Civil War. Everything on this side of the mountain was Confederate, 'cause it had access to Asheville, and to the rest of North Carolina, down east. Marshall was named after John Marshall, the chief justice. It actually started off as a drover town. Marshall is the county seat of Madison County, which was established in 1854.

I'm not really from a family of musicians. My dad doesn't play music, and my mom doesn't play either. But we used to go over to my dad's cousin's house in the early 1960s. His name was Lee Wallin, and he was from a generation before my dad, and he and some others started playing the banjo. I just got interested through them—over at old man Lee's—got interested in playing the banjo.

Once, when I was trying to learn to play the banjo, I was up there at my grandfather's, just fooling around, and he says, "Here, wait a minute. I'll show you a song." So he got the banjo from me and he played "Sally Goodin." Then he just handed it back to me and I never saw him play again!

My dad had a guy who rented his place. His name was Columbus Gunter. It turns out that he was like the premier banjo picker around in this whole area. On Sunday afternoons, we used to go over there and he'd show me some things, you know? He played the two-finger style. That was the style around here, not the clawhammer. It was a two-finger up-picking style. You know Sheila Adams, the ballad singer? She's a cousin of mine. She was learning to play at the same time, but she was more interested in the ballads.

We have a real strong ballad tradition around here. Back in the seventies, Bobby McMillon came up here and stayed for a while. He learned a lot of stuff from the local ballad singers. Cecil Sharp came in through here back in 1916, and he collected more ballads here than he did anywhere else in the nation—right here in Madison County.

I went to college at Mars Hill College, here in Madison County, and got a degree in chemistry. I played music pretty much all along when I was at Mars Hill College, but later, when I went off to pharmacy school at the University of Georgia in Athens, I didn't. The music scene in Athens back then was different from the style of music I play, so I put the banjo under the bed. I figured I'd play it every once in a while, but I didn't have anybody really, that I played with.

At that time, a friend of mine was a licensed pilot, and we got interested in flying these ultralights. Once when I was flying ultralights down in South Carolina, this guy was gonna show me what happens if the throttle kicks back. The problem was, that what he was gonna show me didn't happen! We didn't crash, but we just barely avoided it. It bent the wings—the wings actually touched the ground—and it bent the wheel sprockets up! So I got to thinking, "Boy! I've got a banjo up under the bed! I don't need this."

We used to practice in a little building out there where I had my pharmacy, out the road there. Well, we started drawing other musicians. A lot of other musicians started coming in to play with us, and more people would come in just to listen to us. The jam actually got so big that we couldn't get any more people in there. My uncle Wayne and I had looked at the depot in Marshall, and inquired about it. I said, "Man! That would make a nice place to play music!" But the town had it tied up. Southern Railroad had leased it to the town of Marshall—for a dollar a year. So we let it drop.

Then we heard that Southern Railroad was getting rid of their tax rolls, that they were bulldozing all the depots up and down the line. A black man who lives here, his name is Everett Barnett, worked around the depot. And he got wind that that's what they were gonna do here. Then one day in 1996, we saw them working on it and we wondered, "What are they doing?" Somebody said that they were going to put the county commissioner's offices in there. I thought, "Oh, man, what a waste. That would be a good place to play music." A few days later I saw one of the county commissioners walking up—Jim Crane—and I said, "Jim, what are y'all doing with that old depot building?" And he said, "Why, Jerry, I came to get you to do something." So I told him, "We know exactly what to do."

So they organized the depot as a place to play music. The first performance we ever had there was completely full. It was packed! We were trying to get Josh Goforth to play "Orange Blossom Special" that night, and he didn't want to play it—he thought he didn't play it that well. But when he finally started playing it—just when he started to play—the train came by with its horn blasting! The people in the depot just went nuts! We knew then it was gonna be good. It's been packed ever since.

The dancing that happens there is what makes it, I think. And in the summertime, a lot of people like to sit out on that deck at the depot. There's a nice view of the river from there. It's a good place to be on a Friday evening.

❈ Madison County Heritage Festival and the Bascom Lamar Lunsford Minstrel of the Appalachians Concert

The Madison County Heritage Festival is the first part of a day- and evening-long celebration of mountain culture held annually on the first Saturday of October on the streets of Mars Hill, North Carolina, and on the adjacent Mars Hill College campus. The festival runs between 10:00 A.M. and 4:00 P.M. The second part of the celebration is the Bascom Lamar Lunsford Minstrel of the Appalachians Concert, which is staged in the 1,800-seat Moore Auditorium on the college campus. It runs from 7:00 P.M. to 11:00 P.M.

LOCATION: Take US 19/23 to the Mars Hill exit, approximately eighteen miles north of Asheville. Turn left onto NC 213 going west and ascend the hill into town. Go straight through the traffic light and you'll be on the campus of Mars Hill College. Moore Auditorium will be on the left.

CONTACT: Richard Dillingham, Rural Life Museum, Mars Hill College, PO Box 156, Mars Hill, NC 28754, (828) 689-1424, ‹rdillingham@mhc.edu›; or Madison County Visitors Center, Inc., 72 S. Main St., PO Box 1527, Mars Hill, NC 28754, (828) 680-9031, (877) 262-3476, (828) 689-9351, ‹MadisonTourism@main.nc.us›, ‹www.madisoncounty-nc.com›

❈ Rural Life Museum at Mars Hill College

The Rural Life Museum at Mars Hill College is devoted to the presentation, interpretation, and preservation of mountain culture and history. It is home to the William Barnhill collection of photographs illustrating mountain life in western North Carolina and also an archive of folk recordings. The museum is free and is open Monday through Friday from 2:00 to 4:00 P.M. or by appointment. Guided tours must be scheduled in advance. To schedule a tour, call the number below.

LOCATION: The Rural Life Museum is located one block west of Main St. in Mars Hill. Take US 19/23 to the Mars Hill exit, approximately eighteen miles north of

Bascom Lamar Lunsford was born in Mars Hill and spent much of his life collecting and performing the traditional music of western North Carolina. He also organized the Mountain Dance and Folk Festival and wrote the song "Good Old Mountain Dew." (Photograph courtesy of the Lunsford Collection, Mars Hill College Archives)

Asheville. Turn left onto NC 213 going west and head up the hill into town. Go straight through the traffic light and you'll be on the Mars Hill College campus. The native-stone museum building will be on the right and Moore Auditorium on the left.

CONTACT: Richard Dillingham, Rural Life Museum, Mars Hill College, PO Box 156, Mars Hill, NC 28754, (828) 689-1424, ‹rdillingham@mhc.edu›; or Madison County Visitor's Center, Inc., 72 S. Main St., PO Box 1527, Mars Hill, NC 28754, (828) 680-9031, (877) 262-3476, (828) 689-9351, ‹MadisonTourism@main.nc.us›, ‹www.madisoncounty-nc.com›

BUNCOMBE COUNTY

✣ Shindig on the Green

This series of concerts, held in the heart of downtown Asheville, North Carolina, feature old-time and bluegrass bands, clogging groups, and square-dance teams. Held on the green in front of the City Building and the County Courthouse, the shindigs take place most Saturday evenings beginning the first weekend in July and running through the Labor Day weekend. The music is presented from a small portable stage; an adjacent stage is pro-

JOSH GOFORTH
THAT'S MY GOAL, TO KEEP IT GOING

Born in 1981, Josh Goforth of Marshall, North Carolina, is among the youngest of the musicians to be featured in this book. Josh is currently a music education major at East Tennessee State University.

I was born in Asheville, but my family is originally from Madison County. They live here now. We actually live near Lonesome Mountain. My dad's family comes from that area and my mom's family comes from a different part of Madison County, a community called Big Pine. There are no traditional musicians in my immediate family until you go back to about my great-great-great-grandfather. He was a pretty famous fiddle player named Asbury McDevitt. Down the line that I came from, there was really no musicians until, I guess, me.

When I was in the sixth grade, I was in the middle school in Madison County, and Sheila Adams, who's a great ballad singer and a storyteller and a songwriter, came to the middle school and performed. I was struck by it. I loved that kind of music, and decided to look into it. I entered the middle school band program, playing trumpet. I loved it. I went on into high school and played trumpet and some euphonium, and in the eleventh grade, I got to be drum major of my high school band.

The band program here was failing. There were a lot of great players, but there was nobody to really guide the band. I told our band director that I would be the drum major if he'd let me actually take over the marching band. And he said O.K.! So that year I gave them energy, did everything I could to try to motivate 'em, and I used my musical ear that I'd developed through playing old-time and bluegrass to try to get a band sound that I wanted from them. We went on that year to win thirty-three trophies, all first places. I did it again the next year and ended up teaching general music at the high school. I basically ran the whole high school music program my senior year in high school, and I loved it.

Growing up, I listened a lot to contemporary music, but it was never my big thing. When I found old-time music, it was fascinating to me. Think about its history, about how far it goes back, and how you're actually playing songs that people in England played hundreds of years ago. It goes all the way back to England and Ireland and Scotland. I developed an immediate need for singing ballads and for playing ballads on the guitar. That was my first love. And when I heard fiddle music, it changed that path even more. Then when I heard bluegrass, it changed even more. I've kept playing old-time, kept playing ballads, and then I went on to bluegrass. I love classical, I love old-time and bluegrass, and I love jazz. I love all kinds of music.

A lot of people are getting into bluegrass, I think, because bluegrass is getting to be pretty popular even though there's not that many people who may know about it in other parts of the country. There's a lot of young musicians that really get into bluegrass because of the flashiness. It's a very flashy music, and there's a lot of improvising. I have students who really want to learn bluegrass—bluegrass banjo. The first thing I tell them is get your own style. I mean everybody can't play like Earl Scruggs. Everybody tries to copy Earl Scruggs. That gets boring after a while. I want people, when they hear me, to say, "Oh . . . that sounds like Josh Goforth."

Around here there's a lot of older musicians who sit at home and play. It's just a part of life around here. This area was once so secluded that there was really nothing else to do. So people around here just played music with other people, and it's been carried on up to now. It's a part of life. I'm always impressed with how much things around here *don't* change. Marshall was more of a booming town in the twenties than it is now. There's not been a lot of change in old-time music, either. There's a lot of people coming down here from up north to learn music from our old-time musicians.

I'm very strongly opinionated about outsiders' perceptions of mountain people. I take the word "hillbilly" as a curse word. In the past, mountain folks were thought of as being stupid and dumb, people who didn't know what they were talking about. But their culture and heritage is great. They're seen as being poor and uneducated. I totally disagree with the hillbilly stereotype. I just think it's crazy.

I play now in several bluegrass bands, so I get to play it a lot. My goal in old-time music, really, is to get younger people started in it. There's probably only three players now under the age of eighteen who are playing old-time fiddle at the festivals. That's sad, I think. Once all these older people have died out, there's going to be nobody.

That's my goal, to keep it going.

The Indian Creek Music Company teaches students to play dulcimers made out of cardboard at Shindig on the Green.

vided for dance demonstrations. A roped-off area in front of the music stage is reserved for street dancing. Shindig on the Green is a very popular event in Asheville, and hundreds of people of all ages attend each performance. Another feature that draws a lot of people to this event is the large number of impromptu and lively jam sessions that take place behind the stage and under the trees. The event is free. Music begins at 7:00 P.M.

LOCATION: From I-240 in Asheville, take the Merrimon Ave. exit (exit 5A). Travel south on Merrimon to the intersection with Patton Ave. (marked by the Vance Monument on Pack Square). Turn left onto Patton Ave. and the City/County Plaza will be two blocks ahead on the right.

CONTACT: Leesa Sutton, Asheville Convention and Visitors Bureau, PO Box 1010, Asheville, NC 28802, (828) 452-0152, ‹shindig@springmail.com›, ‹www.exploreasheville.com/music.htm›; or Asheville Convention and Visitors Bureau, 151 Haywood St., Asheville, NC 28801, (828) 258-6101, (800) 257-1300, ‹cvb@exploreasheville.com›, ‹www.exploreasheville.com›

✤ Bluegrass First Class

Bluegrass First Class is a two-day bluegrass festival that features nationally known bluegrass performers. It's held at the Holiday Inn SunSpree Re-

SHEILA KAY ADAMS
IT WAS THE SINGING

Sheila Kay Adams of Madison County, North Carolina, is the heir to a family ballad tradition that goes back to the days of early European American settlement in the region.

I was child of the sixties—the whole nine yards. I listened to Steppenwolf and Led Zeppelin and the Rolling Stones and the Beatles. But when I was at college I started to realize how important tradition is. I also realized that nobody else was learning it.

I was born in Madison County. Born and raised there. My parents were also from there—from a community called Sodom. I'm the great-niece of Dellie Norton, who was one of the renowned ballad singers. When I was growing up, there were eight traditional ballad singers around our home still singing the old love songs. Cass Wallin was one of 'em. So was Inez Chandler. They were all family members. As I got older and started to appreciate my heritage, I got really serious about learning from all of 'em.

I spent a lot of time at my granny's house, and there was music there all the time. Granny was also a really neat storyteller, but it was the singing that was the most important. They would sing an old love song, and then they would turn around and sing a song like "Angel Band" or "We'll Camp a Little While in the Wilderness." They'd sing those right along with the old love songs. If you listen real close to the singing of the sacred songs, especially those old campmeeting songs, you'll see that they've got the same quality as the love songs. Their voices break in the same places. They kinda "feather" the end of a line. Granny would lift her voice at the end of a line when she sang a sacred song, just like she'd do when she sang "Young Emily." She said the purpose of it was to get you back into the pitch that you had started in. There's only a few little pockets left where the ballad singers do it that way.

I remember one time Granny and I went to a round robin. I was seventeen and I had driven all the older ladies to the singing. After they got into this big circle, it was announced that one of the singers had recently passed away. I was out in the lobby smoking cigarettes, and Granny sent for me. "Sealy" was her pet name for me—it's the Gaelic pronunciation for Sheila. She said, "Tell Sealy to come in here." So I went in there and she said for me to sit down. So I sat down next to her and she leaned over and put her hand on my knee. She told me that she had been looking around at all the people in the circle, and she had realized how old they were, and she had thought, "If we don't get some young folks to singing these old love songs, it's gonna all be gone! When these folks here are gone, every song they know will be gone too, unless somebody young learns them." She appointed me.

I remember the first love song I ever learned. I was five years old. It was a ridiculously suggestive thing that goes like this:

> There was an old farmer who lived by the sea,
> A merry old farmer was he.
> He had a fair maiden who laid on the grass,
> Ever' time she turned over, she'd show her fair . . . ruffles and tucks . . .
>   and so on and on.

I learned that one quickly! Granny said, "As easy as she learned that one, she can probably learn the bigger ones." Not too long after that I learned Lord Bateman, which has ninety-six verses. So I fell in love with the old stories. All that violence! All kinds of *nasty* stories. I loved the stories.

> He took her by the lily-white hand,
> And he led her across the hall.
> He pulled out his sword and cut off her head,
> And kicked it against the wall!

There were verses like that all the time. And anytime I heard something like

> How do you like my snow-white pillow?
> How do you like my sheet?
> How do you like my pretty little woman,
> Who lays in your arms asleep?

then I immediately wanted to learn it, because I knew that it was one of those kinda risqué, off-color, love songs. Granny just called them all "love songs." Here in Madison County music is so wrapped up in family that it's really hard to separate the two. For instance, Jerry Adams is my first cousin. And Josh Goforth and I are related. The list just goes on. Now my daughter, Melanie, is taking it up. She's twenty-eight. For a time she strayed away from it and I wasn't sure if she was ever going to come back to it. But Granny kept saying, "She'll come back, she'll come back." She was very fortunate in that she learned from the same people that I did. She learned from Granny and the others.

190

I have always said that mountain people are actually an unrecognized minority in this country. Some of our speech patterns are now being studied by language scholars. They're hunting for pockets here in the mountains where the people are still using some Middle English and Chaucerian styles of speech. Sometimes I tell outside people about that. I say, "Your English has become homogenized. If you think I talk funny, it's simply because my English is a lot older than yours."

People see that what I do is a part of a long tradition, and they really crave it for themselves. A music scholar once told me, "Sheila, are you aware that the tradition that you carry on was ancient by the time of Mozart?" Isn't that amazing? My family has been singing those old love songs, as best we can figure, for seven generations. I'm the eighth generation, and my daughter is the ninth. I can't think of any other family tradition that can beat it, unless it might be a recipe. I think that makes those old folks pretty special. They just loved to sing.

---

sort in Asheville on the last Friday and Saturday of February. The entire hotel is reserved for this event. The music starts at 1:00 P.M. both days and lasts until around midnight. There is an admission fee.

LOCATION: From I-240 West in Asheville, take exit 3B. Follow the signs directing you to the Holiday Inn SunSpree Resort, which is located directly behind Westgate Shopping Center at One Holiday Inn Dr.

CONTACT: Milton Harkey Productions, (828) 277-9199; or Holiday Inn Sunspree Resort, Bluegrass First Class, PO Box 7661, Asheville, NC 28802-7661, (828) 275-8650, ‹www.bluegrassfirstclass.com›; or Asheville Convention and Visitors Bureau, 151 Haywood St., Asheville, NC 28801, (828) 258-6101, (800) 257-1300, ‹cvb@exploreasheville.com›, ‹www.exploreasheville.com›

✤ Mountain Dance and Folk Festival

Downtown Asheville is the setting for the annual Mountain Dance and Folk Festival, the oldest continuing festival of traditional mountain music and dance in the United States. In 1927 the city of Asheville asked Bascom Lamar Lunsford to present a group of musicians and dancers from various Appalachian communities at the city's Rhododendron Festival. The presentation proved extremely popular, so much so that the following year Lunsford mounted a separate event on his own. The festival soon became a model for other folk festivals around the country and inspired the beginnings of the National Folk Festival in 1935. Recent festivals have included both indoor and outdoor stages at various locations in and around Pack Square in the heart of Asheville. The main event now takes place in the

For many years, fiddler Marcus Martin opened the Mountain Dance and Folk Festival with a distinctive version of the tune "Gray Eagle." His son, Wade Martin, carved this image of his father around 1949. (Photograph courtesy of Robert S. Brunk)

Diana Wortham Theatre at Pack Place, in downtown Asheville. There is an admission charge. For information on the exact dates and times for this event, contact the Convention and Visitors Bureau of the Asheville Area Chamber of Commerce.

LOCATION: From I-240 in Asheville, take the Merrimon Ave. exit (exit 5A). Look for the brown Pack Place signs and follow them on US 25 South (Broadway) for three blocks to Pack Square. Pack Place is located at the corner of Biltmore Ave. and Patton Ave. across from a fountain and the Vance Monument. There is a parking garage on Broadway just before you reach Pack Place and another at the corner of Biltmore Ave. and Eagle St., one block south of Pack Place.

CONTACT: Leesa Sutton, Asheville Convention and Visitors Bureau, PO Box 1010, Asheville, NC 28802, (828) 452-0152; or Asheville Convention and Visitors Bureau, 151 Haywood St., Asheville, NC 28801, (828) 258-6101, (800) 257-1300, ‹cvb@exploreasheville.com›, ‹www.exploreasheville.com›

❀ Goombay Festival

The Goombay Festival in Asheville is an annual weekend-long street festival that features music on two stages, dancing, a children's village, and more than sixty vendors. Performances include both popular and traditional music, with an emphasis on African American traditional music such as gospel and a variety of other African, Afro-Caribbean, and African American styles. Goombay brings together diverse ethnic communities of Asheville as no other event does. The festival, which is free and open to the public, is held the fourth weekend of August, from 1:00 to 9:00 P.M. on Friday, 10:00 A.M. to 9:00 P.M. on Saturday, and 1:00 to 6:00 P.M. on Sunday. The Goombay Festival has occurred annually since 1982.

Goombay Festival at the YMI Cultural Center

LOCATION: The festival takes place in downtown Asheville at the City/County Plaza and on the block between S. Market St. and Biltmore Ave. north of Eagle St. Much of the event occurs directly outside the YMI Cultural Center.

From I-240 East, take the Merrimon Ave. exit (exit 5A), then turn left and travel south toward downtown, following the brown Pack Place signs. At the fourth traffic light, turn left onto Patton Ave. (Vance Monument and Pack Square will be on your left before you turn). Continue one block and turn right onto S. Market St. Proceed for one more block and the YMI building will be on your left at the corner of Eagle and S. Market Sts.

From I-240 West, take the Merrimon Ave exit (exit 5A), then turn left under the freeway toward downtown and pick up with directions above.

CONTACT: Rita Martin, YMI Cultural Center, PO Box 7301, Asheville, NC 28802, (828) 252-4614, ‹YMIGoombay@aol.com›; or Asheville Convention and Visitors Bureau, 151 Haywood St., Asheville, NC 28801, (828) 258-6101, (800) 257-1300, ‹cvb@exploreasheville.com›, ‹www.exploreasheville.com›

❀ Old-Time Music and Dance Week at the Swannanoa Gathering

The campus of Warren Wilson College is the location of a weeklong workshop and performance series on traditional music and dance. Old-Time Music and Dance Week is a component of a summer program called the Swannanoa Gathering. Attendance at the workshop is through advance registration only. Enrollment is limited, and the workshop typically fills up months ahead. However, the general public can attend evening concerts on campus featuring the musicians who teach the classes.

Don Petty and Bruce Greene perform for a kids' class at the Swannanoa Gathering.
(Photograph by Sally Council; courtesy of the North Carolina Arts Council)

In addition to traditional Appalachian music and dance, the Swannanoa Gathering offers workshops on other musical styles and traditions, including Celtic Week, Dulcimer Week, Contemporary Folk Week, and Guitar Week.

LOCATION: From I-40, take exit 55 and travel north for a quarter of a mile. Exit onto US 70 and head east approximately one-and-a-half miles to the next traffic light. Turn left onto Warren Wilson Rd. and continue another mile and a half to Warren Wilson College.

CONTACT: Phil Jamison, Warren Wilson College, PO Box 9000, Asheville, NC 28815-9000, (828) 771-3722, ext. 387, (828) 298-3434 during July, ‹gathering@warren-wilson.edu›, ‹www.swangathering.org›; or Asheville Convention and Visitors Bureau, 151 Haywood St., Asheville, NC 28801, (828) 258-6101, (800) 257-1300, ‹cvb@exploreasheville.com›, ‹www.exploreasheville.com›

Monday Night Street Dance in Hendersonville

HENDERSON COUNTY

Monday Night Street Dance in Downtown Hendersonville

This Henderson County dance tradition began in 1918 in honor of returning World War I veterans. It's been going ever since. The dance occurs every Monday evening beginning on the Monday after the Fourth of July and continuing through the Monday of Labor Day. A section of Main Street in the historic downtown area of Hendersonville is blocked off for the event.

The caller, Bill McEntire, has been part of the dance for over fifty years. He invites the audience to join in on the mountain squares and big circle dances that, along with performances by local clogging teams, are the focus of the event. Hundreds of people show up to dance, to watch the dancers, and to enjoy the live music. The Hendersonville Monday Night Street Dance is free. The music lasts from 8:00 to 10:00 P.M.

LOCATION: From Asheville, take I-26 East for approximately seventeen miles. Take exit 18B for US 64 West toward Hendersonville. Within one-and-a-half miles, turn right onto N. Main St. in Hendersonville.

CONTACT: Bill McEntire, Monday Night Street Dance, 262 Charming Pointe Lane, East Flat Rock, NC 28726, (828) 777-6801; or Hendersonville Chamber of Commerce, (828) 692-1413, ‹www.hendersonvillechamber.org›; or Henderson County Travel and Tourism, 201 S. Main St., Hendersonville, NC 28739, (800) 828-4244, (828) 693-9708, ‹www.historichendersonville.org›

✿ Bluegrass Music at the Old Home Place

The Old Home Place is a converted barn located on North Mills River Road in Horse Shoe, North Carolina. There is no fixed seating, so people bring their folding chairs with them so they can sit while they enjoy the music of the local bluegrass bands that play there every Saturday. A small dance floor is provided for those who want to clog or buck dance. Performances are scheduled year-round. There is a charge for adults, but children are admitted free. Refreshments are available. The music starts at 7:00 P.M.

LOCATION: From I-26, take exit 9/Airport Rd. Turn onto NC 280 West, also known as Boylston Hwy. Follow NC 280 West for approximately three-and-a-half miles.

The Old Home Place in Henderson County, North Carolina

Turn right onto N. Mills River Rd. and proceed approximately four miles. A large white sign on the right side of the road marks the Old Home Place.

From Hendersonville, take NC 191 North for nearly seven miles. At the traffic light, take a right onto NC 280 East and go approximately two miles. At the light, take a left onto N. Mills River Rd. and proceed about four miles. The Old Home Place is on the right side of the road, marked with a large white sign.

From Brevard, take NC 280 West out of town to the intersection with NC 191 at the Mills River community. Continue straight for another mile. Turn left at the light onto N. Mills River Rd. Proceed for approximately four miles. A large white sign on the right side of the road marks the Old Home Place.

CONTACT: Bob Presley, The Old Homeplace, Rte. 1, Box 177, Horse Shoe, NC 28742, (828) 891-7704; or Henderson County Travel and Tourism, 201 S. Main St., Hendersonville, NC 28739, (800) 828-4244, (828) 693-9708, ‹www.historichendersonville.org›

POLK COUNTY

✷ Open House at Little Mountain Pottery

The Open House at Little Mountain Pottery combines the passions of potter and musician Claude Graves. The annual event brings together Graves's musician friends from across the country to congregate for a weekend of music. The event features a kiln opening and informal musical performances of old-time, Celtic, folk, and bluegrass music. The event is free and open to the public on the second full weekend of October, beginning at 11:00 A.M. on Saturday and 1:00 P.M. on Sunday.

LOCATION: The Little Mountain Pottery is located six miles from Columbus, N.C., on Peniel Rd. Traveling east on I-26, take the Tryon/Columbus exit and follow signs to downtown Columbus. At the first traffic light in Columbus (the intersection with Walker St.), take a right. Travel two blocks until you reach a stop sign. Turn right onto Peniel Rd. and go another six miles. The pottery will be on the right. Look for the large sign at the driveway entrance. Note: these are curvy country roads, so the drive may seem longer than six miles. Once you reach the Peniel Baptist Church, you are only one mile from the pottery.

CONTACT: Claude D. Graves, Little Mountain Pottery, 6372 Peniel Rd., Tryon, NC 28782, (828) 894-8091, ‹lilmtn@teleplex.net›; or Polk County Travel and Tourism, 317 N. Trade St., Tryon, NC 28782, (800) 440-7848, (828) 859-8300, ‹visitpolk@nc-mountains.org›, ‹www.nc-mountains.org›

REGION EIGHT

TRADITIONAL MUSIC IN THE CENTRAL VIRGINIA HILLCOUNTRY

ROCKBRIDGE COUNTY

❈ Clark's Lumber Company

By day, Clark's Lumber Company near Fairfield, Virginia, is an operating sawmill, a family business that produces the components for building pre-fabricated houses made of logs that are cut from native Virginia white pine trees. On Friday nights, the lumber company office—housed in a large demonstration log cabin—becomes a haven for old-time music and mountain dance. The entire interior of the building where the music is played is finished with beautifully cut and naturally finished white pine lumber that's been made from timber sawed nearby.

Musicians from the surrounding community who have been playing together for years gather for several hours every Friday evening at Clark's, beginning about 7:30 P.M. Fifty or sixty dancers and listeners, some of whom have come from fifty or more miles away to enjoy the event, join them.

Bruce Clark, who is in his early nineties, has been playing old-time music since he was a youngster. He grew up on the land where he still resides, just down the road a bit from the sawmill. It was actually Clark's concern that the traditional music of the region was in danger of fading away that prompted him to start the weekly event in the first place. That was back in 1995. It's still going on today, stronger than ever.

Clark is a tall, lanky, soft-voiced gentleman who talks with a very distinctive central Virginia accent. His son, James, who works with the elder Clark at the lumber company, is lankier still, taller still (he stands over six-and-a-half feet tall), and shares his father's refined speech and good-hearted demeanor. The two of them also share the role of host at the Friday night gatherings.

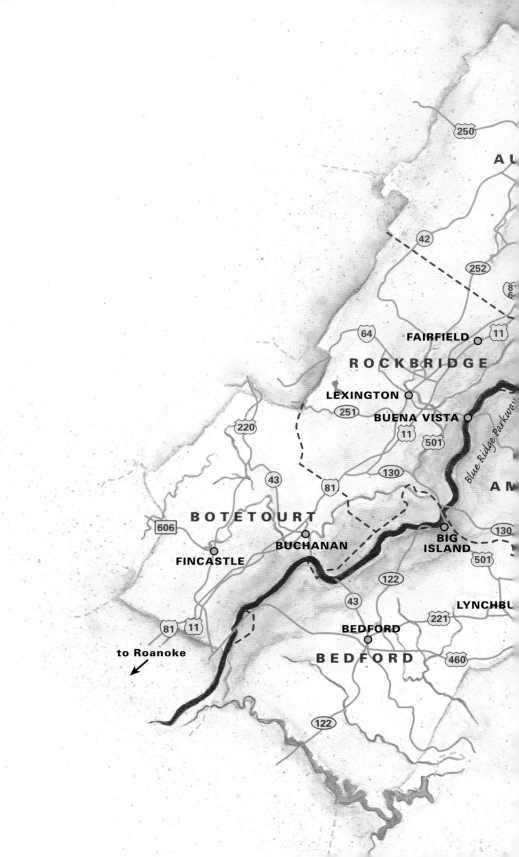

Musicians circle up at Clark's Lumber Company.

To get things under way, the two take turns welcoming all who have come there and making certain that everyone in the place is comfortable. The elder Clark offers a short prayer on behalf of those who are ill, and the younger announces that get-well cards have been placed on a nearby table. He encourages everyone to sign them and to write notes of encouragement to those who are not well enough to attend. Father and son take turns making other short announcements over a PA system that's so small it only slightly amplifies the acoustically played instruments of the assembled musicians. But very little amplification is necessary within the performance space inside the Clark Lumber Company office building.

When the music starts, the sound of Bruce Clark's fiddle rings clear and true throughout the room as he plays along with his fellow musicians, six to ten of them, who use guitars, banjos, bass fiddles, an old upright piano, and, from time to time, an autoharp and a jaw harp. They cheerfully produce renditions of such old-time mountain tunes as "Cotton-eyed Joe," "Old Joe

Clark's Lumber Company is one of the few dance venues in the region where a piano is a featured instrument.

Clark" (reportedly Bruce Clark's direct ancestor), and many other traditional mountain favorites.

Inside an adjacent kitchen area is a table laden with pound cakes, cookies, and other home-baked and storebought sugary treats. Soft drinks and coffee are also provided, free of charge. There's no admission fee, either, but at some point in the evening a contribution basket is passed around the room to help cover the costs of refreshments and utilities. All during the evening, the participants meander from the main room into the kitchen for helpings of snacks and coffee. No alcoholic drinks or smoking are allowed inside the building.

A large, stone-lined fireplace dominates one end of the room, and above the mantelboard is a portrait of Confederate general Stonewall Jackson. There's also a reproduction of a watercolor painting depicting Generals Jackson and Robert E. Lee arriving on horseback at Clark's Mountain, where they've come with their Army of Northern Virginia in search of (or perhaps hiding from) the Union Army. The print is titled *Return to Clark's Mountain*. Both General Lee and General Jackson have Rockbridge County connections, and both are buried in local cemeteries. A third painting is an original watercolor rendering of the Clark family cemetery up on Clark's Mountain, where many of Bruce Clark's kinfolk are interred.

Local artist Bebe Showalter used James Clark as a model for this portrait of Stonewall Jackson.

At about 8:30 P.M., all the band members take a fifteen- or twenty-minute break—all, that is, except Dorothy Findley, the piano player. During break time for the rest of the musicians, Findley cuts loose by herself on the piano, playing a marathon medley of country and ragtime tunes, much to the delight of the assembled dancers, who continue with their fun. After their break, the other band members resume their places and play until, at 10:00 P.M. sharp, Bruce Clark sincerely thanks everybody for coming out and invites them to return the next Friday to enjoy more fun and community fellowship.

LOCATION: From I-81, take the Fairfield exit (exit 200). Then take VA 710 West and almost immediately turn north onto VA 613 on the right. Proceed two miles to Clark's Lumber Yard on the right and pull into the parking lot. The dance is in the log building.

CONTACT: Heather Davis, PO Box 391, Fairfield, VA 24435, (540) 377-6013, ‹mzdavis3@webtv.net›

❀ Concert Series at Lime Kiln Theater

A professionally produced outdoor concert series takes place every weekend from May through Labor Day in a theater located in the ruins of a nineteenth-century limestone quarry just outside Lexington, Virginia. The series features performances in diverse musical styles including bluegrass, old-time, and folk music. This event has been in place for more than twenty years and continues to grow. An admission fee is charged. Season tickets are available.

LOCATION: Coming from the north, east, or south, follow I-81 to exit 188B (US 60 West, toward Lexington). Follow US 60 West approximately four miles through town and go under the bridge at Washington and Lee University. Go four-tenths of a mile past the bridge and make a left onto Borden Rd. (across from the athletic fields). Borden Rd. will bear right through a residential neighborhood, and the entrance to Lime Kiln is two-tenths of a mile down the road on the left.

From the west, follow I-64 East toward Lexington to exit 50 (US 60 East). Follow US 60 East for five miles and make a right just past the Shell Station onto Bell Rd. (VA 666). Follow Bell Rd. to the end, and the entrance to Lime Kiln is just across the street.

CONTACT: Theater at Lime Kiln, 14 S. Randolph St., Lexington, VA 24450, (540) 463-7088, ‹www.theateratlimekiln.com›

❄ Maury River Fiddlers' Convention

The Maury River Fiddlers' Convention is held annually at the Glen Maury Park Campground near Buena Vista, Virginia, on the third weekend of June. This is a competitive event featuring bluegrass and old-time music that awards cash prizes to the winners and provides lots of entertainment for the audience. It starts on Thursday afternoon and runs through Saturday evening.

LOCATION: From I-81, take exit 188 onto US 60 East. Continue to Buena Vista and take US 501 South, which will be on your right. Watch for the sign and road to the campground.

CONTACT: Kim Austin, PO Box 702, Buena Vista, VA 24416-0702, (540) 458-8920, ‹glenmaurypark.com/mrfc›

❄ Rockbridge Mountain Music and Dance Festival

Also at the Glen Maury Park Campground, on the second weekend after Labor Day, there is an annual festival that features bluegrass and old-time music, square dances, clogging workshops, banjo and fiddle workshops, and lots of other musical entertainment. This event was the brainchild of collector and musician Mike Seeger, who lives in nearby Lexington, Virginia. It was Seeger's wish to create an old-time music festival that was supported by regional musicians and staged by the local community without the competitive aspects of the typical fiddlers' convention. Although Seeger no longer plays a leading role in running the festival, he does help out and he does attend. His dream of a community-based and community-operated event has become a reality.

Campground and parking lot picking sessions run continually; the stage events begin on Friday at 8:00 P.M. and end on Saturday night around 11:30.

LOCATION: From I-81, take exit 188 onto US 60 East. Continue to Buena Vista and take US 501 South, which will be on your right. Watch for the sign and road to the campground.

The beauty of the venue and the noncompetitive nature of the event draws many revivalist musicians to the Rockbridge Festival, which was started by Mike Seeger.

CONTACT: Glen Maury Park Campground, PO Box 702, Buena Vista, VA 24416, (540) 261-7321; or Steve Richards, (540) 463-5214; or Toni Williams, ‹williams@rockbridge.net›

AMHERST COUNTY

❀ James River Bluegrass Association Jam Session

This event, which takes place on the second Thursday evening of each month, is part membership meeting and part informal bluegrass jam session. Membership is not required to attend the meeting or to enjoy the music, although memberships are available for $10.00 a year. The meetings are held at the Oddfellows Bingo Hall in Madison Heights, Virginia. They begin at 7:30 P.M.

LOCATION: From Lynchburg, take US 29 North to the town of Madison Heights just north of Lynchburg. Continue until you see the Wal-Mart. The Oddfellows Bingo Hall is one block past Wal-Mart on the right.

CONTACT: Helen Faulconer, James River Bluegrass Association, 208 Pinecrest Dr., Madison Heights, VA 24572, (434) 847-7840, ‹stationbass@aol.com›

❀ Sorghum Molasses Festival

Clifford, Virginia, is the site of the annual Sorghum Molasses Festival. Sorghum is a large, regionally grown grain that is actually native to Africa. Sorghum was introduced into the United States in the early part of the seventeenth century, but it was not grown extensively in this country until around the mid-nineteenth century. To make sorghum syrup, the juices are extracted from the plant by crushing the stalks with a roller mill and then slowly "evaporating" the juice in a large metal cooker, or pan. After a while, a thick, sweet, dark syrup, or molasses, is rendered. Sorghum syrup is a favorite traditional sweetener in the southern Appalachian Mountains and

A molasses "cookdown"

the upper Piedmont. Sorghum syrup poured over hot, freshly baked and buttered biscuits is a favorite breakfast food throughout the region.

The Sorghum Molasses Festival is sponsored by the Clifford Ruritan Club. The festivities include bluegrass bands, regional crafts, and festival food. The event is staged from 9:00 A.M. to 5:00 P.M. on Saturday and from 12:00 noon to 5:00 P.M. on Sunday of the first weekend in October.

LOCATION: From Lynchburg, take US 29 North past Amherst and continue approximately two miles to VA 151. At VA 151, turn left toward Clifford. In Clifford, take a right onto VA 610 and proceed to the Clifford Ruritan Club on Fletcher's Level Rd.

CONTACT: Wayne Crews, PO Box 34, Clifford, VA 24533, (434) 946-2419, ‹wayneL.51@hotmail.com›; or Wayne Crews, 477 Winton Rd., Amherst, VA 24521, (434) 946-2419, ‹wayneL.51@hotmail.com›

✹ WAMV 1420 AM Bluegrass Program

Every Saturday from 12:00 noon to 1:00 P.M., WAMV 1420 AM radio in Amherst, Virginia, broadcasts live bluegrass music. The program features music by regional bands that either contract with the station or volunteer to perform on the show. The public is welcome to watch the live broadcast, but the space is quite small. For more information, call the station.

LOCATION: From Lynchburg, take US 29 North to the first Amherst exit. Turn left onto 29 Business and proceed north to the traffic light in downtown. Turn right onto Second St. and proceed one block. Turn right onto Depot St. and go another block. Turn right onto School Rd. and the radio station is on the right within one block.

CONTACT: Bob Langston, WAMV Radio, 132 School Rd., Amherst, VA 24521, (434) 946-9000

BOTETOURT COUNTY

✹ Town of Buchanan Fourth of July Carnival

A carnival is held on the streets of Buchanan on the days leading up to Independence Day. The festivities include bluegrass music, food, storytelling, and a variety of other entertainments. This is a free event.

LOCATION: Take I-81 to exit 162. At the exit, take US 11 North into the town of Buchanan.

CONTACT: Harry Gleason, Town of Buchanan, PO Box 205, Buchanan, VA 24066, (540) 254-1212

✹ Fincastle Festival

The Fincastle Festival is an annual art show and music fest that's staged the third weekend in September. It has been an annual event for more than three decades. Among the many things featured at this celebration are an art show with cash prizes, craft vendors, mountain music and other entertainment, food and drink, a book sale, and tours of the historic town, which was settled before 1745 and is the seat of Botetourt County. The celebration starts on Saturday at 7:00 A.M. and ends around 5:00 P.M. on Sunday. The main streets of the town are closed to traffic in order to accommodate the festival. This is a free event sponsored by the Botetourt County Chamber of Commerce.

LOCATION: From Roanoke, take I-81 to exit 150. At the exit, take US 11 and follow it to US 220 North. Take US 220 North into the town of Fincastle.
CONTACT: Botetourt County Chamber of Commerce, PO Box 81, Fincastle, VA 24090-0081, (540) 473-8280, ‹tedtowles@earthlink.net›, ‹www.hisfin.org›

❀ Mountain Magic

The Mountain Magic carnival is held in the streets of the small town of Buchanan, which swell to overflowing with local residents and visitors alike every year on the first Saturday in October. The festival features bluegrass and other music beginning at 10:00 A.M. and lasting until around 5:00 P.M. There's also an antique show, crafts, and mountain dancing.

LOCATION: Take I-81 North to exit 162, then follow US 11 North into the town of Buchanan.
CONTACT: Harry Gleason, Town of Buchanan, PO Box 205, Buchanan, VA 24066, (540) 254-1212

BEDFORD CITY AND BEDFORD COUNTY

❀ Main Street Mania and Bedford Centerfest in Bedford

Main Street Mania is an evening bluegrass concert that kicks off a festival held in Bedford on the third Friday in May. Staged at the Farmer's Market, a

Children anticipate a refreshing snow cone at a summer street festival in the Blue Ridge.

Small farmers' markets and fruit-and-vegetable stands are common sights in the region.

covered facility located in the center of town, this event features bluegrass music and mountain dancing starting at 7:00 P.M. and continuing throughout the evening.

Bedford Centerfest starts off a street festival that's held annually in Bedford on the last weekend in September. Centerfest is also staged at the Farmer's Market. Bluegrass music and mountain dancing start at 7:00 P.M. and continue through the evening. Both Main Street Mania and Centerfest are free events.

LOCATION: Follow I-81 to exit 150, then take US 220 South until it becomes US 220 ALT. Follow 220 ALT South and turn left onto US 221 North/US 460 East. Go approximately twenty miles until you reach the outskirts of Bedford. Do not exit onto the ramp that will take you to the bypass toward Lynchburg. Continue straight into downtown Bedford.

From Roanoke, take US 221 North/US 460 East and follow directions above.

From Lynchburg, take US 460 West toward the town of Bedford. When you get to the outskirts of town, US 460 will split into the business and bypass routes. Take Business 460 into downtown Bedford.

CONTACT: W. Scott Smith, Bedford Main Street, Inc., PO Box 405, Bedford, VA 24523, (540) 586-2148, ‹www.bedfordmainstreet.org›

❧ Music Events at the Sedalia Center in Big Island

The Sedalia Center is a regional nonprofit organization that's designed to "ignite and nourish the creative process by offering programs in the arts, culture, environmental awareness, health, and inner development." The Sedalia Center sponsors a series of annual and other regular events that incorporate and showcase Southern Appalachian music and dance traditions.

Oktoberfest is held annually on the first Saturday in October. This community festival focuses on crafts, food, and bluegrass music of the surrounding region. The festivities start at 9:00 A.M. and last until around 3:00 P.M. An admission fee is charged.

The *Community Concert and Fiddler's Workshop* focuses on old-time and bluegrass music during the third weekend in May each year. On Friday evening, beginning at 5:00 P.M., there's a concert of old-time music. Then, on Saturday, music workshops are conducted. There is an admission fee.

On the fourth weekend in June, the *Sedalia Center Bluegrass Festival* is presented, featuring "name" bands as well as regional musicians. An admission fee is charged to attend this event, which starts on Friday afternoon at 5:00 P.M. and ends on Saturday evening at 11:00 P.M.

The *Gospel Festival* is held annually on the second Friday and Saturday in October. The music begins at 5:00 P.M. An admission fee is charged.

The fourth Saturday in October brings the Sedalia Center's annual *Chili Cook Off*. The event, which begins at noon, is a popular local event where festivalgoers are able to taste a variety of homemade chilies while enjoying some bluegrass music.

LOCATION: From Bedford, take VA 122 North for approximately eleven miles. Sedalia School Rd. (VA 638) is next to the Sedalia Country Store. Turn to the left on Sedalia School Rd. and you will see the center.

From Lynchburg, take US 501 North eighteen miles to Big Island. Turn left on VA 122 and go approximately six miles. Sedalia School Rd. (VA 638) will be on the right next to the Sedalia Country Store. Turn right and you will see the center.

CONTACT: Karen Dempsey, The Sedalia Center, 1108 Sedalia School Rd., Big Island, VA 24526, (434) 299-5080, ‹events@sedaliacenter.org›, ‹www.sedaliacenter.org›

CHARLOTTESVILLE

❧ Jam Sessions at the Prism Coffeehouse

The Prism Coffeehouse in Charlottesville has existed for more than three decades now and is a very popular hangout for students in this picturesque college town. Musical offerings at the eatery include weekly concerts and informal jam sessions. The concerts that are presented cover a variety of musical styles including Celtic, Spanish, and African, as well as more regionally oriented genres such as old-time and bluegrass. Weekly amateur jam sessions, which focus on old-time and bluegrass, are held several times a month.

Every second Thursday evening of the month, an event called Acoustic Open Showcase provides an opportunity for "local, regional, and passing-through artists" to perform at the Prism. Every third Thursday at 8:00 P.M. there's Parlor Banjo. Advanced old-time jams are held every third Monday

starting at 7:30 P.M., and beginners' old-time jams take place on fourth Tuesdays at 7:30 P.M.

The Prism Coffeehouse is a nonprofit, volunteer organization devoted to the furtherance of folk, acoustic, and traditional music from around the world. It is a nonalcoholic and smoke-free environment. Many concerts at the Prism are broadcast live on WTJU 91.1 FM radio.

LOCATION: From I-64, exit onto US 29 North (exit 118B). Follow US 29 North for approximately two miles and take the US 250 West/US 250 Business East exit. Follow 250 Business toward downtown; the road will turn into Ivy Rd. Within approximately one mile, turn left at the corner of Ivy Rd. and US 29 Business onto Rugby Rd. The Prism is located in the large white house on the corner of Gordon Ave. and Rugby Rd. Look for the Prism Coffee House sign at 214 Rugby Rd.

CONTACT: Fred Boyce, Prism Coffeehouse, 214 Rugby Rd., Charlottesville, VA 22903, (434) 977-7476, ‹tunes@theprism.org›, ‹www.theprism.org›

AUGUSTA COUNTY

❧ Crawford Brothers' Quartet Anniversary Sing

On the first Sunday in October each year, a gospel music sing at the Robert E. Lee High School Auditorium in Staunton, Virginia, celebrates the singing tradition of the Crawford Brothers Quartet, a noted local African American gospel group. The Crawford Brothers and other local groups perform beginning at 4:00 P.M.

LOCATION: The Robert E. Lee High School is located at 1200 N. Coalter St. in Staunton. From I-81, take the exit for US 250 West/US 250 East (exit 222). Merge onto US 250 West and go approximately three miles to Staunton. Turn right onto US 11 Business and follow it until you reach the intersection of VA 254/E. Beverly St. in downtown Staunton. Turn right onto E. Beverly, go two to three blocks to N. Coalter St., and turn left. The school will be approximately one mile ahead on the right.
CONTACT: John Crawford, 1228 Jackson St., Staunton, VA 24401, (540) 886-8771

❀ East Coast Country Music Championship

Despite its title, this Labor Day weekend event (Sunday and Monday) is actually a downhome regional talent show that includes a wide variety of music. There are categories for bluegrass, country, gospel band, female country vocal, male country vocal, male and female gospel, male and female bluegrass vocal, teen vocal, teen instrumentals, duets, banjo, fiddle, flattop guitar, mandolin, and entertainer of the year. This outdoor event also includes festival foods, baked goods, and a horseshoe-pitching tournament.

LOCATION: The event is held at the Eastside Speedway in Dooms, Virginia. From I-64 near Waynesboro, take exit 96 and proceed north on US 340. Go through Waynesboro and continue north for several miles to the community of Dooms. The speedway is next to the fire station in Dooms.
CONTACT: Mark and Chris Harris, Eastside Speedway, 357 Mine Branch Rd., Crimora, VA 24431, (540) 943-0679

❀ Grand Caverns Bluegrass Festival

Grand Caverns in Grottoes, Virginia, located within Grand Caverns Regional Park, is one of the oldest and most spectacular caverns in the Shenandoah Valley. People have visited these caves at least since 1806, with the sightseers including Thomas Jefferson, who rode over by horseback from his home at Monticello. During the Civil War, General Stonewall Jackson quartered Confederate troops inside the cave. The Grand Ballroom, a room inside the caverns that encompasses five thousand square feet, was the scene of early nineteenth-century dances.

On the second weekend in September, the Grand Caverns Bluegrass Festival fills the cave with the sounds of mountain music. The music begins at 5:00 P.M. on Friday afternoon and winds down on Saturday evening.

LOCATION: Follow I-81 to exit 235. Turn east on VA 256 and proceed to Grottoes. Follow the signs for Grand Caverns.
CONTACT: Cynthia Miller, Grand Caverns, PO Box 478, Grottoes, VA 24441, (540) 249-5705, (888) 430-2283, ‹grandcaverns@rica.net›, ‹home.rica.net/uvrpa›

❀ Oak Grove Folk Music Festival

The Oak Grove Theater, an outdoor facility in Staunton, Virginia, hosts an annual music festival on the first or second weekend of August. This festival presents workshops along with stage performances by regional traditional musicians. The music begins at 10:30 A.M. on Saturday. For the specific date and for more details, call the contact listed below or check the website ‹www.blueridgemusic.org›.

LOCATION: From I-81, take exit 227 to VA 612 West. Travel through Verona on VA 612 and continue approximately two miles. Look for the sign for the Oak Grove Theater.
CONTACT: Fletcher and Margaret Collins, Oak Grove Folk Music Festival, 437 E. Beverly St., Staunton, VA 24401, (540) 886-8391, (540) 828-3011, ‹harouffs@intelos.net›

❀ Gospel Keys Anniversary Sing

This celebration of gospel music features African American quartet singing. It's held at the Oak Grove Baptist Church in Hermitage, Virginia, on the second Sunday in August. The music begins at 4:00 P.M.

LOCATION: Follow I-81 to exit 225 near Staunton. Take VA 275 East, which becomes VA 254. Go approximately five miles to the community of Hermitage. Oak Grove Baptist Church is located off VA 254 in Hermitage.
CONTACT: James Jackson, Oak Grove Baptist Church, 1091 Albemarle Ave., Waynesboro, VA 22980, (540) 943-5029, ‹jackson80_22980@yahoo.com›

Pressing apples to make cider

NELSON COUNTY

✽ Annual Apple Harvest Festivals

This series of annual agricultural festivals includes music in celebration of the Nelson County apple harvest. Three major apple orchards in the county—Drumheller's Orchard in Lovingston, Silver Creek Orchard in Tyro, and Saunders Brothers Orchard in Piney River—participate in the festivities. These events are held in the latter part of September and throughout most of October. Each of the orchards brings in different bluegrass and old-time bands to play during the celebration.

Call the Nelson County Department of Tourism for the locations, dates, and times of each of the festival venues and events.

CONTACT: Dona Duval, Nelson County Department of Tourism, PO Box 636, Lovingston, VA 22949, (434) 263-5239, (800) 282-8223, ‹nelsonco@esinet.net›, ‹www.nelsoncounty.com›

❄ Stelling Banjo Works

Since 1974 Stelling Banjo Works, Ltd., located in Afton, Virginia, has been a manufacturer of handmade banjos, mandolins, and guitars. Each instrument produced is hand crafted using specialty woods and techniques. Tours of the Banjo Works are by appointment only.

CONTACT: Call (800) 5-string for an appointment and for directions.

❄ Nelson County Summer Festival

The Summer Festival, which started in 1992, is a popular community celebration held annually on the last weekend in June at the Oak Ridge Estate, a five-thousand-acre park near Lovingston, Virginia. A variety of music can be heard there, including jazz, blues, bluegrass, and old-time. The music starts on Saturday morning.

Call the Nelson County Department of Tourism for specific times and dates for this event.

LOCATION: From Charlottesville, travel south on US 29 approximately thirty miles to Lovingston. Go three miles past Lovingston and turn left (east) on Oak Ridge Rd./VA 653. Follow Oak Ridge until you come to Oak Ridge Estate. Look for event signs.

CONTACT: Dona Duval, Nelson County Department of Tourism, PO Box 636, Lovingston, VA 22949, (434) 263-5239, (800) 282-8223, ‹nelsonco@esinet.net›, ‹www.nelsoncounty.com›

REGION NINE

WALKING THE KING'S HIGHWAY

Dancing, both social and individual, is a much-loved, much-appreciated, and much-practiced diversion among many people who live in the Blue Ridge. Just as certain as "where there's smoke, there's fire"; in the Blue Ridge, "where there's music, there's dancing." And even though precision team clogging, western-style square dancing, and choreographed line dancing have become extremely popular group dances all across America, in the Blue Ridge you're as likely to see solo individuals expressing themselves through dance as you are to see group dancing.

In the introduction to his book on solo mountain dance, *Talking Feet* (1992), folklorist and musician Mike Seeger wrote, "Mountain dancing had many things in common with traditional ballad singing, solo fiddling, and banjo picking. They were all part of the same everyday life, and existed side by side in the same time and place. They are usually subtle and style is always personal. Dancers, singers, and musicians all learned from, entertained, and danced with family and nearby community members. Although some dancers may speak a similar body language, each has their own brogue, that is, their own style, with moves that differ in varying degrees from those of other dancers."

Appalachian dance has evolved over a period of many years and from a variety of dance traditions—traditions brought in or borrowed from Ireland, Scotland, France, England, Germany, Africa, and Native America. Historically, dancing has been a part of many social and work gatherings in mountain communities. In many places, it is still viewed as a gesture of community hospitality. Newcomers and visitors are invited—in fact are vigorously encouraged—to join in, to have fun, and to contribute themselves to the dance.

Dancing in the Blue Ridge, as in most places, is done only to the accompaniment of secular music. Listen carefully before you get up and dance to a fast-paced fiddle or banjo tune, especially if the group playing the music is a

Demonstration dance teams in southwestern North Carolina
often perform "smooth-style" square dancing.

bluegrass band. Some bluegrass gospel tunes are difficult to distinguish
from secular ones, even for experienced listeners. Often the lyrics of the
song are the only real clue that the song is religious in nature. If you should
happen to start dancing to a gospel tune, some old-timer in the audience
may gently admonish you. It's best to take your cues from other dancers who
know the local protocol.

Customarily, the managers of each Blue Ridge music festival or concert,
especially if it's held out-of-doors, will furnish a specially prepared surface
for dancing. Several sheets of plywood—sometimes three or four—will be
nailed together and laid down side by side on the ground, close to the music
stage, creating a small, low platform just large enough to accommodate five
or six dancers at a time. If more people than that want to dance, they generally just spill off onto the surrounding grass. Many will simply stand up and
dance right where they've been sitting. There are no set rules. If you're
someplace where there's mountain music, and you feel like dancing, then
dance. Chances are you won't be the only one.

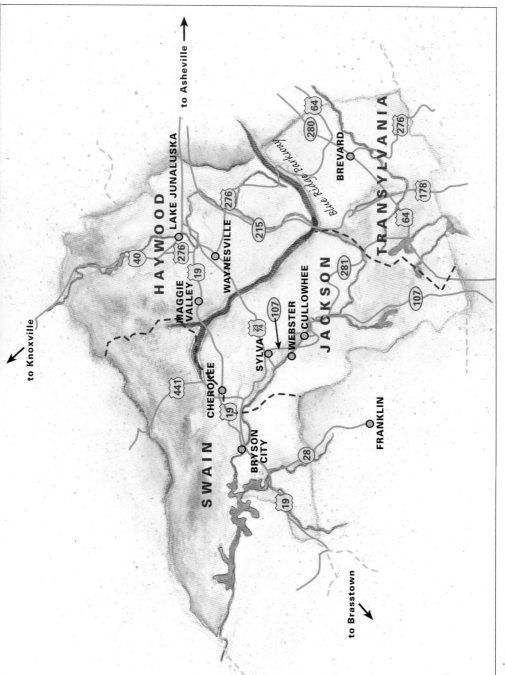

Region 9

Dances at Paul's Family Diner in Cherokee take place outdoors.

Flatfoot dancers at the depot in Marshall, North Carolina

Many music venues are configured specifically for group dancing—square dancing, team clogging—and couples dancing. Traditional square dancing, unlike contemporary square-dance club dancing, is relatively simple. It is almost always performed to the accompaniment of live music by either an old-time or a bluegrass band—unlike contemporary square-dance clubs, which often as not use recorded music. Many traditional mountain dancers in the Blue Ridge believe that dancing to recorded music is a serious affront to the local musicians. And, by the same token, the music of a mountain dance band is considered by many traditional musicians to be incomplete unless it's accompanied by the rhythmic sounds of dancing feet.

The traditional mountain square dance is open to anyone who wants to try. Since there are seldom more than a dozen calls or movements in a traditional dance, lessons are not required, although some callers will provide a brief "walk-through" just before the dance begins, for the benefit of newcomers to the circle.

HAYWOOD COUNTY

Mountain Street Dance

An unsuspecting traveler driving into the town of Waynesville late on a summer afternoon might be puzzled to discover that a portion of Main Street in front of the Haywood County courthouse has been closed to vehicular traffic. Instead of the usual clutter of automobiles and pickup trucks, the traveler will find the street filled with people and will hear the sounds of a live fiddle band. On alternate Friday evenings beginning on the first Friday after the Fourth of July and continuing through the end of August, people go dancing on the street in Waynesville. They've done so now, off and on, for the better part of a century.

In the 1930s, Haywood County resident Sam Queen, who was known as "the dancing-est man in the land," organized the legendary Soco Gap Square Dance Team, one of the very first mountain square-dance and clogging demonstration teams in the country. In 1939 Sam Queen and the Soco Gap dancers performed at the White House for President Franklin Roosevelt, First Lady Eleanor Roosevelt, and King George VI and Queen Elizabeth of England. That legendary performance and the publicity that followed it confirmed what local people believe and hold dear—that their ancestors created a distinctive form of American dance that is an important part of our nation's heritage.

A short while before 6:00 P.M., volunteers led by Joe Sam Queen, the ar-

Soco Gap Square Dance Team
(Photo courtesy of the North Carolina Department of Cultural Resources)

chitect grandson of the famous Soco Gap Dance Team leader, pull sawhorse roadblocks into the intersections at either end of the street in front of the courthouse. They drag metal bleachers from permanent resting places onto the pavement of Main Street and form an elongated open rectangle that is defined by the bleachers on two sides, the folding chairs of dancers and spectators on a third, and an elevated bandstand on the fourth. Then they carefully sprinkle the resulting square with a thick dusting of dry cornmeal to facilitate the shuffling movements of dancing feet. Once these preparations are completed, the fun begins.

From 6:30 in the evening until nearly 10 P.M., Main Street in Waynesville is alive with the rhythmic movements of mountain dance. The bleachers, the grassy courthouse lawn, the concrete sidewalks, and the courthouse front steps are all crowded with hundreds of spectators—people who have come from far and near to dance, to hear lively mountain music, to watch the dancers, and to watch and greet each other.

The mountain square dance, or the Appalachian great circle dance, is the order of the day here. It's a community social dance that has its roots set deep in Southern Appalachian culture and tradition. Mountain square dance, as it's performed on the streets of Waynesville, is part traditional movements and part unadulterated, individualistic creativity. Everyone present is welcomed there by the emcee, or caller, and all are encouraged to join in the dance. Many answer the call.

Young and old are delighted as a snowfall of cornmeal transforms the street in front of the Haywood County courthouse.

The caller yells out for the dancers to "circle up," and the cornmeal-blanketed asphalt immediately becomes crowded with the feet and bodies of scores of dancers. In fact, so many dancers respond to the call that obeying the caller's command to form a simple circle is nearly impossible in the space provided, big though it is. The requested circle becomes something that more generally resembles a badly distorted egg. But soon, after a short welcoming statement from the caller and some simple instructions regarding the form and the symbolism of the dance, the music begins and the dance gets under way.

Among the various participants in the Waynesville street dance, the dancers' skills and knowledge of square-dance movements range from veteran expert to uninstructed novice. And the dancers themselves range in age from toddlers and babes-in-arms to octogenarians. Tall folks, short folks, fat and skinny folks, young and old, athletes and limp-alongs—they all get out there on the street together. It's a sight to behold!

Apparently, there is a mysterious force in mountain dance circles that causes beginners to mistake their left hands for their right. The traditional starting command from the caller (who's the boss of the dance), "all join hands and circle right," nearly always creates momentary grief among some of the more unpracticed participants who, without fail, confidently take off going in the wrong direction. But after a moment of embarrassed laughter, they quickly recover and fall into step with the majority.

Next, the caller orders the circled dancers to execute the "Grand Right and Left." In this simple circular movement, the male dancers circle to the right while the female dancers simultaneously circle to the left. But there's a

The caller leads the dancers through the figures.

catch. The dancers must also weave in and out and touch hands as they travel the circle. So, in going around from start to finish, every man and boy and every woman and girl makes direct hand-to-hand contact with every member of the opposite sex who's there in the circle with them. Again, confusion reigns. But after some hesitation and a few times of weaving "in" when "out" is the way to go, the novices catch on and the action proceeds to the next level—making "squares."

Initially, it's another mess, but a light-hearted one, and the more skilled and experienced dancers patiently assist those who get lost in the fray. Most of the lost are gently led back into place by the hand, while some are more firmly directed home by hands placed from behind on confused shoulders. Very soon, though, sooner than one might predict based on the level of the initial confusion, the dancers find their way and the dance smooths out. Once again the dance, the world, and the streets of Waynesville are set in order.

LOCATION: Follow I-40 to exit 27 west of Asheville. Take US 19/23 South to Waynesville. Get off at exit 102 and follow US 276 (Russ Ave.) toward downtown.

Turn left onto US 23 Business (Main St.). The street dances are held on Main St. in front of the county courthouse.

CONTACT: Ronald J. Huelster, Downtown Waynesville Association, PO Box 1409, Waynesville, NC 28786, (828) 456-3517, ‹dwa@asa-com.com›, ‹www.downtownwaynesville.com›; or Haywood County Travel and Tourism, 1233 No. Main St., Suite 1-40, Waynesville, NC 28786, (800) 334-9036, (828) 452-0152, ‹info@smh.wcu.edu›, ‹hctda@smokeymountains.net›, ‹www.smokeymountains.net›

❀ Maggie Valley Opry House

There are many community organizations, commercial venues, and even local governments in Southern Appalachia that host weekly, and sometimes daily, stage performances showcasing traditional bluegrass and old-time mountain music, demonstration clog team and square dancing, and—in some instances—"hillbilly" comedy routines. These "hometown oprys," as they have come to be known, can differ significantly in character. Those that try to appeal more to a tourist clientele are somewhat reminiscent of the old television series, *Hee-Haw*. But, in fact, *Hee-Haw* was likely modeled after the hometown oprys rather than the other way around.

The Maggie Valley Opry House is owned and operated by Raymond Fairchild and his wife, Shirley. The Opry House show is centered on Raymond Fairchild's lightning-fast bluegrass banjo playing style and the comedy routines of a hillbilly clown named Humphammer.

Nestled between the Blue Mountain Inn and the Country Vittles Restaurant on Soco Road (the main tourist drag in Maggie Valley), the Opry House is a modest building set back behind a gift shop. It's almost hidden from view off the main road. The front section of the building is an open-air porch that serves both as an entryway and as a smoking area. It's there that tour groups count heads and issue admission tickets. Inside are a ticket stall, a concession stand, restrooms, and a performance stage. The rest of the Opry House is one big room furnished for audience seating. Its walls are decorated with posters from events and concerts in which Raymond Fairchild has been featured. Hanging on the walls are numerous autographed photos of country music celebrities who have performed at the Opry House in the past.

Raymond Fairchild himself is a celebrity in Maggie Valley—and beyond. For many years, there was a large sign posted near the edge of town that read "Welcome to Maggie Valley—Home of Raymond Fairchild." Fairchild was born on the nearby Qualla Boundary, the homeland of the Eastern Band of Cherokee Indians. He's been playing banjo professionally since he was eighteen years old.

JOE SAM QUEEN
WALKING THE KING'S HIGHWAY

Joe Sam Queen of Waynesville, North Carolina, is an architect who lives and works in his native Haywood County. He and his son Charlie are from a long line of musicians and dancers.

The street dances here in Waynesville are a traditional thing. They've happened here ever since the time when we first got a good paved road in town, and they danced on the dirt road before that. These little venues really started with the centennial of the town of Waynesville. That was the year my grandfather died. They asked me to bring back some of the old street dances, which we hadn't had in fifteen years or so. We had such a great success of it that we've had them ever since. That was thirty years ago. I've been helping out with street dances here for thirty years. I'm in the third generation in my family to do so.

The dance always starts in a big circle. The circle of joining hands is a symbol of the community. The first movement of the Appalachian American big round dance is the Grand Right and Left. That's where you turn and greet your partner, and then you go right and left all the way around the circle. If you're a country bumpkin, you have eye-to-eye and hand-to-hand contact with all the young ladies of the community — along, of course, with your grandmother, your aunts, your sisters, and everybody else. After the dance gets started, the figures break down into various shapes. All these shapes are little play parties — little parables and stories. Like the one that you usually open a dance with — it teaches people manners:

"How do you do?"

"Fine, thank you."

It teaches you how to embrace your partner and also your opposite-in-the-circles partner. You swing your opposite and then you come back to your own. Then you move along, with your own. My grandfather would say, "You're dancing to the music, with your partner, in the circle." If you can understand those kinds of things in life, then you'll know a lot about yourself as an individual. You learn how to relate to a young lady in a polite way. And you learn how to let her go and to let her dance with another gentleman without jealousy or rage. The symbolism is great.

There is a sense of personal expression in the Appalachian square dance—in the foot work and in some of the moves. We don't have the drum in the Appalachian venue, but we do have the foot, and the rhythm that the foot lends to the set is a part of the music. It's individualistic, but it's also a part of the music. In Europe, the traditions were set—the ways were set, the communities were set, and the traditions were so long and consistent that everybody knew just what they were doing. In America, that was not the case. The American square dance always has a caller. The call itself can be innovative, just like America. The American dance is something of a patchwork gathered from a lot of traditions.

They would have a square dance on special occasions in the Appalachia of the past. At harvest time, at any community gathering or reunion, you'd have musicians and you would gather in the dance. The American dance—the great Appalachian circle dance—has several expressions. The most traditional one is the smooth dance—the large circle with smooth steps, where you don't clog all the time. You only clog when you're doing special things like Walk the King's Highway. Walk the King's Highway—that's a part of the dance that allows you to buck dance, to cut up a little, to show your stuff—to show your individuality. It's very American.

Now we have clog teams. My grandfather was very instrumental in developing the very first organized clog teams. The mountain dance is really a participatory form, and that's the heart of it—it's a social dance. These square dance teams became very popular with the advent of radio, and during the folk revival in the twenties and thirties. They didn't dress up in any fancy costumes; they just wore what they considered to be their social best. My grandfather once brought a dance team out of Appalachia—a very famous dance team. They all went to the White House in the 1930s to dance for the king and queen of England. That was a real threshold for this community which, at the time, was in the throes of the Great Depression. They were all high energy cloggers and dancers out of Maggie Valley and Waynesville—and they danced for the king and queen, who for the first time were visiting America. It was stuff of newsreel importance. It made *Life* magazine, the *Saturday Evening Post*, and everything. It really put my grandfather and his little dance team on the map.

These days you see a lot of dance teams with petticoats, western wear, and so on. That's just the influence of the square dance going west and then ricocheting back this way. Whatever Nashville has done to music, it's done to dance as well. There are no Appalachian folks now who haven't heard western fiddling and seen a certain amount of western dance. I see things now, like line dancing, which excludes those who are not a part of the club. It teaches no social skills. Sociability is the whole point of the Appalachian dance. Appalachian big round dance includes everybody in the community. Everyone joins in, young and old, rich and poor.

One of my grandfather's dance teachers was a black man, John Love. In that generation, the blacks didn't get to enter the circle. It was a segregated community. There weren't a whole lot of blacks here, but they were often the musicians for the dance. They were themselves great buck dancers. But they could only dance on the side. The banjo was really their instrument—and it has really added to the Appalachian musical forms. Nowadays, blacks join the circle—all over the South. That's quite refreshing. We've evolved in America to include everyone. I like to tell my children that if you know who you are and where you're from, then you can go anyplace, meet anybody, and feel at home and a part of it. You're not an outsider to the world if you know where you're from. Instead you're a part of the world.

My belief is that if we can keep our sense of self and place, we will thrive. Appalachia is a bastion of individualism and of community. The people who settled here liked this place—they liked the isolation of it, they liked the peace of it, they liked the magnificence of it. I feel that it's very important for a community to have a sense of place. And for a person to have a sense of place—to belong to somewhere, and to come from somewhere. What you learn from that is so critical to being a world citizen—that you come from someplace and that everybody else does too. That gives you a sense of tolerance, of openness, and of hospitality. I don't come from the best of everything. I come from where I come from. You can start from anywhere and go anywhere.

There are not a lot of places left that have such a strong sense of place, but Appalachia's one of them that does. It's a wonderful place to visit, and to learn to feel that sense. Maybe visitors who come here can take a part of that back home with them, and establish it where they came from—and learn to appreciate their own place.

The show at the Maggie Valley Opry House typically opens with a medley of bluegrass and old-time tunes performed by Zane Fairchild, Raymond's son, on lead guitar. He's joined by Josh Crowe on rhythm guitar and vocals, and Josh's son, Quentin Crowe, sits in on bass. Then—to enthusiastic applause from the audience—Raymond Fairchild comes onstage and joins the group. His extraordinary bluegrass banjo style becomes the focus of the evening's performance from that moment forward. From time to time, the comedian Humphammer joins in with an assortment of jokes and hillbilly musical comedy routines.

Between sets and during intermission, Raymond Fairchild moves to the rear of the three-hundred-seat auditorium. He positions himself behind a table stacked with a huge assortment of tapes and CDs featuring himself or other Opry performers. There he holds forth for fifteen or twenty minutes, greets old friends and acquaintances, and autographs the photos and CDs

Banjo player Raymond Fairchild performs with his band. (Photograph by Roger Haile)

purchased by his fans. Meanwhile, Shirley Fairchild sells soft drinks and bags of popcorn at the concession stand. The nightly routine at the Maggie Valley Opry House runs very smoothly. The performers are professional, the music is well played, and the jokes are corny. It's not a bad show.

Live shows are presented at the Maggie Valley Opry House every night from April through October, 8:00 to 10:00 P.M. The doors open at 7:00 P.M. An admission fee is charged.

LOCATION: Traveling west on I-40, take exit 27 (approximately seventeen miles west of Asheville). Turn right onto US 19 and follow it south to Maggie Valley. In Maggie Valley, US 19 becomes Soco Rd. The Maggie Valley Opry House is located at 3605 Soco Rd., in the center of the valley next to the Country Vittles

Restaurant and Blue Mountain Inn, just across the street from the Soco Garden Zoo. Look for a very small sign near the roadside and a very large sign on the front of the Opry House.

Traveling east on I-40, take exit 20 onto US 276. Follow US 276 East to its intersection with US 19 in Dellwood. Turn right (south) onto US 19 and follow it to Maggie Valley. Pick back up with directions above.

CONTACT: Raymond and Shirley Fairchild, Maggie Valley Opry House, 3605 Soco Rd., Maggie Valley, NC 28751, (828) 926-9336, (828) 648-7941, ‹opryhouse@aol.com›, ‹www.smokeymountains.net/fairchild.html›; or Haywood County Travel and Tourism, 1233 N. Main St., Suite I-40, Waynesville, NC 28786, (800) 334-9036, (828) 452-0152, ‹info@smh.wcu.edu›, ‹hctda@smokeymountains.net›, ‹www.smokeymountains.net›

❧ Music and Dance at the Stompin' Ground

Every Tuesday through Saturday nights, April through October, you can find lots of dance action at a remarkable Maggie Valley establishment called the Stompin' Ground. To see a variety of Appalachian and other American group dance styles performed all in one place and all at the same time, the Stompin' Ground is the place to go.

Built and operated by Kyle Edwards, whose mother was a member of the noted Soco Gap Square Dance Team that danced for the king and queen of England, the Stompin' Ground is a highly popular commercial dance arena. At the entrance is a glassed-in booth where admission tickets are sold. A spacious lobby is furnished with exhibits that interpret the history of mountain dance and showcases that hold the many clogging trophies that have been won over the years by Edwards's son and daughter. There's also a concession stand where soft drinks, popcorn, candy, hot dogs, and gifts can be purchased.

The dance floor itself is enormous—sixty by eighty feet. Seating on two levels accommodates nearly a thousand people. The lofty, well-lit stage, equipped with a professional sound system, is where the house musicians, the Ivy Hill band, hold forth. The band plays a variety of mountain and popular music, ranging from old-time fiddle and bluegrass tunes to contemporary country hits.

As soon as the evening's first music lick is played, the assembled dancers hit the floor with great gusto. Many of the dancers at the Stompin' Ground come dressed in fanciful mountain or western regalia. Couples wearing matching outfits—shirts, boots, scarves, and hats—dance the mountain two-step while the members of organized and well-practiced dance groups, ranging in size from twelve to twenty dancers each, perform square dance,

Stage performance at the Stompin' Ground

Dancers backstage at the America's Clogging Hall of Fame Competition

clogging, and line dancing with exact precision. Audience members are frequently encouraged by the emcee to join in on the dance action, but most are quite satisfied to simply watch the remarkable show unfolding there before them.

Perhaps the biggest dance show of them all occurs each year on the last weekend of October. That's when the Stompin' Ground hosts an enormous clogging competition. At this event, as many as a thousand mountain cloggers literally spend the night performing and standing in line waiting for their turn to dance. Competition occurs all day on Saturday and from 9:00 A.M. to 3:00 P.M. on Sunday.

LOCATION: Traveling west on I-40, take exit 27 (approximately seventeen miles west of Asheville). Turn right onto US 19 and follow it south to Maggie Valley. In Maggie Valley, US 19 becomes Soco Rd. The Stompin' Ground is located at 3116 Soco Rd. Look for signs that identify the location. It's hard to miss the huge painted school bus, parked across the street, that points to the Stompin' Ground.

Traveling east on I-40, take exit 20 onto US 276. Follow US 276 East to its intersection with US 19 in Dellwood. Turn right (south) onto US 19 and follow it to Maggie Valley. Pick back up with directions above.

CONTACT: Kyle Edwards, The Stompin' Ground, 20 Kyle's Way, Maggie Valley, NC 28751, (828) 926-1288; or Haywood County Travel and Tourism, 1233 N. Main St., Suite I-40, Waynesville, NC 28786, (800) 334-9036, (828) 452-0152, ‹info@smh.wcu.edu›, ‹hctda@smokeymountains.net›, ‹www.smokeymountains.net›

❦ Smoky Mountain Folk Festival

The Smoky Mountain Folk Festival, directed by Joe Sam Queen, is held on the grounds of the United Methodist Assembly at Lake Junaluska, near Maggie Valley. The festival, which features regional old-time and bluegrass music, clogging demonstrations, children's performances, and jam sessions, is staged outdoors and onstage in the 3,200-seat Stuart Auditorium at the assembly. The seats in the recently renovated 1913 auditorium are arranged in a semicircle that slopes gently upward from the stage. The hall has wonderful acoustics. Large glass windows on both sides of the auditorium offer vistas of nearby Lake Junaluska. Many festivalgoers watch the stage from outside, leaning their heads and shoulders through the open windows.

In addition to the auditorium, there are two tent-covered performance stages outdoors, one near the lake and the other behind the auditorium. Except for a band that's hired to play for the clog-team demonstrations, no one is paid to perform at this festival. It's simply a gathering of the finest tradi-

Smoky Mountain Folk Festival on Lake Junaluska
(Photograph by Amy Davis; courtesy of the North Carolina Arts Council)

tional musicians from the region, who come voluntarily because they like performing there. The Smoky Mountain Folk Festival is open to the public each Friday and Saturday evening of the Labor Day weekend. The stage show begins at 7:00 P.M. and the children's performances are at 5:00. The out-of-door activities are free. There's a charge for the stage show in the auditorium. Call the Haywood County Arts Council at (828) 452-0593 if you would like advance tickets.

LOCATION: Follow I-40 to exit 27 west of Canton. Exit to the right and take US 19/23 to Waynesville. Take the US 19 exit for Maggie Valley/Cherokee/ Junaluska Assembly. Follow US 19 South for one mile and turn right onto Lakeshore Dr. and into the Lake Junaluska entrance, which is marked by stone pillars on either side of the road. Follow Lakeshore Dr. approximately one mile, keeping Lake Junaluska on your right. Stuart Auditorium, a large, round, white building, will be on your right.

CONTACT: Joe Sam Queen, Smoky Mountain Folk Festival, 71 Pigeon St., Waynesville, NC 28786, (828) 452-1688, ‹jsq@asap-com.com›; or Haywood County Travel and Tourism, 1233 N. Main St., Suite 1-40, Waynesville, NC 28786, (800) 334-9036, (828) 452-0152, ‹info@smh.wcu.edu›, ‹hctda@smokeymountains.net›, ‹www.smokeymountains.net›

❋ Singing on the Mountain

For more than sixty years, an annual gospel singing sponsored by the Salvation Army has been held in northern Haywood County at the Shelton Laurel Mission. Following a morning service in the church building, the singing takes place outside in the surrounding mountainous setting. Typically, several hundred people attend this event. Most are from the local community, but visitors are welcome. The singing occurs on the third Sunday in August from 10:00 A.M. to about 2:00 P.M. There's no charge, but donations are accepted.

LOCATION: From I-40, take exit 15. If you are traveling west from the Asheville/Waynesville area, you will turn right onto Fines Creek Rd. If you are traveling east from the Knoxville area, you will turn left onto Fines Creek Rd. and drive under the interstate. Follow Fines Creek Rd. approximately one mile. Turn left onto Shelton Laurel Rd., a gravel road, and follow it up the hill for a half-mile. At the fork, bear left onto Indian Springs Rd. Follow Indian Springs Rd. for another quarter-mile. Shelton Laurel Mission will be on your left at the red Salvation Army sign.

CONTACT: Sherman Cundiff, Singing on the Mountain, Salvation Army, PO Drawer 358, Waynesville, NC 28786, (828) 456-7111; or Haywood County Travel and Tourism, 1233 N. Main St., Suite 1-40, Waynesville, NC 28786, (800) 334-9036, (828) 452-0152, ‹info@smh.wcu.edu›, ‹hctda@smokeymountains.net›, ‹www.smokeymountains.net›

SWAIN COUNTY

❋ Smoky Mountain Jamboree

The Smoky Mountain Jamboree takes place at the spacious theater of the Saunooke Village Shopping Center in Cherokee, North Carolina. This stage show features a variety of music ranging from bluegrass and old-time to gospel, with even a little rock'n'roll. The show is hosted by an emcee, and a house band performs the music. At times, songs are presented and performed in the Cherokee language. The jamboree is open to the public on weekend evenings during April, May, and November and every night of the week from June 1 through October 31. The theater seats about three hundred, and most of the people in the audience are visitors to the area. The show begins at 8:00 P.M. There is an admission charge.

LOCATION: From US 74, take US 441 North (at exit 74) toward Cherokee. Continue on US 441 North until it intersects with US 19 in Cherokee. Turn right (north) onto US 19 and go to the next stoplight at the Kentucky Fried Chicken and the Long John Silver Restaurants. Turn left and continue to the second traffic light. Turn right and go across the bridge. Saunooke Village will be on your right across from the Best Western motel. Look for a sign for the Smoky Mountain Jamboree.

CONTACT: Rick and Sandy Morris, Smoky Mountain Jamboree, PO Box 822, Whittier, NC 28789, (828) 497-5521, (828) 497-6717, ‹smokymtnjamboree@aol.com›; or Swain County Chamber of Commerce, 16 Everett St., Bryson City, NC 28713, (800) 867-9246, (828) 488-3681, ‹chamber@greatsmokies.com›, ‹www.greatsmokies.com›

❊ Bluegrass Festivals at the Happy Holiday RV Park and Campground

The North Carolina State Bluegrass Festival is held at the Happy Holiday RV Park and Campground on the third weekend of June, and the Cherokee Bluegrass Festival is held there on the third weekend of August. Both festivals run for three days—Friday, Saturday, and Sunday. Both feature nationally known bluegrass and country recording artists. Previous festivals have included performances by Ricky Skaggs, the Osborne Brothers, the Lewis Family, Ralph Stanley, and a host of other "name" musicians. Performances run from noon until around 11:00 P.M. each day. There is an admission fee for the festival. Camping is additional. Call the festival promoters at (706) 864-7203 for details.

LOCATION: From US 74, take US 441 North (at exit 74) toward Cherokee. Continue on US 441 North until it intersects with US 19 in Cherokee. Turn right (north) onto US 19. The Happy Holiday RV Park and Campground is located on the left approximately four miles east of Cherokee.

CONTACT: Happy Holiday RV Park and Campground, (828) 497-7250; or Swain County Chamber of Commerce, 16 Everett St., Bryson City, NC 28713, (800) 867-9246, (828) 488-3681, ‹chamber@greatsmokies.com›, ‹www.greatsmokies.com›

❄ Bryson City Depot

The historic railroad depot in Bryson City, North Carolina, is the location for seasonal performances of traditional country, bluegrass, and old-time music. The Bryson City Depot is a charming historic building that's still a destination stop for daily excursion trains on the Great Smoky Mountain Railway. Concession stands line the side of the depot nearest the tracks. When rail travelers arrive at the depot from their originating station in Dillsboro, North Carolina, they're greeted by the sounds of live mountain music. These performances are staged for the tourists who travel on the Great Smoky Mountain Railway, but they're also open to anyone else who happens by at the time. The music lasts for about an hour, beginning at noon and ending around 1:00 P.M. Call ahead for the performance schedule.

LOCATION: The Bryson City Depot is located in the town's downtown historic district, near where Everett St. crosses the railroad tracks. Take US 74 West to exit 67 near Bryson City. Go into Bryson City and take a right onto US 19. Turn left onto Everett St. and follow Everett to the railroad tracks.

CONTACT: Diane Newalan, Great Smoky Mountain Railway, PO Box 397, Dillsboro, NC 28725, (828) 586-8811, ‹www.gsmr.com›; or Swain County Chamber of Commerce, 16 Everett St., Bryson City, NC 28713, (800) 867-9246, (828) 488-3681, ‹chamber@greatsmokies.com›, ‹www.greatsmokies.com›

JACKSON COUNTY

❄ Mountain Heritage Day

When Dr. H. F. Robinson was installed as chancellor of Western Carolina University in Cullowhee during the fall of 1974, he requested that a barbeque and square dance be held to conclude the day's activities. The celebration proved so popular that the chancellor promised to hold a similar event a year later. The university expanded the activities and presented the first Mountain Heritage Day in 1975 as a tribute to mountain heritage and to commemorate the nation's upcoming bicentennial.

Organizers did not anticipate the enthusiasm of residents of southwestern North Carolina for Mountain Heritage Day. The celebration has grown from a rather modest event featuring a few performers and crafts artists to a large multifaceted festival showcasing traditional music, dance, occupational skills, crafts, and foodways. It is not uncommon for Mountain Heritage Day to draw between thirty and forty thousand people, depending on the weather.

The Queen family, headed by matriarch Mary Jane Queen (far right), performs annually on the Traditional Music Stage at Mountain Heritage Day.

The largest performance venue, the Belk Stage, presents a good mix of regionally known bluegrass, old-time country, and gospel music, along with clogging and smooth-dance groups. This stage is located near the Midway, a huge area with over two hundred craft and food booths. The crafts are handmade, if not traditional, and the food is regional fare—ham biscuits, cider, barbecued chicken, Cherokee fry bread, and beans and cornbread. Contests take place throughout the day, including a dog show, a cat show, an old truck and tractor show, a horseshoe-pitching contest, a chainsaw competition, and contests for baked goods and preserves.

Smaller performance venues and some first-rate crafts and occupational-arts demonstrations are found next to the Mountain Heritage Center, a museum and research center that collects, interprets, and disseminates knowledge about Southern Appalachia and its people. Crafts traditions showcased in past years include quilting, cornshuck doll making, and basketry. Occupational skills demonstrated, such as tobacco curling or whiskey making, will be less familiar to many in the audience.

The Traditional Music Stage is housed nearby under a tent with hay bales for seats. Local musicians from Jackson and surrounding counties perform here and at the smaller Circle Tent, which is reserved for more informal music sessions. A Religious Music Stage gives attendees an opportunity to hear some unique mountain sacred song traditions such as shape-note singing from the *Christian Harmony* hymnbook.

The Mountain Heritage Center itself is an attraction. A permanent exhibit entitled Migration of the Scotch-Irish People describes the links between the Scotch-Irish who found their way to western North Carolina in the eighteenth century and their descendants. The center also preserves a large number of historical artifacts that are used in exhibits and conducts educational outreach programs with schools and community groups.

Mountain Heritage Day is free and open to the public from 8:00 A.M. until 5:00 P.M. on the last Saturday of September. Stage performances begin at 9:30 A.M. On-site parking is limited, but free shuttles from outlying lots run throughout the day. The attendants who help park cars are highly efficient.

LOCATION: Take US 23/74 to exit 85 at Sylva. Follow US 23 South into downtown Sylva and turn left on NC 107. Take NC 107 South for approximately seven miles until you come to Western Carolina University (on your left) in Cullowhee. Look for signs directing you to the event.

CONTACT: Mountain Heritage Center, Western Carolina University, Cullowhee, NC 28723, (828) 227-7129, ‹www.wcu.edu/mhc/mtnhrtdy.htm›

❀ Shape-Note Singing at the Cullowhee Baptist Church

Shape-note singing made its way into the South in the early nineteenth century, when itinerant singing instructors used the system of shaped notes to teach sightreading and harmony to residents and congregations in rural communities. Later, southerners began to compose and arrange hymns in the shape-note tradition for themselves. Some shape-note hymnals use a scale containing four shapes, while others use a seven-shape notation. Shape-note singing is unaccompanied by instrumentation of any kind. The music is created entirely by the human voice—the "sacred harp." Often, the notes are sung by name before the actual words of the hymn. This style of hymn singing is sometimes called "fa-so-la" singing.

The hymnal used by the congregation at the Cullowhee Baptist Church uses the seven-shape notation system. The group sings from the *Christian Harmony*, a hymnal published in Alabama and referred to as the "black book." The hosts of the singing at Cullowhee have extra hymnals to loan to visitors, and offering to share a hymnal with others is a prevailing and friendly gesture on the part of the singers. Visitors are genuinely welcome to attend shape-note singings as listeners, but ideally they should not join in the singing until they are familiar with the tradition. Newcomers will not be expected to sing or to lead songs unless they indicate that they are interested in doing so.

Song leaders set the pace for the group by "beating time."

At shape-note sings, participants typically share a potluck dinner that consists of primarily home-cooked and sometimes storebought foods. Visitors who want to eat with the church community should always bring along suitable food items to contribute to the general meal. Anything that's typically served at a church covered-dish supper would be a suitable offering. The annual shape-note sing at Cullowhee Baptist Church is observed on the first Sunday in February from noon until 3:00 P.M.

LOCATION: Take US 23/74 to exit 85 at Sylva. Follow US 23 South into downtown Sylva and turn left on NC 107. Take NC 107 South for approximately seven miles until you come to Western Carolina University (on your left) in Cullowhee. There will be a traffic light at the WCU entrance. Turn left onto campus and then take an immediate left again. The road curves right up the hill to another traffic light. Turn left on Central Dr. Proceed for one-fourth of a mile. The church is at 148 Central Dr., on the left just beyond the library.

CONTACT: Etheree Chancellor, Christian Harmony Shape-Note Sing at the Cullowhee Baptist Church, Cullowhee Baptist Church, PO Box 37, Cullowhee, NC 28723, (828) 293-9024; or Jackson County Chamber of Commerce, 116 Central St., Sylva, NC 28779, (800) 962-1911, (828) 586-2155, ‹jctta@nc-mountains.com›, ‹www.mountainlovers.com›

✻ Christian Harmony Sing at the Webster United Methodist Church

Another annual shape-note sing takes place at the 1881 Webster United Methodist Church in the town of Webster, North Carolina. This sing happens on the Saturday before the third Sunday in April, unless that day happens to fall on Easter weekend. Visitors to the sing at the Webster United Methodist Church should observe the same civilities as those described above for the Cullowhee Baptist Church sing. The Webster Methodist Church sing starts at 11:30 A.M. and continues until around 3:00 P.M. The church is located in Webster's historic district. Visitors are welcome.

LOCATION: Take US 23/74 to exit 85 at Sylva. Follow US 23 into downtown Sylva and turn left onto NC 107. Travel south on NC 107 for approximately two miles until you come to NC 116. Turn right on NC 116 toward Webster. Webster United Methodist Church is the small white frame church on the left at the top of the hill. Parking is located just past the church in the lot of the stone school building.

CONTACT: Will Peebles, Music Department, Western Carolina University, Cullowhee, NC 28723, (828) 227-3260, ‹wpeebles@wcu.edu›; or Jackson County Chamber of Commerce, 116 Central St., Sylva, NC 28779, (800) 962-1911, (828) 586-2155, ‹jctta@nc-mountains.com›, ‹www.mountainlovers.com›

CONTACT: Dan Huger, 9 Cedar Cliff Rd., Asheville, NC 2905, (828) 274-8890, ‹dehuger@mindspring.com›

TRANSYLVANIA COUNTY

�֎ Thursday Night Jams at the Silvermont Mansion

At the extreme southern end of the Blue Ridge region of North Carolina, in Brevard, an unusual and entertaining jam session takes place every Thursday night at the Silvermont Mansion, a community center owned by the Transylvania Board of Commissioners and operated by a volunteer group called the Friends of Silvermont. The Silvermont Mansion is a massive, three-level, early twentieth-century (1917) brick house with an impressive colonnaded front portico and generous front and side porches. A set of broad front steps and a massive entry lead into a central hallway flanked on either side by a pair of spacious formal parlors. Silvermont Mansion is about as unlikely a place for a mountain music jam session as can be imagined.

The Silvermont jam began back in 1981 when a trio of local traditional musicians were asked to play out on the front porch of the mansion. News of the session quickly spread by word of mouth throughout the community, and the number of participating musicians who showed up to play in the weeks following eventually grew large enough that the session was moved inside to one of the front parlors. And there it is now, every Thursday evening, year-round.

The Silvermont Thursday Night Mountain Music Jam Session is unusual—not only because of its elegant surroundings, but also for its interesting form. The musicians—typically, between fifteen and twenty-five of

Musicians and listeners enjoy the fellowship at the
Silvermont Mansion Thursday Night Jam Session.

them—set up folding chairs in a large circle inside the left front parlor of the
house. Within the circle is a single microphone on a stand. As each musician
takes a turn leading a song, the microphone is passed along, person to person, in a clockwise direction. Each player is expected to choose and an-
nounce a tune or song, start the piece, and lead the group as the chosen
song is performed. So the evening goes, tune after tune. Meanwhile, non-
players who are there to listen sit in folding chairs out in the hallway or in an
adjacent connecting dining room. Some audience members flatfoot or clog
a little whenever a particularly bright tune is played. The music ranges from
bluegrass to old-time to country to gospel. Since this session is truly open to
all who want to participate, there's even an occasional jazz or classical
player in the mix. Generally, when that person's turn comes to lead, most of
the other players just sit quietly back and enjoy the nonconformer's solo performance.

Music at the Silvermont Mansion is held on Thursday evenings year-
round beginning at 7:30 P.M. The players perform until around 10:00.

LOCATION: Traveling west on I-26 from Asheville, take exit 9 and follow NC 280 West to Brevard. On the outskirts of town, US 280 will merge with US 64 and US 276 and become Broad St. Follow Broad St. in downtown and look for the courthouse. At the courthouse, turn left on Main St. (also called US 276 South). Continue south on Main St. for approximately one-fourth of a mile. Silvermont Park will be on the right at the point where the road narrows to two lanes.

CONTACT: Rick Pangle, Transylvania County Parks and Recreation Department, 1150 Ecusta Rd., Brevard, NC 28712, (828) 884-3156, ‹recdept@sitcom.net›; or Brevard/Transylvania County Travel and Tourism, 35 West Main St., Brevard, NC 28712, (800) 648-4523, (828) 884-8900, ‹waterfalls@citcom.net›, ‹www.visitwaterfalls.com›

❈ Tuesday Night Jam at Celestial Mountain Music

Another jam in the Brevard and Transylvania County area worthy of attention is the Tuesday night old-time music session at Celestial Mountain Music, a restored 1892 storefront on West Main Street in Brevard. Celestial Mountain Music is a great resource in the area for acoustic music, particularly old-time. The sessions there are free. They get started at 7:00 P.M.

LOCATION: Traveling west on I-26 from Asheville, take exit 9 and follow NC 280 West to Brevard. On the outskirts of town, US 280 will merge with US 64 and US 276 and become Broad St. Follow Broad St. in downtown and look for the courthouse. At the courthouse, turn left on Main St. (also called US 276 South). Celestial Mountain Music is in the third building on the right. There are several areas designated for parking.

CONTACT: Mary Gordon, Celestial Mountain Music, 16 W. Main St., Brevard, NC 28712, (828) 884-3575, ‹celestial@citcom.net›; or Brevard/Transylvania County Travel and Tourism, 35 W. Main St., Brevard, NC 28712, (800) 648-4523, (828) 884-8900, ‹waterfalls@citcom.net›, ‹www.visitwaterfalls.com›

❈ Bluegrass Concert at the Ecusta Union Hall in Brevard

This annual bluegrass concert features a number of popular bluegrass bands, including the Lewis Family and Jim & Jesse and the Virginia Boys. The concert is held in March. The Ecusta Union Hall, where the concert is held, is owned by the Ecusta Paper Processing plant, which is the largest employer in Transylvania County. The music starts at 8:00 P.M. An admission fee is charged. All visitors should call in advance for details.

JOHN C. CAMPBELL FOLK SCHOOL

The John C. Campbell Folk School at Brasstown, North Carolina, was founded in 1925 as a collaboration between two progressive educators and an Appalachian community. Olive Dame Campbell, Marguerite Butler, and the people of Brasstown created a unique institution that seeks to encourage people in two kinds of development: inner growth as creative, thoughtful individuals and social development as tolerant, caring members of a community. Throughout its history, the school has worked toward these goals through performing arts, agriculture, and crafts rooted in the traditions of Southern Appalachia and other cultures of the world.

Autoharp class at John C. Campbell Folk School

The John C. Campbell Folk School has been designated as a "historic district" by the National Register of Historic Places. The school's twenty-seven buildings are the scene of many services to the community, a variety of special events, and an internationally known instructional program. The 372-acre campus has fully equipped craft studios, a sawmill, meeting rooms, a covered outdoor dance pavilion, a nature trail, a craft shop, a vegetable garden, rustic lodgings, and one of the best dance floors in America.

The school hosts weekly music concerts on campus at the Keith House, featuring local bluegrass and old-time bands, ballad singers, and gospel groups. The performances are presented free of charge every Friday night at 7:30 P.M., except for the week of Christmas. The Friday night concerts are enhanced by a responsive audience that's a mix of local residents, students enrolled at the school, and visitors, and by the warmth of the Keith House, which is constructed with natural wooden floors, walls, and ceilings. The acoustics are excellent.

Community contra and square dances with live music are held at the school twice a month—usually (but not always) on the first and third Saturdays, from 8:00 to 11:00 P.M.

For more than twenty-five years now, the Campbell Folk School has produced an annual Fall Festival, and attendance at this event now numbers in the thousands. The festival showcases traditional music, dance, foodways, arts and crafts, vintage occupational and home skills, and more. It's held on the first full weekend in October.

LOCATION: The John C. Campbell Folk School is located seven miles east of Murphy, North Carolina. From Murphy, take US 64 East past Tri-County Community College. Turn right onto Old 64 and follow the signs to the school.

From Hayesville, take US 64 West for approximately eight miles. Turn left onto Settawig Rd. and follow the signs to the school.

CONTACT: David A. Brose, John C. Campbell Folk School, One Folk School Rd., Brasstown, NC 28902, (828) 837-2775, ‹www.folkschool.com›

LOCATION: Traveling west on I-26 from Asheville, take exit 9 and follow NC 280 West toward Brevard. Just north of downtown Brevard, near the junction of NC 280 and US 64/276, you will come to the community of Pisgah Forest (not to be confused with Pisgah National Forest just to the west). Cross the bridge over the Davidson River and turn left at the next light. Continue about one mile and you will come to the Ecusta plant. Turn right on Morris Rd. You will see Ecusta Union Hall (Local No. 1971) on the hill to your right.

CONTACT: Mary Ruth Stamey, Bluegrass Music Association of North Carolina, South Carolina, and Georgia, 705 Morgan Mill Rd., Brevard, NC 28712, (828) 884-3225, ‹mrstamey@citcom.net›; or Brevard/Transylvania County Travel and Tourism, 35 W. Main St., Brevard, NC 28712, (800) 648-4523, (828) 884-8900, ‹waterfalls@citcom.net›, ‹www.visitwaterfalls.com›

PHOTOGRAPHER'S NOTE

My work began on a rainy day on the first weekend in June at the Mount Airy Fiddlers' Convention in Surry County, North Carolina. Three days later, anxious to "keep the work in gear," I traveled ahead to the Bluff Mountain Music Festival a hundred miles away, near the Tennessee border. The following week, a visit to Sims Barbeque down near Granite Falls, not far from I-40. Three trips during June and July to the Marshall Depot in Madison County, North Carolina. Silvermont Mansion on a Thursday evening, Old Fort Mountain Music in McDowell County on Friday night. Then up to the weekend venues in the Virginia mountains, and down to Roanoke for a Wednesday night old-time jam at Mill Mountain Coffee. Somewhere in between all these venues, I met and photographed the musicians profiled in this guidebook.

Never in my life have I been treated with such kindness. There were times when I simply was not prepared for the generosity. I was fed lunch on a regular basis, offered a place to stay if I did not have one already. I can't imagine anything like this happening in the more urban areas that I've called home.

In late July, as I realized that I'd be finished with this work all too soon, I began to feel a very real sense of sadness. I would have to resume a normal life again. Give up camping in beautiful places like Price Lake in Watauga County, North Carolina, and return to a world where the communal experience and spontaneous, live music were rare.

August came quickly, and with it one of the big events of the season, the sixty-fourth Annual Galax Old-Time Fiddlers' Convention in Galax, Virginia. For diehards, this is reputed to be the one to see. On the other hand, I had heard that crowds can be heavy and campsites are completely loaded from one end of Felt's Park to the other before the first note is played. Food and craft vendors and sellers of musical instruments line the main walkway shoulder to shoulder. And if it rains, as I've been told it does nearly every year, mud adds significantly to these challenges. I didn't really know what to expect, but I was ready for anything.

In the late afternoon of my third day at Galax, I remember feeling the weight of my camera bag over my shoulder as I weaved through the campsites and along the footpath. It had been a great summer—almost nonstop. I had planned well and worked hard, listened to a lot of music, met so many wonderful people over the past few months—it all felt like it had gone by too quickly. This reflective state of mind was suddenly interrupted when I recognized one of the musicians featured in this book. He was jamming with some other players, fellows I had met a few times at the Old Helton School in North Carolina the month before. They were together again, gathered in a spot they had claimed for themselves beside somebody's camper, spreading the full force of their energy to a growing crowd. I quickened my step and raised a hand in greeting. They glanced up from their instruments and nodded at me, smiling, and in that moment I felt a kinship with these musicians. It was a feeling I will never forget. And as their music gained momentum, I watched the crowd and could see on the faces of friends who gathered that same level of feeling, proving again how this music, wherever or whenever it may be played, is always a shared experience that can define, and at the same time transcend, the given moment.

My experience at Galax would later give me cause to think of what is truly at the root of all this great music: community. By that I mean friendships or family bonds that last a lifetime, or rather *make* a lifetime. I believe this is why mountain music sounds the way it does. Go listen. Feel it for yourself.

I would like to gratefully acknowledge all the bluegrass and old-time musicians, fans, and music venues in western North Carolina and Virginia who appear in this publication. I would also like to thank June Thompson, Barbara Lau, Lesley Williams, Starr Markham, Wayne Martin, Beverly Patterson, Molly Matlock Parsons, Katherine Reynolds, Fred and Cathy Fussell, Roddy Moore, Sally Council, Amy Davis, Melanie Rice, Jack Bernhardt and Lisa Napp, Denver Butson and Rhonda Keyser, Greg Hershey, Jay Chatterley, Jo Lea Chatterley, Leonard Gutnik, the North Carolina Folklife Institute, the Blue Ridge Institute in Ferrum, Virginia, David Perry at the University of North Carolina Press, B&L Photo in Carbondale, Illinois, JW Photo Lab and Southeastern Camera in Raleigh, North Carolina, Barr's Fiddle Shop in Galax, Virginia, the Center for Documentary Studies at Duke University, and Northwest Airlines.

Cedric N. Chatterley

INDEX

Page numbers in italics refer to illustrations or illustration captions.